MR. PINK

The Inside Story of the Transylvania Book Heist

Chas Allen

MR. PINK

The Inside Story of the Transylvania Book Heist

By Chas Allen

Cover Design By LJ Graphics

Published by:

Allen Brothers Publishing

838 East High Street Suite 258

Lexington, KY 40502

Copyright 2010 Charles Allen

Copyright © 2010 Charles Allen. Copyright claimed in all chapters, exclusive of U.S. Government information.

First Printing 2010

Printed in the United States of America

ISBN-13: 978-0-615-40716-6

Keep in mind:
This story is based on the true-life experiences of the author. Anything not experienced first-hand was derived from conversations, statements, and police reports involving those with first-hand experience. To protect the rights of the innocent as well as the guilty, some names, characters, places, and events have been changed. For more information go to **www.WhoIsMrPink.com**

To Blake and Sydney

"Everyone has in him something of the criminal, the genius, and the saint."

-Carl Jung

Chapter 1: Interrogation

"What would you say if I told you we could make twelve million dollars in one day?"...

Those were the words that had started it all, and nearly two years later, those were the words that still echoed in my mind as I waited to be questioned by the F.B.I..

I was locked in a holding cell, somewhere within the federal building of Lexington, Kentucky. A light bulb glowed from the ceiling of my cell and a quiet hum of electricity filled the air. A round, glass fixture surrounded the bulb and was covered with dust that seemed to choke the life and vibrancy from the lone source of light. The plain walls of the cell, the tile floors, the ceiling, the door, and a small wooden bench that sat along one of the walls, were all colored by a shade of yellow like an eerie penumbra of the sun. I assumed that the bench was placed there to provide me with some small amount of comfort as I waited, but I wasn't sure whether anything could comfort me anymore. Not after what I had done. And not while I was preparing to face the consequences. All that I could do to cope with my worries, my anxieties, and my fears, while I waited for the inevitable interrogation, was pace. I paced back and forth across my cell, again and again, still hearing the words, "twelve million dollars"... and wishing that I never had.

I wasn't alone within the federal building. There were at least seven others, that I was aware of, who had either been arrested or brought in for questioning. They were my friends, my roommates, and my girlfriend. Half of them knew nothing of why we were there and the other half knew too much. A few wrong words from the right person had the power to change the course of my life forever, and I wasn't ready for change. I was twenty years old then, a sophomore in college, and I had never imagined that my choices would lead me so deeply into the hands of the law. I had been raised better than that. Or, at least I thought I had. I believed that people like me didn't belong in prison. That was the arrogance in me talking, of course. It was a side of me that I didn't like to acknowledge, but knew that it existed. A side of me that believed because I was born into a life of privilege, I was entitled to extra privileges in life. And in the past, it had proved true. The appearance of wealth, a few well-placed family ties, and a bit of my own charm had kept me out of a few minor scrapes with the law. But I didn't fool myself into believing that those things could save me anymore.

There was a knock on the door of my cell and it resounded from the walls like a knock on a coffin.

"Mr. Allen?"

"Yes?"

"It's time."

The door opened and white light spilled into the cell. A bear of a man approached, then stood before me. He wore a stand-alone moustache and his shirt-sleeves were rolled past the elbows to reveal thick forearms and what almost seemed to be a coat of brownish-grey fur that covered his arms, the backs of his hands, and his knuckles.

"I'm only going to say this once." He warned. "I'm not going to put you in cuffs, because we aren't going far, but if you try anything stupid, I'll make sure you regret it. Understand?"

I had never liked people who tried to exert their authority over others. And from the moment he spoke, I didn't like him. I understood his words well enough, and they irritated me like a blanket sprinkled with fiberglass, but under the circumstances, I could do nothing but swallow my pride and nod my head in agreement.

He took my arm above the elbow in a grip like a steel vice and led me from the cell into a large, cluttered room. It was like a labyrinth of four-foot high dividers. There were dozens of cubicles, each complete with a computer, phone, swivel chair, and enough government employees to man them all. We walked through the heart of the labyrinth and I could feel the eyes that watched me from within their work-stations. And that was when I saw her.

My girlfriend, Claire, was sitting alone in an empty cubicle. Her back was turned and her dark hair slid over her shoulders like a gentle, but deep, creek. I wondered how she, who sat there as innocent as the day we met in high school, could have been pulled into my wrongful affairs. More often than not, it isn't our own pain that hurts us the most; it's the pain that we cause the ones we love. And seeing her there, like that, tore at the strings of my heart. I couldn't forgive myself then, and still to this day I don't forgive myself, for the pain and heartache that I unintentionally caused her, and countless others.

I hated to do it, but I forced myself to look away and kept walking. I scanned the office for anyone else who had been brought in for questioning, but found no one. I felt a tug at my elbow and I was pulled toward a door. We stopped, but the man's grip didn't. He knocked twice and the door opened.

Inside the room, two agents were standing in near darkness.

"Take a seat." One of the figures announced, insisting that I inch past them in the already cramped room.

I felt the iron-grip release my elbow and a fresh wave of anxiety rushed through me as I did as I was instructed. I stepped into the room, sat down, and the door closed behind me, taking the white light with it. It took a few seconds for my eyes to adjust, but when they did, I realized that I was trapped. The only exit from the room was blocked by two F.B.I. agents, one man and one woman and they had me backed into a corner with nothing but the stool that I sat on and the short table that separated us.

The man was the first to speak. "My name is Special Agent Markum," he said, "and this here is Special Agent Williams." I took Markum to be the one in charge. He wore a black hat with his agency's letters written in white. It was difficult to determine the color of his hair. Anything that showed above his ears had been cropped to his skull. From his pale complexion and freckles though, I assumed it was red. He wasn't a large man, but what he may have lacked in stature he overcompensated for with the intensity of his demeanor. It was his eyes, his glossy black eyes that held me captive in that room. He stared at me from across the table with the eyes of a serpent, stalking its prey.

His sidekick, Special Agent Williams, as he had introduced her, had blonde hair, an attractive face and the restless expression of someone who dreaded that she would have to do her job.

"Before we get started," Markum said, "I'm required by law to read you your Miranda Rights…"

All I had to do was stay calm. I can beat this, I reminded myself. All that

I needed to do was act like I didn't know anything, answer some questions, then go home. I knew that they only had an arrest warrant for two of my friends. I was almost certain that there was no evidence against me, almost.

"You have the right to remain silent. Anything you say can and will be used against you in the court of law. You have the right to an attorney. If you cannot afford one, the court will appoint one for you. Mr. Allen, at this time, would you like to speak to an attorney?"

"An Attorney? No, why would I need an attorney?" I asked in mock disbelief.

"It's only procedure." He reassured me. "I'm required by law to ask." Markum stacked some papers in his hands and laid them on the end of the table. "So, are you ready to get started?"

I flashed the most charming smile that I could manage. "Yeah, sure. I don't mind answering a few questions for you."

"Okay, great. Do you mind if I jot down a few notes while we talk?" He asked, playing along with my jovial charade. He attempted to sound as if we had known each other for years.

"No, sure, go ahead."

"Alright, let's get started then." He pulled a pen from his chest pocket, clicked it once, and held it ready above the page. "Mr. Allen, do you know why you have been brought here for questioning today?"

"Well," I began slowly, trying to form a passable answer in my head, "I've heard a few of the officers say some things, but other than that, no, not really."

"So you're telling me that you have no knowledge of the stolen property that we recovered at your residence this morning?"

"No." I lied. "I didn't know anything about that until today."

And he started writing, jotting notes on his paper.

"Mr. Allen, is it true that you are the current owner of the house that you and your roommates reside in?"

"Yes, well ugh, not completely, I own half and my dad owns— "

"Are you aware then," he interrupted, "of the penalty for harboring stolen property?"

"No, I don't think so." I muttered, feeling the temperature of the room beginning to rise. I had to fight to suppress the heat that had flushed through my face, but I was fairly sure that they hadn't seen it. Over and over I repeated to myself to just relax… relax.

"Tell me about when you went to New York." He questioned, bulldozing ahead. "Tell me about the meeting with Christie's Auction House."

How did he know about that, I wondered? How much did they actually know?

"In New York? I've never been to New York." I lied.

"So, between December 19th and December 23rd, you weren't staying at the Hilton Hotel in New York City?"

"No. Like I said, I've never been to New York."

And he was writing. His pen was flowing on the paper. "Mr. Allen, are you aware of the penalty for lying to a federal agent?"

His words flicked over me like the flames of a grill, slowly roasting me, outside and in. I was barely able to respond, but somehow, the words came out. "No, I don't think so, why?"

"Because unless you start answering me truthfully, that is exactly what will happen to you." He tensed his arms as if he were restraining himself from crossing the table.

"Mr. Allen?" The blonde asked, directing my attention. "Do you mind if I call you, Chas?"

"Sure." I offered reluctantly, wondering how she knew my nickname.

"Okay, good." She replied with a sincere smile. "Chas, I really think it is in your best interest to start answering his questions. We can only help you, if you help us. So please, will you help us by answering honestly now?"

She made a good effort, but I had a vague idea of what she was implying.

I looked back and forth between them in silence until Markum had composed himself enough to take the lead again.

"Okay, Mr. Allen, we're going to try this one more time. If you don't start giving us some answers, I'll make sure you spend the next twenty five years of your life behind bars. Is that a clear enough picture for you?"

I nodded. I tried to swallow, but my mouth was too dry.

"Good. Now that we're on the same page, I want you to tell us what happened on December 17th"."

"I don't know what you're talking about."

"That's it!" Markum exploded. "That was your last chance!" He grabbed the stack of papers and slammed them on the table.

"Chas," Agent Williams said. "They already talked. We already have enough information to convict you. Names, dates, times. Everything."

I couldn't believe what I had just heard. It didn't make sense. If what she had said was true, then something had gone wrong, terribly wrong. I thought that it might be a lie meant to trick me, but something in the pit of my stomach told me otherwise. I was too stunned to move. I wasn't even sure if I was still breathing while I waited to hear their next words.

"It's true." Markum said. "One of your buddies already wrote and signed his own affidavit. He already talked. Both of them did. Here, look, we've got something for you." He pulled several pages of papers from the stack and slid them along the table.

In bold, capital letters I saw my name, and I knew it was a warrant for my arrest. It was something that I had known was possible, but it was something that was impossible to prepare for. I felt the course of my life shifting, irrevocably, as I stared at the warrant.

I knew that I was not going home that day. I was not going back to the comfort of my king-sized bed, to the comfort of Claire, and to the comfort of the life that I had left behind, only moments ago. No, there was no comfort where I would be going.

Special Agent Markum quickly pulled the warrant away. His black eyes gleamed with victory as he looked at me with a smug grin.

"So, tell us, Mr. Allen. Who is Mr. Pink?"

"I want to speak to an attorney."

Chapter 2: Attorney Interview

A door opened and a man stepped into the room. From my seat behind a perforated partition of glass, I first noticed his height. He was a tall and slender man with blonde hair. It was short in length but lay neatly as if it had been trained to perfection with a comb. He wore a tailored black suit with a white shirt and red tie. He seemed to exude an air of professionalism.

He sat down and introduced himself through the glass. He held a business card so that I could read his name and his title of attorney at-law. "Hi, Charles. My name is Harvey Bird."

"Any relation to Larry?" I asked, half serious.

He gave an easy smile. "No. I used to play basketball, but that was years ago." He admitted.

"That's okay. If you spent all of your time playing basketball, then honestly, I'd be worried about your qualifications as an attorney."

He laughed. His face and his whole demeanor seemed so relaxed, so open and honest that I instantly felt like I could trust him.

"You can call me, Chas, by the way." I offered.

"Okay, well Chas, I was contacted by one of your family members. Your mother asked me to come down here to speak with you. I have read the police reports and the statements that have already been made, and I am here to advise you and give you legal counsel. What that means is that anything you and I discuss will be held strictly confidential. Everything that you say is protected by attorney-client privilege. Are you familiar with that?"

"I think so." I glanced around the partition that divided us.

"That also means that there are no monitoring devices in this room. No wires, no cameras, just you and me. Anything that we discuss will not leave this room."

I nodded, feeling slightly more at ease.

"So, before I can properly give you any legal advice I need to hear your side of how things happened. And like I said, I've already read up on the case, but for some reason, I just don't get it. Working criminal defense, I've represented all types of clients, and I hope you don't mind my saying, but you don't exactly fit the profile. I know your family. I know you went to a private school and I know you're enrolled at a good university. In my experience, most people commit crimes out of necessity. But in your case, you seem to have never wanted for anything, and from the looks of it, you had every opportunity in life that a young man could hope for. So my question is, why? Why did you do it?" He looked at me expectantly, but patient.

"Well, for starters, Mr. Bird, just because something appears to be a certain way, it doesn't necessarily make it true."

He stared at me through the glass, perplexed. He spoke after a moment of thought. "If I am going to be able to help you, I need you to tell me how things happened. And if my experience has taught me anything, it is that the how always begins with the why. So please, Chas, trust me to do my job and help you the best way I know how."

I felt like he was trustworthy, but still, I had learned that if given to the wrong person, trust could be a dangerous thing. My deepest and darkest secrets were safely locked away within my own mind and I was apprehensive to let them free. But, I was desperate for help.

"You want me to tell you about the crime?"

"Yes. And also anything else that could possibly pertain to the case. I usually find that it is best to cover all of the bases first so that there are no surprises later."

"Do you mean like any other crimes?"

"If you feel it pertains to the case, then yes."

I released a deep sigh and sat back. I could feel my conscience weighing me down. I knew that I needed to let him help me. And he had said that anything I say wouldn't leave the room. I decided that for better or worse, I would have to trust him.

"I don't even know where to start." I said, hopelessly.

"The beginning is usually a good place."

I smiled and gave a slight laugh, knowing that I had made the right decision. I thought back to a better time, a time before my life had spun out of control, a time when life seemed easy.

"Okay, that's where I'll start then."

Chapter 3: The Beginning

Long before I was born, there were ties between Lexington, Kentucky and Las Vegas. Cocaine runners, politicians, dirty cops, thoroughbred owners, and gamblers alike used the ambiguity of the small city to mask their illegal activities. Unlike the city of sin where debauchery was as visible as the bright lights of the strip, Lexington was a place where a person's actions could hide behind a good reputation and stay hidden.

When I was in high school, a friend, nicknamed Deuce, had introduced me into the world of underground gambling. We were both sixteen years old at the time, tall and slim, but we looked older than the ages on our new driver's licenses. Deuce had a cow-licked tuft of light brown hair that he wore short, buzzed to keep the unruly mane in check. My dark brown, almost black hair was clean-cut and my budding facial hair was nothing more than dark stubble, but I hoped it would make me seem older for what I was about to do.

Deuce drove me to a large apartment complex and led me through what seemed like a maze of turning and twisting sidewalks tucked between short, squat, two story brick apartments. He opened a door that was as plain as any of the other hundred that we had passed. We entered a building and climbed a flight of stairs, knowing the security cameras on the wall watched our every move. He knocked casually on a heavy steel door as I stood beside him feeling a mixture of emotions. I was both nervous and excited as we waited for approval from whoever was on the other end of the cameras. Finally, an electronic lock clicked open and we were allowed in. Deuce addressed the crowd that was huddled around a poker table in the poorly lit room. "Hey everyone, this is Chas. He's with me today."

From that point on, I became a regular, coming and going once or twice a week. It gave me the chance to practice playing blackjack and poker on a much higher level than only playing among friends. This was as close to Vegas as I could get at sixteen years old and I loved it. There was something about the thrill of the high stakes that I enjoyed. I had enjoyed business at an early age, trying to follow in the entrepreneurial footsteps of my father, but something about cards was different. Maybe it was the money; the excitement of winning or losing more in a minute than most people earned in an entire day. Maybe it was the thrill of watching money change hands in an instant, based only on a combination of a person's skill and luck. Or maybe it was the risk, knowing that what I was doing was considered illegal. Either way, something kept me coming back.

When I graduated high school, I decided to stay in town for college. By the time I began classes as a freshman at the University of Kentucky, the underground casino had been a part of my weekly routine for years. One particular afternoon I had been sitting across from the dealer at the blackjack table and was focused on the cards being dealt. I was alone at the table as the dealer and I were playing heads up against one another, just me against the house, as I preferred to play.

"Hit me." I said as I tapped the plush green felt.

The dealer was a guy named Slim. He had long hair and his arms were sleeved with tattoos. He was behind the blackjack table and he only had a king revealed. I had jack-five, or fifteen, so I decided to hit and take another draw, but the odds were in my favor. We were almost at the end of the shoe and most of the high cards were gone. I was hoping for a six on my next pull to give me a perfect twenty one.

"Come on, Slim, let me get that six!"

He pulled out a card and slid it on top of my jack-five. The new card was a three.

"Shit!" I blurted. "Eighteen, oh well, I'll stay where I'm at."

In my pocket, I felt my phone vibrating anxiously, but I ignored it.

The dealer flipped over the last card that was hidden under his king. It was a two, which gave him a total of twelve and at least one more draw. Slim spoke in a methodical and cigarette burned voice. "Dealer has twelve. Dealer hits." He pulled the next draw from the shoe and dropped it on the overturned cards. It was a five. The hand was over. "Dealer has seventeen. Dealer has to stand. Eighteen wins."

Slim pushed my winnings across the table to match my bet. I was playing with twenty five dollar chips and I had four of them riding on that hand. With that win, I was up almost four hundred dollars for the day.

My phone was still vibrating, insisting to be answered, so I checked the caller-ID, and saw that it was Luke.

"Hey, Slim, go ahead and cash me out for today." I said, pushing my chips across the table, then sliding one directly to him. "I've got to take this call."

Usually, the owner of the underground casino didn't allow people to talk on their cell phones while they were still inside, but he had seen me around enough not to care. His nickname was Bullfrog and it fit him well. He spent most days with his massive body hunched over a stool as he watched the poker, black-jack, and roulette tables from the monitors at his desk. Most people called him Frog for short. He was a decent enough guy, but he was the type that you knew you didn't want to end up being on his bad side. He had built a reputation that he was ruthless when it came to handling cheaters and collecting debts. Slim and some of the other employees served a greater purpose than only dealing the cards. They were mostly ex-cons who he had hired as a form of muscle.

I picked up a stack of bills and stepped away from the table as I spoke into the phone. "Hello?"

"Hey, man, where are you?"

Luke knew that I went to the casino once or twice a week, but he never wanted to come along. He wasn't much of a gambler. Even though I was only talking to Luke, I didn't want to say where I was over the phone.

"Oh, I'm just finishing some stuff that I had to do. Why? What's up?"

"I'm at my place just drinking some beer with a few of the guys. I think some girls are on their way over, so swing by whenever you get done."

"Alright, man. I'll be there in a little while."

"Alright. Oh, and do you think you could pick up a bottle of Crown while you're out?"

I had a good day at the tables and I felt like celebrating. "Yeah, no problem. What about Sprite? Should I grab some of that too?"

"No, just the Crown. I've still got some leftover from last night."

"Alright, man, I'll see you in a minute."

"Later."

I ended the call, but I continued to hold the phone to my ear as I took a good look at my surroundings. I had seen them countless times before, but I felt compelled to study them at any opportunity in case I was ever in a situation when I needed to escape in a hurry. There were two cameras in the room that seemed to cover various angles. One was mounted on the ceiling above the table to watch the cards and any players that would be seated around the action and the other was in the back corner of the room which faced an open doorway. There were no paintings hung from the plain taupe walls and there were no sofas or chairs to lounge in aside from the stools at the table. My eyes were drawn to the only window in the room and I thought it was odd that it led to a small balcony, an overhang little more than an ellipse of concrete protruding from the second story. There were no seals, no wires, or any other signs of a security system on the window. The pane was lifted and fresh autumn air was drifting into the room.

I hung up the phone and made my way through the hallways that branched from room to room in the cramped apartment. Some of the walls had been knocked out to combine two apartment units in order to accommodate the makeshift casino, but space was still scarce. From outside of the building it would be impossible to guess that within the complex there could be a gambling operation of such magnitude hidden within those walls. The place had Vegas style tables and chairs, and they required players to play with their own customized clay chips. It was a small operation, but it brought in plenty of cash.

It was said that some nights, Frog would close the place and walk out with a bag full of money in his hand and a loaded pistol on his hip. It was all tax free money that he had illegally beaten people out of, but he was smart about it. He had kept his business low key for years and he slowly filtered his money into the real estate market. After years of patience, he had made millions of legitimate dollars and owned properties all over Lexington. Like the makeshift casino, he too had been converted to hide within a greater realm. He was able to cast a shadow over his nature as a gangster to pass as a businessman.

I nodded to some of the regulars that were playing poker and walked over to Frog. He looked lost in thought as he systematically watched the panel of security monitors in front of him. I clapped him on the back to get his attention. "Hey, Frog, I'm headin' out."

He pulled his eyes away from the monitors and looked me over with a lazy glare. "Congratulations, kid, ya did well today. How much did ya beat me for?" He said, half jokingly.

"Oh, I don't know. I guess I did alright. The cards were falling my way today. And like I've always said, I'd rather be lucky than good at anything."

"Yeah... Lucky." A deep chuckle rose from his throat, but it seemed to exhaust his air supply. He took several labored breaths to recover from his outburst, then washed it down with a swill of bourbon.

I tried not to, but I glanced down and saw the loaded shotgun leaning against his knee. I didn't even realize what I was doing at the time, but I was playing a dangerous game. I guess I enjoyed the challenge. The black-jack was the easy part. As long as I kept my count and made the right plays, then the odds were slightly on my side. Staying below the radar was the hard part. I only came by the casino once or twice a week and I would only play with the twenty five dollar chips. It was usually slow. On most days I would win a few hundred dollars then call it quits. Other days I would lose fifty or even a hundred, which I didn't mind, because I wasn't trying to attract any unwanted attention from Bullfrog while he watched from the monitors. I thought he was an alright guy, but I knew better than to cross him.

Before I looked away, I realized that there was a cabinet door hanging open on its hinges within the interior of Bullfrog's desk. I had never noticed it before, which made me even more curious. I tried to see through the shadows to whatever was inside. It was hard to tell, but it seemed to be some sort of box. I could see a corner where the edges came together in a point. Toward the center there was a small circle, which almost glowed in contrast to the otherwise dark interior. Then I understood what it was that I was looking at, or at least I thought I did. It was a cashbox. It was probably where the money that exchanged hands across the tables was stashed during the casino's open hours. Maybe it was even stored there over night. But that would depend on how careless Bullfrog was. Either way, I decided that I would have to look into it further. Then my gaze was drawn back to the shotgun resting against his knee and I realized that I shouldn't push my luck.

He watched me as I pulled my eyes up from the gun to meet his glare. He broke the awkward silence. "Alright, kid, I'll see ya later. Take it easy on me next time, will ya?" He turned around to push a button that unlocked the door.

I laughed nervously, because I couldn't tell if he was joking or serious. "Alright, Frog, I'll see you soon." I walked through the heavy security door, went down the stairs, and out a second door that led to sidewalks criss-crossing through the apartment complex. I weaved through a pattern of memorized turns until I found my car and drove away. I made a quick stop at the liquor store to pick up a handle of Crown Royal Whiskey. I was only eighteen, but buying liquor wasn't a problem. I flashed the elderly lady behind the counter my fake-ID, paid in cash and I was on my way.

Over at Luke's place, a crowd of people had already gathered by the time I showed up. His apartment at Greg Paige was small, but it was somewhere for everyone to party. Most freshmen at the University of Kentucky lived in the dorms, so most parties that my friends and I had were either at Luke's apartment or at my house, which was on the edge of campus. There wasn't much space to move around in Luke's apartment, but that was the least of our worries. The living room and kitchen were open and there were two bedrooms and a bathroom in the back, so we were able to make due with what we had.

When I walked through the front door, the music hit me like a wave. ACDC was playing full-blast and people were shouting and laughing over the music. Luke was the first to see me.

Aside from my girlfriend, he was probably the person that I spent most of my time with. We had gone to high school together at Lexington Catholic, but we hadn't grown to be close friends until the start of college. From his chubby appearance and shaggy blond hair that hung over his eyes, it was hard to believe that he was an athlete. In high school, he had played football and all of the drinking of the college lifestyle had caused a few extra pounds to cling to him without the constant exercise and practice. But he was trying to slim back down. We worked out together a few times a week lifting weights and played racquetball on the off days at the Johnson Center.

"Chas! Where you been, man!" He stood from his seat on the couch, caught my open right hand and pulled me in for a one-shouldered hug.

"I had a few stops to make, but I didn't come back empty handed!" I pulled the handle of Crown from a brown paper bag. "Where are all the cups? I'm ready to crack this thing open!" I set the bottle on the counter and let him make the drinks while I went around and greeted everyone else at the party. A lot of the crowd was friends of ours that went to high school in Lexington and stayed in town for college. Others, we had met around campus. I scanned the party for my girlfriend, Claire, but I didn't see her. I had talked to her earlier that day and she had said that she and her best friend Rachel were going to be at Luke's party that night.

"Chas! Come get your drink!" Luke shouted through the crowd. I could tell that he was already drunk, which meant that I had a lot of drinking to do to catch him.

I walked through the jumbled mass of bodies and grabbed my drink. I held my blue plastic cup up next to his for a toast. "Clinkies!" I cheered.

We touched cups and I took a long pull from the drink. Crown and Sprite—my favorite. As I lowered my cup, I looked around the room and saw one of my best friends walk through the front door.

"Devon!" I yelled. "Get over here, man!"

He was slightly over six feet tall—about my height—with a sharp angular face, a lanky body, and long black hair that he usually tied back in a pony tail. He loved to play soccer and spent hours in the university's practice facilities, which caused us to hardly ever see him. He wanted to make sure that he maintained his scholarship and his spot on the varsity soccer team, but his goals didn't prevent him from having a good time and partying often. He claimed that his drinking and drug habits didn't interfere with his soccer, but I knew better than to believe him.

Devon made his way through the crowd and said hi to people along the way. He came over and grabbed each of us for a hug. "It's good to see you, boys! It's about time you threw a party, instead of those sausage-fests you usually have!" We laughed and Luke punched him in the shoulder to return the sentiment.

"Grab yourself a drink." I offered. "I brought plenty of the good stuff tonight."

"Yeah and there's Sprite in the fridge." Luke added. "Help yourself."

Devon poured himself a tall drink, which was typical. Any time he was given something for free he would push the limit of someone's kindness. I didn't mind, I had grown used to his habits over the years. After our cups were filled, the three of us talked between drinks and stood back as if observing the party from a distance. People at the party were playing drinking games with a deck of cards on the kitchen table, some were dancing in the living room, others were taking shots on the kitchen counter, the potheads were smoking outside, and the couples were sneaking off to a bedroom or bathroom to hook up. It had all of the signs that it would shape into a typical weekday night.

When Claire walked through the front door, I was already three sheets to the wind. She was the type of girl who didn't like it when I drank too much. She drank occasionally, but rarely compared to my habits. She had always excelled in school and was taking pre-med classes at UK, whereas my major was business. I wasn't nearly as dedicated to school as she was, because for some reason, I was more interested in business opportunities in daily life, rather than learning about them in school. When I went to class, the teachers couldn't seem to maintain my interests while I was there. I never studied as Claire did, but my test grades didn't suffer.

As she walked across the room, I walked to meet her in the middle. I caught her eye and she smiled. It was sincere and it was her smile that meant she was happy to see me. And as with any of her smiles, it was still able to make my heart race. She had a naturally athletic build and was tall and thin with dark brown hair that she always straightened and let fall over her shoulders. In some lights her eyes were deep blue and in others they were bright green, but usually they were a combination of the two. They were an aquamarine with color and life like the ocean. She was beautiful, but more than that, she had a genuine heart and she was the only person that I felt I could share my thoughts, my problems, and my successes with.

"Hey, Baby." I smiled and opened my arms. I could tell from her eyes that she had already had a few drinks herself.

"Hey!" She walked into my arms and gave me a kiss, letting her lips linger for a moment on mine.

"What's up, Ray?" I gave Rachel, Claire's best friend, a quick hug. They had been inseparable since they met in middle school when Claire had moved to Lexington. Rachel had curly black hair and a personality that loved to party.

"If you girls want a drink, I have plenty. Claire, I know you don't like Crown, but I've got Crown Royal and Sprite, then we've got some Jim Beam cooling in the freezer, and some beer in the fridge. Get whatever you want."

"Okay, I guess we'll have a beer."

"Hey, Luke!" I yelled into the kitchen. "Hey, grab a couple of Bud Light's!"

He walked over with the beers in hand and gave them to the girls. "Do you girls know how to play quarters?" He asked. They looked at him in response as if he had insulted their intelligence. Luke smiled at Rachel in apology. "Okay then, the teams are me and Rachel against you two."

I looked at Claire who shrugged in agreement. We each found seats at the kitchen table. I laughed to myself as I watched Luke make sure that he took the seat closest to Rachel. I slid some loose change across the table to Claire and let her have the first toss. She steadied herself, took aim, and bounced a quarter against the table top. The quarter landed in a glass of beer and I watched with amusement as Claire cheered. She smiled mischievously and pointed to Rachel. "I choose Ray!" And Rachel willingly complied by downing the glass of beer.

My attention was drawn across the party as I noticed someone standing in the doorway of Luke's roommate's room. I knew that his roommate was out of town for the weekend and the door was locked. It was Devon who stood in the doorway and he quickly fidgeted with the lock as he looked over his shoulder. I began to stand from the table and call him away from the door, but I decided to let him do whatever it was that he was doing. The door opened and Devon stealthily slipped inside the room.

I turned my attention back to the table and to the game of quarters where Claire and I were playing against my best friend and my girlfriend's best friend. It was easy to lose track of time while the four of us were together. It was almost as if we were having our own private party. It wasn't until we stopped playing that I realized that the rest of the party was dying down and most of the crowd had already left.

Luke, trying to be discrete, stood from the table and slipped off into his room. I thought the alcohol had caught up to him and he was sneaking away to go crawl into his bed. I took the hint and decided that it was a good time to leave. He was probably hoping that Rachel would take the hint as well and follow him into his room.

Claire had decided to stay at my house for the night, so we said goodnight to Rachel, who refused a ride back to the dorms, and the two of us got in my Jeep, a grey Grand Cherokee. We were both drunk, but I had enough practice driving that way to not worry about it. I knew where the campus police held road blocks and set up speed traps, so I took the back-roads on the outskirts of campus and we made it home without any hassles.

Throughout the entire night, Claire and I had been driving each other crazy, crazy in the best kind of way. We had been flirting, stealing kisses here and there, and whispering into each other's ears. When we got to my house, we went straight to bed. The alcohol had drowned our inhibitions and allowed us to forget the stresses and the tensions of everything else in the world. For that night, all of our problems melted away and the only thing that mattered was us, and the moment we were in.

Chapter 4: Day After, Hangover

I was in desperate need of some electrolytes. Some beta-carotene, guarana, caffeine, taurine—something. I needed something to help me get rid of my hangover and I didn't care what it was. I was dehydrated and my head was throbbing. I had just dropped Claire off at her car and I needed to make a pit stop. I pulled in to a gas station and bought an energy drink and a couple of Gatorades.

On the way to Luke's apartment I drank the energy drink, hoping that it would help ease the pain, but I knew that it would take a few minutes for the caffeine and the sugar to kick in. I pulled into a parking space near Luke's building and found his apartment door unlocked, so I let myself in. I went back to his room and found him sitting at his desk listening to rap music on his laptop, loud.

As I walked through the door, I noticed that he was playing some old school rap that happened to be one of my favorite groups.

Wu Tang Clan ain't nothin' to fuck with! ... Wu Tang Clan ain't nothin' to fuck with!

Over the music, I yelled "Introducing!....Tha Riza, tha Giza!... Tha Ghost. Face. Killah!!"

Surprised, Luke spun his chair around to face me. He turned the volume down then saw the Gatorade in my hand. His eyes lit up like a man in the desert who had just spotted an oasis. "Did you bring one of those for me?"

I looked down at the half-finished plastic bottle I was holding. "Does it look like I brought one for you?"

His hopes were shattered. His shoulders slumped and his optimistic smile turned into a scowl. He turned his chair to face his laptop. "Thanks a lot asshole."

I pulled an extra Gatorade from behind my back and hit him in the head with it, then dropped it in his lap. "Your Welcome – asshole."

He sighed with relief as he opened the bottle. It was almost empty by the time he turned his chair back to face me.

"Have you heard from Devon yet today?" I asked.

"Yeah, he should be on his way over here to pick up that ugly-ass bicycle of his. Can you believe that guy? He actually wanted me to drive all the way over to Transy to pick him up from Ethan's dorm. It's not my problem if he's too broke to buy a damn car.

I laughed. "So how's he planning to get over here?"

"Ethan's dropping him off."

"Huh, where did he go last night? I looked up and he was gone."

"I don't know, I guess Ethan picked him up." Luke answered dismissively, and then hit a button on his laptop and the volume came back.

M-E-T-H-O-D Man! ... M-E-T-H-O-D Man! ...

"Hey, hold on, turn that down for a minute." I said, taking a seat on his bed. "What happened with you and Rachel last night?"

He turned the volume down, but remained facing the computer screen. "What do you mean?"

I laughed. "Come on, man. You know exactly what I mean. Did you hook up with her, or not?"

"Well," he hesitated, "not really."

"Not really? How do you not really hook up with her? It's one of those things that you either do or you don't."

He spun his chair around to face me. "We were about to, but she left." He said as if he was exasperated by the thought of last night, and slightly embarrassed.

"Ohhh, that sounds like a big no to me!"

"Shut up, man. It's not funny." He leaned over and punched me in the leg, then pulled his arm back to swing again.

I couldn't keep myself from laughing. "Alright, alright, I'll stop. But, you have to admit it's kind of funny."

He didn't smile.

I hadn't heard the front door open, but Devon popped in the room wearing his backpack and his usual charisma. "Hey, boys!" He said with a smile. "What's going on in here?"

Ever since I had met Devon in high school, he had always carried himself in a unique way. He would occasionally adopt some European words into his vocabulary and he typically dressed in a stark mismatch of colors, but he always managed to wear them flamboyantly, or at least, proudly. As he occupied the doorway, he wore blue jeans, a pair of leather sandals, and a bright yellow polo shirt with the collar popped.

"Hey, Devon." Luke said. "I thought we lost you. What happened to you last night, you just disappeared."

"Yeah, Ethan came by to get me because they were having a hall party over at Transy."

"I bet that was fun…" I said sarcastically.

Devon gave me a sideways glare, then turned back toward Luke. "Hey, let me get the laminator. I've got to head out. Where did you put it?"

"What do you need it for?"

"What do you think I need it for? Come on, man, I'm kind of in a hurry, so where is it?"

"What's the rush?" I asked.

"I've got some people waiting on me back at the dorms."

With a huff, Luke stood from his desk chair and opened a closet door. He shuffled some clothes around on the floor and pulled something out from under a pile in the back corner. He handed Devon a box that was slightly larger than a football. "Here, don't do anything stupid with it. I want it back in one piece. And I expect my cut." He added.

Devon responded with a sly smile. "Of course you'll get your cut. It's me you're talking to here." He unzipped his backpack and stuffed the box inside.

They had been in business together since the semester began about a month ago. Back in high school they had acquired a knack for making fake I.D.'s – which was why I never had trouble buying alcohol – so it was only natural that their skill was carried over into the college market where there was an abundance of underage drinkers. Even though they were only freshmen, they had become the go-to guys for anyone that needed a high quality fake I.D.. It was amazing what they could do with a scanner, Photoshop, and a laser printer. They were charging an outrageous price of eighty dollars per license, but they had more business than they could handle. People were lining up to buy from them because they could provide something that no one else could, a hologram. It was the one thing that every vendor examined on a driver's license to check for authenticity.

They couldn't do it alone though. They had help from an art student at the local private college, Transylvania University. He was a childhood friend of Devon's named Ethan, who was beyond gifted at anything artistic. Transylvania had given him a full scholarship and he was the top student in their highly renowned art program. So when Devon had asked him if he could create a hologram for his fake I.D.'s, it was no problem. For Ethan, that was simple. With a dab of golden-foil paint, a thin brush, and the steady hand of an artist, he was able to recreate Kentucky's insignia flawlessly on each card.

The three of them were making good money with the I.D.'s, but it only seemed to be enough to cover their expenses, especially Devon. He was always trying to scrounge together enough money to buy his next bag of weed, the occasional bottle of Goldschlager Liquor, or any form of pills or pain killers that happened to be available at the time. He knew his habits weren't helping him as a soccer player, but he wasn't willing to quit—or even slow down. For his sake, I hoped he could.

"Okay, boys, that's it for me. I'm off to the dorms." Devon said as he slung his back pack into position over his shoulder and walked toward the door.

"Hey!" Luke yelled after him. "Make sure you take that piece of crap bicycle with you!"

"I know you're not talking about Speed Racer like that!" He yelled back to us as I laughed, thinking about the scrap metal that he called a bike. It was a hand-me-down from another era. His dad had given it to him and it was one of the few things that Devon actually owned. He didn't have a car, so he rode the old racing bicycle everywhere. I had to admit that it fit him perfectly. It was like an ornament to his already peculiar sense of style.

"Hey, Devon, hang on a sec." I said before he slipped out of the apartment.

Devon popped his head through the open gap in the doorway. "What's up?"

"Hey, did you go in The Donny's room, last night?"

"Maybe…"

"What the hell, Devon?" Luke asked, slightly offended. "The Donny's out of town and I locked his room so that people like you wouldn't go in there."

"People like me?"

"Yeah, people who steal shit. So let's hear it. What did you take?"

"Nothing. You boys are overreacting. It's not a big deal, trust me."

"If it's not a big deal then just tell us." I replied.

"Fine. If you really want to know, I took a blank check from his checkbook."

"Damn it, Devon! Put it back!" Luke insisted.

"It's too late for that. I cashed it before I got here. But it's not a big deal. It was just forty bucks. The Donny won't even notice that it's gone."

"Still, man, you're stealing from my roommate and I'm not cool with that."

"Alright, alright. It was a one time thing, 'cause I'm trying to save up some money for this trip. But don't worry about it. It won't happen again."

"And the same goes for my roommates, Devon." I added. "Stealing *anything* from *anyone* who lives in my house is off limits. Understand?"

"Yeah. But I gotta run. I'll see you boys later."

Devon's head disappeared from the doorway, and he was gone.

I had a few other errands to run, so I stood to leave. "Well, I'm out of here too, Luke. I'll call you later if anything's going on."

"Alright, later."

I was feeling much better than I had when I first showed up at Luke's. The fluids were finally catching up with me and my headache was fading. I walked out and could hear the music from Luke's laptop as he turned back to whatever he was doing earlier. I climbed into my Jeep and drove the short trip down Alumni Drive and was at my Mom's house within a few minutes.

I noticed that my mom's black BMW X5 was in the driveway as I pulled to a stop. I stepped out of the Jeep and went around to the side door of the house. All of the lights were off. It was the middle of the afternoon, but the house was dark, which worried me, because I knew that my mom spent most afternoons alone while my brother and sister were in school. My brother was three years younger than me, a freshman following in my footsteps at Lexington Catholic High School where I had graduated, and my sister was in her first year of middle school, and three years younger than my brother. I walked into the house and was greeted with excitement from our family's two black Labradors. Their happy demeanors quieted my worries, because I knew they wouldn't let anything happen to her as long as they were in the house with her.

"Hello?" I yelled into the quiet two story house. "Is anyone home? Mom? Are you here?" But no one responded aside from the echo of my own voice within the spacious rooms.

I walked downstairs through the large, open room where I once lived. It was a rec-room with tiled floors, a pool table, and a foosball table, a wrap around bar along one wall and an entertainment center along another. My room, which had become my brother's room, was in the back corner.

He had left the layout the same. Bed, nightstand, TV cabinet, and dresser. One wall had remained exactly as I had left it. There were built-in shelves that held my life's achievements that my brother called, The Wall. There were rows of trophies and medals and a gold state championship ring. Game-balls and autographs from famous athletes. My sports career, my childhood spent in basketball gyms, baseball diamonds, and soccer fields was alive on that wall. I had told my brother that he could take it down and box all of that old stuff up, but he had said that he wanted to leave it there as a reminder of me. I even noticed, as I walked through my old room, that my brother had blended his achievements and trophies in with my own along The Wall.

I went into a storage room that was connected to my old bedroom and found my safe, where I had left it hidden above an air vent. The safe was small, heavy, and fire-proof. I pulled it down from above the vent. I unlocked it with a small key from my key-ring and opened it to the reassuring sight of my personal savings, a stack of neatly pressed fifty dollar and one hundred dollar bills. My savings began at the age of twelve when my dad had helped me start a lawn care business. I mostly provided upkeep for the properties that his real estate company owned or managed. But each year the lawn care service continued to grow. I eventually hired friends as laborers and operated the service as a manager. Under my dad's guidance, I also became a licensed apprentice of real estate appraisals, and learned the personal property and estate auction business working for the Thompson & Riley auction house of downtown Lexington, a company which he co-owned. At the age of sixteen, I bought my first rental property, thanks to the willingness of my dad to co-sign on the loan. The first property was used as collateral to purchase the next property, and the next, until two years later, we owned three rental properties together. Upon my graduation of college, he had promised to relinquish his share of ownership as a gift for the future.

But the equity that accrued from the rental properties was intangible without my dad's signature and the modest stack of bills that I kept squirreled away in my safe after several years of hard, honest work was something that I could hold within my hands and spend or save as I desired. And I was proud of the money I had saved. Flipping through the bills, I made sure that everything was still there. It was. I counted thirty of the one hundred dollar bills and stuffed them into my pocket. I re-locked the safe and slid it back into its hiding place.

Before I left the house, I stopped in the kitchen for a snack. I opened the refrigerator and couldn't believe how bare it was. I couldn't seem to find anything substantial. I noticed a bag of salad, some old fruit that was bruised and hardly edible, a few boxes of Chinese take-out, and the usual condiments of butter, mustard, ketchup, mayonnaise, and pickles.

I heard a door open behind me, followed by my mom's voice, which sounded tired but sincere. "Charlie, what are you doing here?" She asked, standing in the darkened doorway wearing a robe and slippers. I could tell that I had just woken her from a nap. She wasn't wearing any make-up, but she had never needed to. She had always been beautiful in an effortless sort of way. She was petite and slim with light brown hair and soft brown eyes.

"Hello, Mom." I said, trying to not be overly judgmental about what she was wearing or about how late in the afternoon she had slept, because more than anyone, I understood how hard the divorce had been on her. I knew all too well how often she put a smile on her face for the benefit of the rest of the family, but truly, behind the facade I knew things were falling apart. Our way of life was changing and there was nothing that could be done to stop it. For some reason though, I felt compelled to try.

"I was trying to find something to eat, but you don't have anything." I complained.

"Sure we do. What do you want, I'll fix you something."

I swung the refrigerator door open so that she could see. "Mom, there's nothing in there."

"Well, you have to check the cabinets too. There's plenty to eat. You just have to look around." She insisted in her slight southern drawl.

I opened the six-foot cabinet doors that once held row after row of food. It too, was deserted.

"Mom, there's no food in there either. What have you guys been eating?"

"We've been eating fine. We must've just run out." She said, and from the pain in her voice, I knew her words weren't as true as she wanted them to be.

"Then go to the grocery."

"Don't worry about it, I will."

"No. How about this? Let's go right now. Come on, I'll go with you." I suggested, attempting to motivate her.

"No, Charlie, its okay."

"Come on." I pulled her toward the doorway. "You go on up to your room and get dressed. I'll take you out to lunch, and then we can go to the grocery."

She tried to pull back, away from the door. "Charlie, stop it!" She demanded.

"No, come on, we're going!" I insisted as I continued to pull.

"Stop it, I can't!"

"Yes, you can! We're going!"

Forcefully, she jerked herself away. "I can't go!" She blurted, then began to sob. I watched as her eyes welled with tears. "I don't have any money!"

It had been almost a year since my dad had walked out on us. I could still vividly remember the night when he left. My mom had stood up for herself and confronted him about an inner-office affair. He packed his bags, and on the way out the door, he stopped and shook my hand. He looked at me with eyes hazel and green like a reflection of my own. He told me to take care of my mom, brother, and sister, and I shook his hand with a firm grip, looked into his eyes and promised him I would. Then he left, and as he walked out the door all the money we were accustomed to went with him. My mom had worked as his partner, managing several companies and keeping the books for nearly half her of life, and because she refused to work in the same office as his mistress, who was also his secretary, my mom was unemployed, heartbroken, and flat broke.

She had burned through the credit cards and any stray bank accounts that she was aware of, until he realized what she was doing and cancelled and closed them all. She had saved a frugal amount of money to last our family through any dry spells while the divorce and litigation wore on, but her savings must have run dry.

"What? I thought you had some saved up." I asked.

"It's all gone." She cried. "And your father is trying to freeze me out. Everything's late, the house payment, my car, the utilities – they're all past due." She held her face in her hands, ashamed. I looked around. The only light in the whole house was the glow of the open refrigerator door. I wondered if the lack of money was the reason for the darkness.

She must have read my thoughts, because she answered my unasked question. "To save money, I turn all the lights off until Blake and Sydney get home from school. Please don't tell them though." She begged. "I don't want them to worry."

Furious, an anger rose within me like a mercury thermometer left under the sun on an August afternoon. I couldn't believe that anyone, least of all, my dad, would be so cruel to his own family. There had to be an explanation for his actions.

"Why hasn't Dad given you any money? I thought the court ordered him to pay for everything until the divorce is final."

"They did, but he won't do it. He said he wouldn't give me anymore money until I agreed to his terms."

"Terms? What terms?" I asked, confused. The divorce proceedings had been dragging on for almost a year. Both sides were ready for it all to be over, but neither wanted to budge when it came to their demands.

"He wants me to sign a deal, so he doesn't have to go through the court and the attorneys anymore."

"Then sign it." I answered simply.

"I can't. Charlie, I've worked too hard. You don't understand. I've worked for your father for twenty years and never even asked for a paycheck.

I've helped him get to where he is today, but he won't give me what I deserve."

"What's his offer?"

"He wants to give me this house and enough money to pay our expenses for a few months, but he's mad at me because I want half. I have to think about you kids! This is about our future! I'm forty-three years old! I'm too old to start over! I've worked half of my life for nothing! And that's what I'm going to be left with—nothing!" She cried. "What did I ever do to deserve this?"

It hurt me to stand there and watch her cry, knowing that there was nothing that I could do to make her pain stop. I knew the game that my dad was playing and I despised him for it. He would stall his court ordered payments as long as possible in order to freeze her into submission. His tactics and his cold heart made me ashamed to be his son. I knew that I couldn't stop my mom's pain, but if I could make things easier, at least in some small way, then I was determined to be the man of the house in the absence of one.

She broke my train of thought with the sound of her deflated voice. "What am I supposed to do, Charlie? Just start flipping hamburgers at McDonald's?"

I laughed softly. "No one's going to be flipping hamburgers, so you don't have to worry about that."

She chuckled as she wiped the tears from her eyes. "But, what am I supposed to do?"

"Just do whatever you have to do and don't worry about all of the other stuff. The four of us – me, you, Blake, and Sydney – we're the core of this family, we'll make it. We always do."

She hugged me then, and spoke through a sniffling nose. "I know we will. We always do."

"Alright, Mom, how much do you need?"

"No, Charlie, don't worry about it. I'm fine"

"No, you're obviously not fine. I'm serious. Tell me how much money you need to get caught up."

"It's okay, the banks have been helpful. I told them the situation and they haven't been charging us any interest."

I cut her off. "How much?"

"Twenty-five hundred, but you don't need to worry about all of this. Hopefully your father will help us out soon."

"Don't count on it." I answered quickly. I pulled the money from my pocket and set it down on the counter. "Here, that's three thousand. The extra five hundred is for groceries."

She stared at the money apprehensively as if it was wrapped in razor-wire. "Charlie, where'd you get all that cash?"

"Don't worry about it. I've been saving up for emergencies too." I had, but I knew my meager savings wouldn't last against the accumulated monthly expense of an upper middle-class family. I knew I would have to find a way to make more money than lawn care, live auctions, residential appraisals, or even gambling could offer.

"Charlie, that's a lot of money to be just carrying around."

"It's no big deal, just go put some clothes on and lets go get some lunch."

She walked to her room to get ready, and left me there as I waited in the glow of the empty refrigerator, contemplating what the future would hold.

Chapter 5: Casino Royale

When the car pulled up, I was nervous.

I stood on the curb with my back toward my house, but I could still hear the noise. The bass from the music, the guys yelling, and the girls screaming all jumbled together to make one unmistakable sound; the sound of a college party. It was a typical weekday night. Ever since I had bought the one and a half story tan brick house on Beaumont Avenue and started classes, it seemed like every night ended the same way. A few people would come over and we would have a few drinks. Then more people would lead to more drinks. I was still only in my first semester, but I was already tired of the monotony.

The party was getting too loud. We had elderly neighbors who liked to sleep early, and on most nights, we made that impossible. We would be lucky if they didn't call the campus police and ruin the fun for everyone. The cops would show up and force us to turn off the music and send everyone home. Let them come, I thought. My roommates, Alex and Brian, would have to deal with them for a change, because I had other plans.

The dark green Lexus had stopped silently in front of me. The windows were tinted, but I knew the driver was watching as I walked around to the passenger side and opened the door. I took one last look at the party, then slid into the car.

It was Luke who was sitting behind the wheel. I quickly noticed from his demeanor that he was all about business tonight. There was no hint of the usual pessimistic glare. His round face was set in a mask of determination and his shaggy blonde hair was hidden under a black toboggan, which matched his black sweat suit. He pointed to a duffle bag at my feet.

"Your clothes are in there."

I glanced down and gave him a slight nod of acknowledgment. "I'll change when we get there."

He understood, and the car crept away from the party. Neither of us looked back. I let my thoughts drift away as we rode closer to the decision that had already been made. I thought about changing my mind. It wasn't too late, I could still turn back, we both could, but I remained silent as the homes and the downtown neighborhoods passed us by. I didn't know whether or not I would be able to look myself in the mirror tomorrow, but I decided that I would have to try.

"Is this it?" Luke asked, breaking my concentration.

We were slowly approaching a large apartment complex. "Yeah, just park down the street though."

Luke found a secluded stretch of curb that was shrouded in the darkness of the overcast night like pale skin beneath a cloak, and parked. He cut the headlights and let the car idle as we prepared ourselves. I took the duffle bag from the floorboard and emptied the contents into my lap. I was relieved to see that everything was there. I kicked off my brown oxfords and stripped out of my khaki pants and blue button-down shirt. I replaced them with black sweatpants, a hooded sweatshirt, and a pair of sneakers. I filled my pockets with a few essential items. In my left pocket, I placed a flashlight and into my right pocket, I stuffed a thin compactable bag. Luke was carrying a few other important items, but I knew that I didn't need to ask if he had them. I pulled a pair of black leather gloves over my hands, then pulled a black toboggan over my head. As Luke's was, the toboggan was also a ski mask with holes cut for the mouth and eyes, but it wasn't time to pull them down yet.

We rolled the windows down and sat in silence as we observed the area. It was after two o'clock in the morning and most people seemed to be asleep or secluded within the solitude of their apartments. We waited for several minutes and didn't see or hear signs of anyone coming of going within the complex. I knew that it wasn't likely that we would be able to reach our destination without someone noticing us, but we wouldn't take long and we were relying on the cover of darkness to conceal us.

Without words, we both knew that it was now or never. Luke rolled up the windows and I turned toward him. I couldn't see the expression of my own face, but I imagined that it was probably similar to the expression that Luke looked back at me with. He seemed calm and revealed no outward emotion other than determination, but his eyes spoke the truth. They were wide open, alert, and attentive. I knew that he was suppressing the butterflies that were flittering in his stomach just as I was. I felt that a little nervousness could be a good thing at times. I thought it might even help us focus. I held my hand in front of my face to see if it was shaking. It wasn't, my hand was steady.

"Check your hand, Luke. Is it steady?"

He held a black gloved hand out toward me and it remained motionless.

"Good." I chuckled wryly at the absurdity of the circumstance and the cloak-and-dagger attitude that we had each assumed. "We're both steady. I guess that's a good thing."

"Yeah, you ready to go?" He announced flatly.

"Yeah, let's get this over with."

We pulled our masks down and lifted our hoods so that our faces were nothing more than shadows. I felt safe hidden behind the black fabric, although my eyes seemed vulnerable and naked for what I was about to do, like two open windows to my soul, but it was too late to turn back. We stepped out of the car and left it quietly humming along the curb behind us.

For protection, I lifted the Saint Christopher medallion that hung from my neck and kissed it for good luck. Within the solitude of my mind, I prayed to a dear friend who had passed away and asked him to watch over me and bring me safely through the night, so that I may live to see the next day. I let the medallion fall back inside my shirt to hang close to my heart and stepped ahead of Luke.

I led the way through a memorized pattern of dimly lit sidewalks. I could feel the adrenaline pulsing through me and I could hear the faint sound of my footsteps increasing in speed. I tried to keep my head tilted down and straight ahead, while my eyes darted from side to side, searching for anyone who may happen to walk by or glance out from a window. I didn't notice anyone, and kept moving forward. In what seemed like an eternity later, we reached the building that housed Bullfrog's casino.

Everything within the building looked dark, almost as if it were deserted. I could hear the muffled sound of cars off in the distance, driving along the road even though the hour was beyond late. The wind was blowing gently and seemed to whistle through the grass as slight gusts buffeted between buildings. I attempted to make my foot falls light and hoped they were drowned out by the other ambient noises as we made our approach.

There was an unmarked door that I knew to be the maintenance room. A week prior, I had wandered through the complex in search of the individual power supply that ran into each apartment, but I couldn't find them. I knew that every building that connected to the city power grid had an accessible meter for utility usage readings. If the meters weren't outside I knew that they had to be somewhere within the buildings. To find the maintenance room I spent an afternoon in the county clerk's office researching the layout of the complex. It was a trick that I had learned as an appraiser.

As I stood before the maintenance room, under the glow of the security light, I was thankful for what I had learned, but I felt exposed and out in the open under the light. I was eager to get inside, so I tried the door, only to find it locked.

"Shit." I whispered.

Within an instant, Luke was by my side with a box cutter in hand. He slid the blade down the crevice in the door until he found the bolt. He worked quickly, trying to wiggle the blade behind the lock and push it back in place. My eyes alternated between watching his progress and scanning the windows and doors for any sign of movement. There was a blue glow, flashing in one of the second story windows across from us.

Then I heard it. Something metal had snapped and fallen to the concrete path with a high-pitched clang. "Fuck!" I heard Luke grunt in frustration and I realized that it was the razor blade that had snapped. "Here." He said, handing me a crowbar. "See if you can make some space."

I stepped in front of him and wedged the bar in the door. I pushed side to side, feeling the wood creak and fracture under the pressure.

"There, try it now." I whispered impatiently.

He clicked a new blade into place and I pulled back, giving him room to maneuver. It wasn't long before he held the bolt back and was able to pull open the door. I took one last glance over my shoulder to check if anyone was watching, then eagerly ducked inside. We clicked our flash lights on as I shut the door behind us.

The room was eerily quiet like a vacant concrete tomb. Our flashlights failed to cut through the complete darkness, forcing us to scan the room slowly. Along the walls, we found clusters of electricity meters that were grouped in fours. I stepped closer to take a better look and was relieved to see that they were each labeled by the corresponding apartment number. I glanced through them quickly and found the rapidly spinning meters of apartments 212 and 213. Even after hours, Bullfrog's homemade security system seemed to be working overtime.

"Let me see that box cutter." I whispered. Luke handed it to me and I hooked the razor under the tight metal band that held the meter in place. I pulled the razor up sharply and the band sprang loose. It clanged and clashed like a tiny circus as it clattered against the floor, and I cringed warily at the sudden noise. I felt certain that someone outside of the maintenance room could have heard the crash of metal and concrete. I didn't waste any time as I did the same to the next band, but didn't let it fall, then returned the cutter to Luke. I took a firm grip around one of the whirring meters and braced myself as I pulled it out of the socket as if I were unplugging a giant outlet. The whirring instantly died and I felt myself exhale. If everything went as I expected, there would be an electricity outage in apartment 212, followed shortly by an outage in apartment 213. We left two lifeless meters lying on the floor as we made our way to the door.

I glanced out into the open air and saw not a soul. We stepped out into the night and walked briskly as we crept through the grass, hugging close to the building's brick wall. We kept moving until we reached the back of the building.

"This is it." I said quietly as I looked up to a small, second story ledge. The small sliver of concrete was just big enough for a person to stand. I assumed that the ledge was intended to hold window gardens, but for the moment, it served a greater purpose. Luke placed his foot in my hands and stretched upwards as I boosted him toward the ledge. He grabbed a firm hold

and scrambled upright. I watched as he reached for the window. I wasn't
entirely sure that there would be no alarm system, but I hoped that my plan to
cut the power would disable any of Bullfrog's active security systems. I
watched Luke pull against the window and sighed in relief as it slid open.
Somehow, it wasn't even locked. We had reluctantly planned on cutting the
glass or even breaking it if we had to, so I took the unlocked window as a good
sign. But I was torn, because a part of me believed that the seeming stroke of
luck could have been a fluke and we were unknowingly climbing into further
danger.

     I watched as Luke slipped through the open window and I knew that
it was too late to second guess myself. I prepared to make the jump. The ledge
looked to be between nine and a half and ten feet high. I had played basketball
long enough to know that I could reach it. I just needed to concentrate and get
a good jump. I took a few steps back and let the adrenaline of the moment push
me upward. My hands caught the concrete ledge and I hurried to pull myself
up until I was crouched outside the window.

     In a panic stricken instant, I saw a hand reach out for me. My breath
caught and my heart skipped a beat, two beats, then I realized that it was only
Luke. I let him help me crawl through the window. We fumbled through our
pockets until we found our flashlights. They flicked to life with two beams of
light. I panned the bare room revealing the taupe walls, the blackjack table,
and the empty stools. I knew where the cameras were mounted and I attempted
to avoid looking in their direction. I had to hope that the electricity supply had
been cut. If they were battery operated, then there would be nothing that we
could do but rely on our disguises.

     I crept forward, one hesitant step after another. There was an odd
stillness in the air. I could hear nothing but the breath escaping from my lungs
and the beat of my heart pounding against the wall of my chest like a deranged
prisoner. I stopped. I listened closer. The apartment was filled with a stagnant
silence like the basement of a funeral home or like a hospice center, long after
all of the patients had checked out. I continued forward and let the flashlight
guide my steps. The beam crossed the roulette tables, the poker tables, and
then illuminated Bullfrog's desk. I tried to swallow, but my throat was dry as
cotton.

I approached the desk apprehensively. I crouched, looking to find the compartment that I had seen weeks earlier, hoping that my suspicions about what was kept inside were true. I found the compartment and reached back for Luke to hand me the crowbar. I placed it in the crevice and pushed violently against the wood. I slid the bar deeper until it found purchase. I shoved again, grunting with the effort. The wooden cabinet groaned in vain like an old man realizing the end was near, then I heard a loud crack. The wood splintered around the lock and the door swung open.

Luke shined his flashlight into the dark interior. Exactly where it had been before, I saw the metal box. I lifted it. It was heavy. I shook the box gently and heard a rustling sound and the sound of something shifting against the metal.

"Jackpot!" I whispered to myself. I pulled the black compactable bag from my pocket and shuffled the box inside. I turned toward Luke. "Let's go."

We both stood and checked our pockets. We had everything that we came with and everything that we came for. It was time to go. We made our way through the dark apartment the same way we had entered. I handed the bag to Luke as I crawled out through the window. I glanced toward the ground and the surrounding windows. I saw no reason to stop. I dropped to the grass below, landing harder than I expected. The bag was tossed down to me as I waited for Luke to jump. He closed the window behind him and dropped to the ground.

I walked as fast as my legs would carry me through an alternate maze of sidewalks. I was vaguely aware of Luke's footsteps behind me. I wasn't worried about the police attempting to track us down. But I was acutely aware, as I walked away, that the only person that would be after us was Bullfrog. He would seek his own justice and impose his own punishment, which was something that I could live my entire life and never hope to experience. Our only option was to not get caught. A thrill entered my heart as I found Luke's car still humming quietly in the street. The Lexus looked better to me than it ever had before, like an oasis in the desert after weeks in the sand, like food for the starving, like homes for the homeless, and like freedom, because as thieves, it was our escape. We each slid through the doors and sped away.

I went to work on the metal box as Luke navigated the car through neighborhoods and side streets to avoid traffic and an undesirable run in with the law. It took several minutes to wedge the crowbar into the seams, but eventually the box gave way. I opened the ruined lid and used my flashlight to look inside. Luke was still driving, but his eyes weren't on the road; they were glued to the inside of the box just as mine were. What I noticed first were the envelopes. I thumbed through them, then tore one open. I was amazed to find a stack of bills inside. It was what I had hoped for and what I had truly expected to be in the box. But seeing it and holding it in my hands was still a surprise.

"How much is in there?" Luke's excited voice asked.

"I don't know." I said, flipping through the bills. "There's probably a few thousand just in this one envelope!" I piled the envelopes into my lap and realized that the box was not yet empty. Lining the bottom of the box, there was an assortment of casino chips. They were high-dollar chips that had been custom designed only for use at Bullfrog's casino. The values were higher than I had ever seen used. Each chip was labeled with a number greater than one thousand. I could hardly believe my eyes. I felt an impulsive desire to keep the chips, because I knew they had to amount to a small fortune, but I knew better. They were only redeemable through Bullfrog, and under the circumstances, that made them worthless. I set the box filled with thousands of dollars of unredeemable chips in the floorboard and I turned my attention to the envelopes. I tore each one open and stuffed the money into the black bag.

"Hey, man." I pointed to a storm sewer on the side of the road. "Pull over up there."

The car came to a stop and I opened the glove box where I knew there was a lighter. I held a stack of torn envelopes in my hand and lit them on fire.

"What the fuck, man!" Luke shouted. "Get that shit out of my car! You're gonna burn my seats!"

"Hold on. Let it burn a little more."

I watched carefully as the flames licked the white paper, quickly devouring the evidence.

"I'm serious, Chas, open the door!"

I popped open the door and held the paper near the mouth of the sewer drain until I could feel the heat from the fire through the tips of my gloved fingers. Finally, I let them go and watched the sparks drift off into the sewer. I took the box from the floorboard and looked at the chips one more time. I hated to do it, but it had to be done. I dumped the contents of the box into the sewer and watched with a heavy heart as thousands of dollars of worthless clay chips sank into the filth.

"Why the hell did you do that?" Luke asked, shocked.

"They were only good if Bullfrog paid for them and I wouldn't want to be caught trying to cash them in. Would you?"

"Oh."

I shut the door and we drove away. "Are you sure you don't want to try to cash them in?" I joked, finally feeling a wave of relief that our escape was almost finished. "Because if not, we could still turn back and you could fish them out of the sewer." I smiled, but he didn't laugh.

We found a dumpster several neighborhoods away and tossed the empty metal box inside. When we pulled into the driveway of my house, I noticed that the party had died down, but there were a few stragglers still hanging around. Luke and I had changed out of the sweat suits and back into our regular khaki and button-down attire. We took the back way into my house and went straight up to my room and locked the door behind us. Even though I had left the party only an hour ago it felt like it was in the distant past.

I emptied the black bag and let the contents fall on the bed.

I was speechless as I stared blankly toward the pile of money lying in front of me. It was mostly loose cash, but some stacks were bundled with rubber bands.

"How much do you think it is?" Luke asked.

I let a smile slide across my face. "I don't know. Let's count it."

We dug into the pile and began counting. We went through it several times and finally, we agreed on a number.

"Fifty-Six thousand, three hundred dollars! Can you believe it! That's like a Porsche piled up right there!" Luke said, trying to contain his excitement. I was also trying to contain my own excitement, but I knew that we shared the emotion for different reasons.

I split the remaining pile in half. I took my cut and gave him his. "There, that's over twenty-eight grand in cash! For each of us!"

We both counted our share to double-check the math, and for a brief moment I was happy. It wasn't a deserved happiness. I didn't earn it in an honest way, but I knew that I would have to live with my decision. I would have to live with whatever the consequences would be. It was my first attempt at crime, and unlike honest work, the repercussions for failure could potentially cost me my life. In that moment, I only felt the success of my decision. I reasoned with myself that maybe it wasn't truly a crime that I had committed. Maybe because the money had already been obtained through illegal means, then I was only stealing from someone who stole from others. But my conscience wouldn't let me believe that. I knew what I had done was wrong, but what it had come down to was the question of Bullfrog or my family, and given the choice, I would always choose my family. I smiled and thought that maybe everything would be okay after all.

Chapter 6: Party On

The music was so loud that I could hardly hear myself think. It was old-school funk night at my house and James Brown was screaming through the speakers.

I feel good!... Like I knew that I would!... I feel good! . . .

Between the music and the alcohol in my system I couldn't think clearly, but for some reason, I had the impression that I felt good, and that seemed to be the only necessary thought at the moment.

My house was filled with people and most of them were crammed into one small room in the back. There was a beer-pong table at the center of everyone's attention, where Luke and I were defending our status as the only unbeaten team of the night and also as the only unbeaten team of the semester.

Every house played by their own rules, but the basics of the game were universal. At my house, two people would stand on each side of a ping-pong table. Each team had ten plastic cups in the shape of a triangle in front of them. All twenty cups were filled halfway with beer and the object of the game was for each team to throw or bounce a ping-pong ball into the opposite team's cups. When a team made a shot, one of the opposing players had to chug whatever was in the cup. A throw was worth one cup and a bounce was worth two. On offense, a team would have two shots, one for each partner. If a ball was thrown then the other team was unable to play defense, but if it was bounced then the other team could attempt to block the shot with their hand. Defense wasn't difficult, but if a team didn't pay attention to the game they could fall behind quickly. There was only one other thing that the defending team could do to prevent a shot from going in. If a ball was spinning around the rim of the cup, someone could blow the ball out, before it splashed into the beer.

The first team to get rid of all the other teams' cups, making them drink beer in the process, was the winner. The winning team then stayed on the table to play the next challengers, while the losers had to chug the remaining cups from the winner's side.

Luke and I had already won several games and were refilling the cups to play again when my phone rang. I checked the caller I.D. and saw my brother's number on the screen.

"Hey, Luke!" I said, trying to talk over the music and all of the commotion. "Hey, I'm going to sit this next one out! I'll be back in a few minutes!"

I nudged my way through the crowd, through the Beer-Pong room, through the kitchen, into the living room where I found the door to my room. My room, shaped long and narrow like a shotgun-ranch, was the entire top floor of the one and a half story house. The walls were lined with antique furniture that I had bought through my family's auction house. There were pictures of friends and family standing in frames atop the available wooden surfaces, then in contrast to the mature furnishing of my room, there were also posters scattered along the walls displaying my favorite movies and icons of cinema, along with several hundred DVD's towering in racks on either side of my Xbox and flat screen TV. I hurried through the door and ran up the straight set of stairs that opened into my room.

I opened my phone as I tried to catch my breath. "Hello?"

"Hello?" My brother answered back.

"Bubble O!"

"Hey, what are you doing?" He asked.

"I've got a party going on at my house right now. Why? Is everything alright? Where's Mom? Where's Sydney?" I demanded, my voice almost rising to the point of panic. My sister, Sydney, was only eleven and Blake had recently turned fifteen. If anything went wrong, I felt that it was my responsibility to try to help them.

"Mom's out with her friends and Sydney's sleeping over at a friend's house." He answered easily.

"So, everything's cool?"

"Yeah. I'm just looking for something to do tonight. Jake and I were wondering if we could come hang out with you."

Blake and his friend were both freshmen in high school. By that age, most kids had already started drinking. I reasoned that if he was going to drink, regardless of what anyone told him, then I would rather let him drink with me where I knew he would be safe than to let him stumble through the experience anywhere else.

"Of course, man." I answered. "Do you need a ride over here?"

"Yeah, we don't exactly have licenses."

"I might not exactly have one either, if I get pulled over tonight." I paused, considering my options. I had been drinking for several hours, but I didn't feel drunk. I believed that I could make the short drive for my brother's sake. I decided that I would. "I'll be there in a few minutes. Be ready to go when I get there."

I ended the call and looked to the staircase where I heard someone running up to my room. A head, then a whole body appeared, and I realized that it was Luke.

"Hey, what are you doing up here?" He asked.

"Nothing, I'm getting ready to leave."

"Why? Where are you going?"

"Nowhere, I'm just going to pick up my brother."

He seemed relieved. "Are you picking him up from your mom's house?"

"Yeah, why? Do you want to go?"

"No, I was just wondering if you could do me a favor."

"Sure, what's up?"

"When you're over there, could you pull some of my money out of your safe?"

I had agreed to keep Luke's take from the casino hidden with my own and I wasn't surprised that he already wanted to make a withdraw. "Sure. How much do you want?"

"I don't know. Maybe thirty five hundred?"

I laughed. "Alright, I gotcha. I'll be back in about ten minutes."

We both walked down the stairs. He stepped back into the party as I cut through the crowd and out the front door. People were huddled in small groups on the porch and I could smell the pungent aroma of marijuana along with a hint of cigarette smoke as I walked through their self induced fog.

I stepped into my Jeep Grand Cherokee feeling, but not quite acknowledging, a desire to be reckless. I drove into the street with the windows down and the moon roof open to the clouds of the night sky. I allowed the pedal to creep toward the floorboard as if it were being pulled by an unknown magnetism. My Jeep careened down the side streets of once quiet neighborhoods as I held the wheel like a captain who had resigned the fate of his ship to the mercy of the winds, leaving nothing in my wake but the roar of an engine and the low rumble of music in the air.

I don't practice Santeria!

I ain't got no crystal ball!

I had a million dollars,

But I, I spent it all!

Somehow, I survived the ride and my brother and his friend, Jake, were waiting on the porch when I screeched to a halt in front of the house. Jake was a football player with buzzed hair and a body too big and developed for his age. There was no reason to wonder why he had been asked to play for the varsity team as a freshman. He and my brother were such good friends that Jake had become like a brother to me also.

I watched as my brother, and my assumed brother, walked eagerly to the car. Jake jumped into the back seat and Blake took the front. Sitting there, I knew that he and I looked almost identical. We had many of the same features; hazel eyes, a quick and easy smile, a thin, athletic frame, though his hair was a brown several shades lighter than my own and he stood a few inches shorter than me.

"Hey, hang out here for a minute." I said as I stepped out of the car. They looked confused, but didn't respond.

I jogged to the side of the house and paused outside of the garage. I pressed the code into the keyless entry pad and waited as the door was lifted and light from within spilled onto the driveway. I hurried downstairs to where my safe was hidden. I pulled it down and opened it to find two thick, neatly separated stacks of money, one larger than the other. I removed thirty five of the hundred dollar bills from the smaller stack and ten from the larger. I stuffed them into my pocket, locked and returned the safe, then hurried back to my car where Blake and Jake were still patiently waiting.

I pushed the pedal down, consciously driving with care now that I was not alone. Within a few minutes, we made it back to the party. I pulled easily into my driveway and parked.

"Hey, before you two go in there." I said "If anybody asks, especially girls, you tell them that you're freshman in college, not high school. Got it?"

They both laughed and agreed.

"When you two see Luke, do me a favor and tell him to come up to my room."

They nodded.

"Alright, cool. You two go on in and have fun! There's beer in the fridge."

Timidly, they got out of the car and walked through the gaggle of smokers on the front porch and into the house.

Before sliding out of the car, I touched the medallion around my neck to thank my unseen protector for watching over me. Then I kissed my fingers and touched the wood grain of the steering wheel, thanking my car for a safe ride, because despite my unanswered feelings, I was glad to be home.

I took my time winding back through the party. I stopped to speak several times, but of nothing important. I made my way to my room where I waited for Luke.

It was only a few seconds before he jogged up the stairs and was standing on the far side of my long and narrow bedroom. He crossed the distance with an expectant expression on his face. I pulled two stacks of money from my pocket and gave him the larger of the two. He took the stack and counted what I had given him as I opened my wallet to stuff the smaller stack inside.

"It's all here, thanks." He said, after he finished counting.

"No problem, man. Hey are you sure you want to carry that much on you tonight?"

He paused, thinking it over. "What else could I do with it?"

I shrugged. "I don't know. I guess you could stash it up here somewhere. No one's going to be in my room, so it's probably the safest place for it."

"Alright." He reluctantly agreed. He walked to my dresser and pulled out the bottom drawer. He unfolded a pair of pants so that he could hide the money in one of the pockets. "There, I'm going to leave it here until—"

He stopped talking in midsentence and looked beyond me. I turned my head to find Devon standing only six feet away. I wasn't sure why, but he startled me. I hadn't even heard him come up the stairs.

He entered the conversation with a sly smile. "Hey, boys. Looks like I'm right on time."

I greeted him with a smile of my own. "You sneaky bastard, I didn't even know you were up here!"

Luke quickly refolded the pants that contained his money and stuffed them into the drawer and slid it closed. He was probably hoping, as I was, that Devon hadn't been there long enough to see what he had hidden.

"Where'd all that money come from?" Devon asked with an edge more blunt than a twenty pound bowling ball, toppling our hopes of avoiding the unnecessary.

"It's a long story." Luke answered. "I'll tell you about it later. For now, let's just go back down to the party."

I shot Luke a loaded glance to warn him against sharing the story, but I wasn't certain whether he understood my intentions. The three of us left my room together and I turned out the lights and shut the door behind us. I grabbed another Bud-light from the fridge. I wasn't sure how many I had had that night, but it didn't seem to matter. I wasn't drunk yet and there was more than enough beer left in the house and several hours remaining of the night. I closed the fridge and noticed a Post-It note stuck to the door. Written with barely legible handwriting, it read:

That's the only thing you feel is connections between people. – Devon

Isn't that a pleasant reminder, I thought derisively to myself. I was accustomed to seeing similar messages from Devon's infinite storehouse of wisdom scattered throughout the house.

I squeezed my way into the back room that had originally been a sun-room, but had quickly evolved into the beer-pong room. It was hard to see the wood paneled walls and the half dozen large windows for all of the people that were packed within the room. The floor was a bay colored tile that the endless cups of spilled beer couldn't stain. There was just enough space in the room for me to bring a pool table with me when I bought the house. The old slate table was an antique that had white side panels and legs with brass trim. It had come from a house that my dad and I had bought and the previous owners had left behind. Within my house, it hosted the occasional game of pool, but it was mostly used as a flat surface to hold the addition of a ping-pong table top.

I maneuvered myself through several people to stand along the side of the table. I realized that Blake and Jake were in the middle of a game of beer pong, and they were winning. Standing across the table from them were two girls that I had seen before, but couldn't remember their names. One was short with long brown hair and a low-cut tube top that barely prevented her breasts from falling out. The other girl was thinner and taller than her partner and had copper tinted hair tied back in a ponytail. In front of the two girls there was only one cup remaining on the table and Blake's team still had three.

It was the brunette's turn to shoot. She whispered something in her partner's ear then smiled and winked at the boys across the table. She leaned over the table seductively, letting her cleavage nearly topple out onto the table as she lined the ball up and prepared to throw. Blake and Jake's eyes were glued to her chest as she had planned. She threw the ball and in the same instant her partner bounced another ball toward the three remaining cups.

The first throw missed long, but as the second ball bounced and was heading toward the cups, the boys were still too mesmerized to even attempt to play defense. The redhead's shot fell into one of the cups, scoring two. It was a bold move, utilizing the bounce and shot combination to potentially score three and win the game, but the brunette had missed, concentrating too hard on throwing off her opponents rather than on the throw. Blake and Jake each had to remove one cup from the table and drink it.

Each team had one cup remaining. Between the two of them, all that Blake and Jake had to do was make one of their next two shots to win the game. I had a feeling that if they missed on the opportunity, the girls wouldn't. I watched Jake take aim and let the ball fly. The ball hit the rim of the cup then bounced from the table and fell to the tile floor. The redhead retrieved the ball while the brunette positioned herself behind the last remaining cup. As Blake tried to focus she let her breasts hang seductively above the target. My brother's eyes widened, looking as if the last thing on his mind was beer-pong, then I saw a smile crawl across his face. He threw the ball high, way above the cup, but he hit his target. The ball banked off the girl's breast and dropped into the cup.

The room erupted with laughter. The girl could hardly believe what had happened. She tried to protest that it was unfair, but the crowd wouldn't stand for it. The rules allowed any shot that landed in the cup as fair game. There was nothing that she could do but drink her loses and move out of the way.

I stepped to the table claiming the next game against the two youngsters who had just won their first game.

"Hey, Luke!" I yelled over the crowd to no response. I pushed my way into the kitchen to find Luke and Devon huddled together in a private conversation. "Hey, Luke!" I interrupted. "Come on, man. We're on the table!"

He held up an impatient finger.

"I'm going to get everything set up, but hurry your ass up, I'm not going to wait long." I turned to the refrigerator as they turned back to their conversation. Luke's face held the rigid lines of concentration as if he were choosing each word carefully while whispering to Devon whose features were unresponsive, but for a thin smirk. I pulled three beers from the refrigerator and returned to the beer-pong room.

At the table, I reorganized the ten cups into a triangle and divided the three beers evenly among them. "Bubble O!" I yelled across the table. "Are you two ready to play against *me*?" I pointed to myself as if I was a champion prize-fighter.

"You're goin' down!" Jake yelled, giving enough answer for them both.

"Alright, let's go. I'll play without Luke until he gets here. It's your throw first."

As Blake prepared to take the first shot, Luke stepped to the table to stand beside me. I had an idea of what he and Devon had been discussing, but I needed to know for sure.

"What was that all about?" I whispered loud enough so that only Luke could hear.

"What do you mean?" He answered dismissively.

The beer-pong game didn't seem important any more. It took only any instant, but I could feel a flash of anger at his blasé attitude toward my question. I hesitated, measuring my words, then turned from the table to face Luke directly. "When I walked up, you and Devon were talking about something. What was it?"

On the table, Blake threw the ball and it splashed into the front cup. Luke fished the ball out, dropped it into a clean water cup, then chugged the beer.

"He was asking about the money, so I told him." He answered with beer on his breath.

"What!?" I exploded. "What that fuck is wrong with you!?"

Luke's eyes darted around the room, noticing the unwanted attention that I had attracted. "Shh!" He pleaded.

I heard Jake's shot bounce on the table and land in a cup. He knew we were distracted and he had taken advantage of it. Luke pulled the ball out, dunked it into the water cup, then rolled both of the ping-pong balls back across the table. Their two made shots earned them each an extra turn. Luke took one cup from the triangle and handed me the other. "Here, I'll tell you about it later. I didn't have any choice, but you'll understand why."

I took a deep breath and tried to restrain the tension in my voice.

"You shouldn't have told him."

"I couldn't help it. What's the big deal though? It's just Devon."

I trusted Devon. But with some things, it was better to leave them unsaid. It was like entrusting the supervision of an infant to a junkyard dog. No matter how loyal the dog might be, when food became scarce, it would eat anything to survive. It would only be following its nature, so the dog wouldn't be the one to blame when it attacked. The one responsible would be the one who ignored its nature.

"We'll talk about this later." I stated flatly.

I turned back to the table to see Blake throw the ball and miss just short of a cup. Jake took the next shot and tried to bounce the ball again, but I swatted it back at him. I wagged my finger over the table. "Nope, not anymore! You guys got lucky the first time, but it won't happen again." I could feel the tension easing itself away as I playfully taunted my little brother and his friend.

Luke and I were down seven cups to ten, but it didn't take long for us to rally our way back into the lead. The game moved along as each team made shot after shot, forcing the four of us to drink cup after cup. In the end though, our experience caused Luke and I to pull away from the youngsters and eventually win the game. I passed our two remaining cups across the table for them to drink.

"Bubble O, that was a close game. I think you and Jake have been practicing at home or something. You had us worried there for a minute."

I could see the glazed look in each of their eyes as they drunkenly took the cups and forced more beer down their throats. Blake looked across the table and smiled with pride at his accomplishment. I was glad to see that he was having fun. It looked like the two of them had already had more than enough alcohol for the night, and I considered telling them to slow down, but I thought better of it. They wouldn't understand their limitations until they experienced them on their own. They stepped from the table and meandered through the crowd until they disappeared within the mingled mass of bodies.

Luke brought three fresh beers from the fridge and we refilled the cups for another game. The two girls that had lost against my brother stepped to the table to challenge us.

The game began, but seemed to stretch on without any excitement. Luke and I won the game by a four cup margin. We slid the cups across the table to the losers and I stepped back from the table. I had played enough, so I wanted to go check on the youngsters to see how they were doing.

I slapped Luke on the shoulder. "That's it for me, man. I'm bored. I'm going to go walk around for a minute."

He nodded in agreement and we both walked into the kitchen. A friend, named Patton, caught me by the arm and pulled me to the side. He was short and wore his blonde hair spiked with gel.

"Whoa, easy Patton!" I laughed. "You might poke somebody's eye out with that hair!"

"Ha. Ha. Ha." He said sarcastically. "Chas, seriously though. I need to talk to you about something."

I grabbed another beer from the refrigerator. "Why? What's up?"

"I think you might want to say something to that kid with your brother. He just came up to me and asked me to punch him in the face."

"What!? Why would he do that?"

"I don't know, man, but he's going around asking everybody he sees. You might want to go talk to him."

"Alright, I will. Thanks Patton."

I walked into the living room, and sure enough, Jake was yelling in some guys face, trying to pick a fight. The guy that Jake had chosen was about his size with carrot-orange hair and freckles. The guy seemed to be annoyed but filled with profound consternation at the cause of Jake's anger. I stepped between the two of them, and pulled Jake out of the room and into the kitchen. I could feel the crowd's eyes follow us as we walked away.

"Jake, what are you doing man?"

"Why won't any of these pussies take a swing at me?" He slurred.

His breath reeked of whiskey.

"Did you take some shots?"

He didn't respond. He watched me with a belligerent glare.

"Jake you need to chill out, man. This isn't the place to pick a fight. You're here as a guest in my house and you're embarrassing me."

"Fuck you!" He pushed me away, laughing.

He was testing my patience. I leaned closer to his ear. "Jake, stop it! I brought you here because I thought you could handle it, but you're acting like a little kid!"

"Then do something about it!"

I looked to my brother, who stood by my side, to see if he had any suggestions.

He only shrugged.

"Fucking hit me!" Jake yelled.

"Shut up, Jake. I'm not going to hit you."

"Are you scared? Watch, I can take a punch!" He balled his fist and threw a right hook into his own jaw.

People began to gather in a circle to watch the circus Jake was performing.

"Damn it, Jake! Stop it!"

"Then make me stop!" He said, laughing.

I set my beer down on the counter. "Alright, fine Jake. I'm going to hit you. It's not as fun as you think."

"YEAH! Here we go! Bring it on!"

He braced himself. He had a cup of beer in one hand and he stuck his jaw out to absorb the blow.

"Jake, I'm not going to punch you, because I don't want to hurt you. I'm going to slap you hard enough, so you'll remember to never do this shit again."

"Slap me!? What? Are you a girl or something!?"

He looked around the room for laughs and he found a few scattered chuckles.

"Okay, Jake. That's real funny. Are you ready?"

"Bring it on!"

He tensed his body, waiting for the impact.

In my best impersonation of Dave Chappelle when he impersonated Rick James, I looked around the room and spoke as if I was behind the bar of the China Club in downtown New York. "I'm Rick James! It's a celebration Bitches!" I turned back to Jake who was watching me. "Hey, Charlie Murphy! I've got a joke for you! What did the five fingers say to the face!?

"What?" Jake answered, confused.

"Slap, Bitch!"

I swung my open palm across his face, hard.

His head spun so fast that snot flew from his nose. Beer sloshed from the plastic cup in his hand and splashed against the wall. The cup fell to the floor, bouncing noisily against the hardwood as the room waited in silence for his reaction.

Jake slowly turned toward me and the rest of the crowd. One side of his face was bright red from the impact; the other side was red from embarrassment. His eyes were watering. Snot dribbled from his nose. Then a goofy grin spread across his face. "Holy shit that hurt!" He said with embarrassed laughter. Everyone that had gathered in the room burst into laughter, realizing that he was alright.

"Come on, Jake." I put my arm around his shoulder. "Let's get you cleaned up."

On my way to the bathroom, I turned back to the crowd in the kitchen. "Drink up! It's a celebration bitches!"

In the bathroom, I wet a clean washcloth and handed it to Jake. "Here you go, buddy. Are you alright?"

"Yeah, I'm okay, thanks." He said, still embarrassed.

The slap seemed to have knocked the alcohol out of him, giving him an instant dose of sobriety.

"Hey, Jake, can you do me a favor?"

"Yeah, sure."

"Don't ever do that stupid shit again. There's no reason to go looking for a fight, especially here. Can you promise me that?"

Sheepishly, he chuckled. "Yeah, I'm sorry. It won't happen again."

"Alright, good." I smiled. "And another thing, I think you've had enough to drink. So for the rest of the night I want you to take it easy, got it?

He nodded.

"Let's go back out there and just have fun. There are already too many tough guys. You don't need to be another one. You're here to have fun, not to fight, alright? So, go have fun."

"Okay, I'm sorry, I will." He walked out of the bathroom and back into the party. His pride was slightly bruised, but it was better than someone actually hurting him. I was glad that no one took him up on his original demand. He was big for his age, but he would learn eventually that size won't always determine the outcome of a fight. I hoped that he, and also my brother, had learned something that night.

I left the bathroom and went upstairs to my room. I wanted to make sure that I inflated the air mattresses so that Blake and Jake would have a place to sleep. When I stepped into my stairway, I could see the lights glowing from my room.

I had turned the lights off when I left, and had expected them to stay off until I returned. I rose above the threshold, hoping to find an intruder. Clothes were scattered across the floor. There were empty drawers thrown from my dresser. And in the center of it all, I found Luke.

"What the hell are you doing!?" I demanded.

He didn't pause; he continued rummaging through my clothes. "I can't find it!" He yelled.

"Find what?"

"My money! It's gone!"

I glanced around my bedroom to see if anything else was missing. My computer, my entertainment system, my standing racks of DVD's, my TV, my Xbox – everything that a thief would steal remained untouched. The only thing missing was Luke's money.

"Are you sure you checked the right pocket?" I asked.

"Yes! It was right here!" He shook a pair of pants at me.

"Who would have been going through my dresser?"

Then before he could respond, I knew the answer. "Where's Devon!"

He shrugged. "I don't know."

I ran down the stairs and back into the party, searching for Devon, but he was nowhere to be found. I asked throughout the crowd and no one seemed to remember seeing him leave. It was as if he had been there only moments ago, but had vanished. I ran outside the house and into the street, but there was no sign of him or his bicycle. I assumed that it would be a waste of my time if I tried to track him down at his dorm room. He would expect us to come after him there.

I stood under the weak glow of a street lamp and looked out into the darkness. I knew that Devon was out there, somewhere. He couldn't hide forever, so his only option was to run. But where could he go?

Chapter 7: Amsterdam Bound

The line was long at the airport security gate. Guards were taking their time to examine each passenger that walked through the international terminal. Devon tapped his hand-me-down dress shoes on the carpeted floor, waiting for his turn. He wore a black trench coat that hung below his knees, a green sweater, and black pleated slacks. His lucky red scarf was tied precariously around his neck. He was sweating, not from the climate controlled temperature of the terminal, but from his nerves that were fighting against him. In his mind, he was no longer Devon Koli. He was acting the part of Harry Ballsani, an international consultant in fine arts and antiquities. If anyone thought otherwise, he had the forged passport to prove it.

"Next." An airport security officer announced as though he had said the word for the thousandth time of the day.

Devon stepped forward and held his breath, trying to exude an aura of calm.

"Passport please." The man requested.

It was a stolen passport that Devon carried. He had replaced the original picture with his own and had doctored the pertinent details to fit his purpose. Devon pulled the fake documents from his coat pocket and handed them to the officer. There was nothing more that he could do, but remain casual and prepare to run at the first sign of trouble.

The man examined the passport. He looked at the picture then looked to Devon who claimed to be a twenty-six year old man by the name of Harry Ballsani. The reflection of the government seal flashed as he twisted the passport in the light. He stamped the book and handed it back to Devon, who sighed with relief.

"Here you go Mr.... Mr. Ballsani, have a good flight."

Devon walked away to meet his plane, triumphant.

Twelve hours later, he landed in Amsterdam. A country with a reputation of lawlessness, freedom of drugs, sex and a cesspool of black market traders. For the next few days, Devon was right at home. He spent his first night in Amsterdam snatching a few hours of sleep in a cheap motel before the dawn.

The next morning, he woke ready to explore the city. He dressed himself, wearing the same outfit that he had arrived in, the day before.

He took to the streets and his shoes clacked on the cobblestone pavement as he moved along. The clothes that he wore gave him an extra boost of confidence. In addition to his usual arrogant demeanor, his attire allowed him to effortlessly assume the role of Harry Ballsani, the dealer in fine arts and antiquities.

The town was quaint. Every building was no more than three stories tall. The people that he passed were polite enough, not showing outright distaste for a young American, but Devon did what he could to hide his true nationality. He tried to give off the impression that he was European, but his efforts weren't convincing. His walk gave him away. His pigeon-toed strut, with his shoulders thrown back and his head held high, was too cocky to be European.

He noticed a bustling coffee shop, busy with customers, and decided to walk inside. He stepped to the counter to place his order, but couldn't decide. There were too many choices. Behind the counter were samples of Northern Lights, White Widow, AK-47, Blueberry, Skunk Bud, Bubblegum, an assortment of Hydroponics, and countless other strains of marijuana from around the world.

A young, pale-faced cashier stood waiting for Devon's order. "Vat vould ju like, zir?" He asked in a thick Dutch accent, with a regal air as if he was impressed by his own ability to communicate with the traveling American.

"Umm, I can't decide. What do you recommend?" Devon asked, amused by the man's accent.

"Vell, ze Jack Herer iz very guud, Et iz a locul favurud."

"Alright, let me get a joint of Jack Herer then." Devon looked around the coffee shop to see what the Europeans were eating. "Umm, and let me get some waffles and a small cup of coffee."

"Vould ju like ze short stuck, or ze tull stuck?"

"Of what?"

"Ze vuffles."

"I'm sorry, one more time, what did you say?" Devon asked, toying with him, enjoying the garbled English.

"Ze-Vu-FFles . . ." The cashier clarified as if he was speaking to someone who was unfortunately slower than others.

"What? Truffles?"

"No… Vu-FFles!"

"Oh, the waffles." Devon finally relented, noticing the line that had formed behind him. "Okay, I'm probably going to be pretty hungry after I smoke this joint, huh?" Devon elbowed the guy standing in line behind him. "Huh? You know what I'm talking about!" The guy only stared at him in response, bewildered, not understanding his gesture. Devon answered his own question. "Well… maybe not." He turned back to the cashier. "Alright, let me get the tall stack." He finally announced.

The cashier filled Devon's order and Devon took his food, his coffee, and his joint, then snatched a book of matches before stepping away to find a seat. He went outside toward the street. He found an open table where he could watch the passersby as he enjoyed his breakfast. He struck a match and lit his joint with a puff. The smoke had a strong odor, and a distinct taste. He enjoyed being able to smoke out in the open. It was as if for the first time he felt free to do what he wanted to do. But still, he couldn't shake a nagging paranoia that prevented him from feeling completely free. He felt the American paranoia that at any moment as he was enjoying his breakfast and enjoying his smoke in the open air, a police officer would catch him and arrest him, charging him with possession of marijuana. But then he reminded himself that he was in Amsterdam, a liberal country that allowed its citizens to be freer than his own. So he took his time, savoring the freedom to smoke openly, then finished his meal.

He moved on, walking along the streets, guiding himself aimlessly as he soaked in the ambiance of Amsterdam. He turned onto a block and saw red signs illuminating the windows. He took his time perusing the sights. Scantily clad women gestured from the windows for his attention. He saw all types of women. Some were beautiful. There were blondes and brunettes and redheads. Some looked as though they had seen better days, their faces rough as leather. Some seemed too exhausted to move, let alone hustle for more customers. He mused that the city was somewhat like an all you can eat buffet at a lousy Chinese restaurant. You could consume your fill of pleasure around every corner, but as you walked away, you were left wondering what was actually inside the won-tons.

Devon walked on, because he had business to attend to. He pulled his mind back to the task awaiting him. He had to stay focused. He had one of the most important meetings of his life within the next few hours. Through a customer who had purchased artwork from Ethan, Devon had been given the email address of a dealer in Amsterdam who operated in legal, and not-so-legal, transactions. After several emails back and forth, the dealer insisted that he meet Devon face-to-face, in Amsterdam, if they were to conduct business. They were to meet at a coffee shop. To properly recognize one another, the dealer would wear a green scarf and Devon would wear his lucky red scarf.

When the time came, Devon found his way to the meeting place. He was nervous. He didn't know what to expect, but he knew that he had to present himself as a professional, despite his young age. He was known to the dealer only as Walter, another alias intended to disguise his true identity. Devon strolled into the café and spotted the man in the green scarf. He was tall and thin with his blonde hair pulled back into a ponytail, similar in fashion to how Devon's own hair was confined. Seated around the table were three heavy-set men. All were dressed in well tailored suits. They spotted Devon's red scarf, spoke amongst themselves, then waved him over.

Devon introduced himself. "Hi, I'm Walter." He shook each of the men's hands firmly.

The man with the ponytail looked hesitant to speak, clearly disturbed by Devon's youth, but proceeded none the less. "Hello, Walter." The man spoke in clear English with a hint of European eloquence. "I'm glad to finally meet you in person."

"Yes, thank you for meeting with me today. I'm glad to finally meet you too."

"So, Walter, did you bring the items that you had mentioned?"

"The items?" Devon stammered, caught off guard. "You wanted me to bring them today? No, I didn't know that you needed to see them." He was nearly at a loss for words, but he had managed to keep talking.

The dealer eyed Devon with unmarked disdain. "How am I supposed to buy the items if I have not inspected them? Did you at least bring photo-copies or pictures of the items that you intend to sell?"

Devon was beginning to feel foolish. He was out of his league and he knew it. But he was determined to recover the ground that he had already lost with his newfound associates.

"Gentlemen." Devon said, gesturing with his hands for everyone to remain calm. "There will be plenty of time to inspect everything during our next meeting. But." Devon leaned closer to them for an effect of secrecy. "Let's just say that I may not necessarily have the merchandise in my possession at the moment. But. Let's just say that they are somewhere safe and that I will have them soon."

The seasoned dealer didn't flinch. He had been through the game before. "I understand." He said with a knowing nod. "When we meet again, I will expect to view the items."

"Don't worry, you will."

"Good, I only have one last question to ask of you. Can I expect the collection to be complete?"

"Yes, I will make sure it is."

"Excellent." The dealer reached into a pocket within the lining of his jacket and withdrew a card. "When we last spoke, you had asked me to make you an offer. I hope you will find the amount that I have written on this card to be agreeable." The dealer stood and extended his hand. Devon took the card, and inspected the proposed amount. For once in his life, he was speechless. The dealer smiled. He gripped Devon's hand and shook it firmly. "I will look forward to our next meeting."

Chapter 8: Confrontation

It was three days later when Devon resurfaced. Luke and I had searched the campus end to end and all over Lexington without finding so much as a lead in any direction. Devon didn't own a cell phone, and never had, so it was tough to track him down even at times when he wanted to be found. When he wanted to disappear, all he had to do was walk away.

We had grown accustomed to using Ethan as if he were Devon's personal answering machine. I called Ethan's phone in search of Devon, but only found Ethan's voicemail. His voicemail recording was as short and to the point as his personality. "This is Ethan, leave it." His flat monotone voice said after the beep. I left a message for him to tell Devon to call Luke or me as soon as possible.

It was three days after I had left the message when Devon called from Ethan's phone. He said he had something that he needed to talk to Luke and I about, so we agreed to meet with him, expecting a confession. We decided to meet on campus at the ninety degree turn by the dorms.

Luke and I parked there, Luke sitting behind the steering wheel of his Lexus and me riding shotgun, waiting for Devon to show up. I looked through the tinted windows to the scenery outside of the dormitories. There seemed to be girls everywhere, and not just average, run-of-the-mill girls, they were attractive girls. They were one of several reasons why I was proud to be from Lexington. It was a city of horse racing tradition, Kentucky Wildcat basketball, and girls, gorgeous girls by the thousands. I watched as they walked by our car in groups, like clusters of mobile advertisements for their sororities. Each a different brand of beauty with Greek letters stretched across their pastel T-shirts. Theta, Pi Phi, Chi Omega, Tri Delta, and so on the letters went. And where there were sororities, there were fraternities. I was rushing Sigma Alpha Epsilon, or SAE, because it was the biggest fraternity on campus. It had the reputation of being the most prestigious, the most exclusive, and the best, so naturally I looked at it as if it were my only choice. Luke, Deuce, and four other friends of mine from Lexington were also pledging with me.

In the distance, I noticed Devon strolling in our direction. He was wearing his soccer team warm-ups with a backpack slung over his shoulders. As he came closer to the car, I thought that something seemed different about him. There seemed to be something darker about his features, almost as if there was a shadow cast over him in the light of day. I assumed the change was merely his feeling of guilt for having been caught after he stole from a friend.

Devon opened the door to the backseat and slid into the car. He shut the door and sudden silence followed. We each sat quietly for a moment, gauging the weight of the elephant that was smothering our words. I could almost taste the tension in the air. It was the kind that you could pull into your lungs with each breath.

Luke shifted the gear into drive and reentered the flow of traffic. As we drove through campus I saw students going in and out of the library. There were pick-up games in play at the basketball courts. The tennis courts were packed. The gym was open. Girls crossed the street on the way to hit the treadmills and guys headed to the weight room. We however, were on our way to the back of a secluded parking lot.

Luke found a spot and parked under the shade of several ash trees. No one spoke. The radio was off. The only sound was the soft hum of the engine. The leather of Devon's seat creaked as he shifted his weight. Luke's hands gripped the wheel tightly at ten and two while he stared blankly out the windshield.

Finally, Luke spoke. "Devon, why did you do it?" He punched the dashboard and turned in his seat to face Devon. "Why'd you steal my fucking money, Devon!?"

"Oh, I see." Devon chuckled. "That's what this is all about! Bravo! Let's hear it then."

I turned toward the backseat. "What? You think this is a joke!? Think about it, Devon, only the three of us in this car even knew the money existed, let alone where he was hiding it." I pointed to myself. "I didn't take it. Luke didn't steal it from himself." I moved my pointed finger directly in front of Devon's face. "So, that only leaves you!"

Devon was appalled. His mouth dropped open and his eyebrows

bunched together to make one gargantuan brow. "I don't believe this! Of all people, I never thought you two would do something like this! I knew you thought that I actually *stole* your money. Do you really think I didn't expect that? But look at this! This is bollocks! I never thought that you would turn this situation into something like *this!*" He waved his arms and looked out through the tinted windows. "You're actually going to bring me into an empty parking lot to confront me!? What kind of friends are you!?"

"What kind of friend are you!?" Luke snapped back. "Cut the bullshit Devon! Just admit it, we know you took it!"

Devon laughed sarcastically in response. "You know what? I was waiting for the right time to tell you something that could change your lives, but screw you two! Friends? HA! You two are like brothers to me! But, I'm not going to sit here and put up with this…."

Luke looked him square in the eye. "Devon, this is the last time I'm going to say it. I know you took it. Just admit it." Luke moved closer, watching to see if Devon would flinch. "Devon, did you take my money? If you did, just tell me."

Devon didn't budge. He didn't hesitate for an instant. He looked directly into Luke's livid stare. "I can't believe you." He glanced over at me. "Either of you! This was supposed to be a time to celebrate! I guess I should have told you sooner so it wouldn't come to this, but now I see what kind of friends you really are! So, just fuck off! Both of you!"

I had heard enough. He wouldn't give us a straight answer and he insisted on turning the blame toward us. I raised myself higher and hunched over the headrest of my seat. "Get out of the car, Devon!" I yelled. "I'm not going to play word games with you! If I can't even trust you in my own house – in my own room – then we have nothing left to talk about!"

We stared at one another. His eyes seemed to plead for understanding, yet they held a smug, stubborn resolve that irrationally irritated me beyond control. My pulse quickened and I breathed furiously, every fiber of my being teetering on the tipping point of violence. He didn't speak, so I spoke for him. "If you don't get out, I'm going to jump over this seat and *break your fucking face!*" I threatened.

Devon saw the intent in my eyes and stepped out of the car. I wasn't sure whether I would act on my threat, because although I believed him to be disloyal, I still believed him to be a friend. I was glad he chose to leave, so that I wouldn't be forced to discover the truth. He slammed the door shut, and immediately, Luke popped the transmission out of park and into drive. The tires squealed as they found traction and we sped away, leaving Devon to walk home, alone. His voice was all that trailed behind us. I could barely hear his words, but it sounded like he yelled a threat that I didn't understand. Something about how we had just made the biggest mistake of our lives. It would be years before I understood what he meant.

Chapter 9: Check

I was sitting on the couch in my living room as one of my roommates, Brian, held out his bank statement and pointed to a black and white copy of a check. It was written for forty dollars, cash, and the signature was an illegible scribble on the lower line. "Hey do you recognize this handwriting?" He asked.

I couldn't deny it. I would recognize the distinct chicken-scratch anywhere. It was on Post-it notes all over the house, giving us "important reminders".

"Yeah." I answered. "I think I might have an idea of who it might be, why?"

Brian's appearance was deceiving. His protruding eyeballs surrounded by ever-present circles of blues and purples made him seem like he might be a little slow. He smoked pot all day – everyday – so his mind was working with a handicap. Somehow, he still managed to out-smart his own looks.

"I was missing some checks." He said. "They weren't in my checkbook, so I went to the bank and found these two checks that were cashed, that I know I didn't write. One for forty bucks and one for fifty."

"Where was your checkbook?"

"I always keep it in my room, but my door is always open when we have people over. Anybody could have gone in there and took 'em."

I knew there was only one person that could have stolen his checks. It didn't bother me when Devon stole from unsuspecting kids who had the misfortune to live in his dormitory. I had even given him a ride to the grocery store on campus that didn't ask for I.D. so that he could cash the checks. The money had come from random people and as long as his victims were faceless, I didn't mind. But he stole money from Luke and now from my roommate. He had gone too far. His lack of morals had crossed a line and I knew I couldn't trust him, and if I couldn't trust him, I no longer owed him anything, especially loyalty.

"That's Devon's handwriting." I said, nonchalantly. "He stole your checks."

"That *mother-fucker*! Are you sure!?"

"Yeah, man, I'm positive. Have you not seen the Post-it notes scattered all over the house? Devon wrote those."

Brian walked away in search of the notes I spoke of. He came back with a stack of yellow squares in his hand. He slammed them down on the coffee table in front of me. I leaned forward on the couch to read the note that was stuck to the table-top.

"Don't Forget! – Smoke Weed!"

– Devon

It was one of Devon's important reminders. Underneath the words there was a pitiful little stoner doodle of what looked like a blunt. The next note was more philosophical in nature. It read:

"The person who allows the law to control his life,

who says the possible isn't possible because it is illegal,

is leading an inauthentic life."

– Søren Kierkegaard

The next:

"The bite of conscience, like the bite of a dog into a stone, is a stupidity."

– Friedrich Nietzsche

"Nietzsche?" Brian asked. "Kierkegaard? Where the fuck is he getting this shit from?"

"Books." I answered sarcastically. "You should try them sometime. You might learn something." I glanced back to the table to read the last note:

"Men are more ready to repay an injury than a benefit,

because gratitude is a burden and revenge is a pleasure "

– Tacitus

The final message sent an icy chill down my spine. The tone seemed to contain a darkness that reminded me of what I had seen in Devon the day on campus, over a week ago. Something had changed within him, but I couldn't quite grasp what it was. He was different somehow. A vague notion that I could relate to the changes within Devon crossed my thoughts, then I dismissed it as quickly as it had appeared.

"This is bullshit!" Brian yelled. "I can't believe that bastard would just rob me like that! I'm going to go file a police report on his bitch-ass and make him pay me back."

He might have deserved a lot of things, but a police report was not the way to go about it. I explained to Brian the process. He wouldn't be arrested. He would go to small claims court – eventually. Both of them would waste their time and maybe even spend more money on an attorney than the amount taken to begin with. The only people that win in court are the judges and attorneys. It is impossible for them to lose. They get paid just to be there.

What Devon needed was to be taught a lesson. He needed to be beaten at his own game, and more than anything, he needed to discover what it felt like to be the victim. Whether the victim exacted immediate retribution, or whether it came much later, or from an unrelated source such as karma, when it was least expected, the victim would have revenge.

Chapter 10: Racer X

It was three o'clock in the morning and I was dressed in black. Luke and Alex, who was my other roommate aside from Brian, walked quietly by my side. The three of us slipped through a large gap in a chain-link fence that led from my backyard into the UK practice field for the track team. It was a short-cut that led to the dorms. Luke and Alex both wore backpacks and beneath my sweat suit, I wore a set of bolt cutters strapped to my waist.

We moved stealthily through the field as the light from the moon casted long shadows in our path. We hopped another fence into the baseball stadium and made our way under the grandstands and into the parking lot. It was the same parking lot where we had left Devon stranded during our last encounter. The three of us stayed under the shadows of the trees that obscured the edge of the lot, then wove through the empty cars that seemed as still as tombstones, until we reached the first dormitory building.

Devon's building was one of the smaller dorms on the outer circle of campus housing. Alex's original idea for retaliation was to surprise him at his dorm room and beat the crap out of him. He thought that would teach him a lesson. I disagreed. I believed in the logic of an eye-for-an-eye. I thought the best way to teach him a lesson for stealing would be to steal from him. I realized I would be teaching him a lesson that I also needed to learn, but I reasoned that the rules were different among friends than among strangers. The other guys agreed with the eye-for-an-eye strategy, but there was a problem. Luke, Brian, Alex, and I couldn't think of anything that Devon owned that was worth stealing – until an idea rolled into our thoughts like Lance Armstrong in the Toure De France.

"Are you guys ready?" I whispered. I peeked my head around the corner of the building. "The camera is going to be behind us when we walk out, so keep your back to it and don't look up. On the way back, keep your head down and your hoods up. We ready?"

"Yeah, man, this is nothing. Let's just do it already." Luke answered.

I looked at Alex. "You ready?"

"Yeah, let's give this bastard what he deserves."

We turned around the corner walking at a quick pace. I withdrew the bolt cutters and held them close to my body so they wouldn't be seen by the camera. It would only be a student, or at most, a campus security guard that was sitting behind the entrance desk, possibly paying attention to the security monitors, but most likely not. Either way, we didn't want to take any chances.

Along the bike-rack of Cannondales and Gary Fishers and Giants, there it stood, Speed Racer, a turd among titans. It was Devon's only means of transportation, his prized possession. It looked pitiful standing there beside the other expensive bikes with their fresh coats of paint and sturdy frames. Sadly, it was locked tighter to the rack than any of the others. There was a chain woven through the frame, the front tire and the rack. The whole apparatus was fastened together with a thick padlock that claimed to be unbreakable.

I put the bolt cutters to the padlock and quickly realized that the spot where the lock unclasped was too narrow to cut. I couldn't get a good angle at it, but it wasn't a problem for long. What most people didn't realize about a lock and chain combination was that the lock was only as strong as the chain. I moved the bolt cutters to the chain and watched as it slid through the metal like a switchblade through warm butter. I handed the lock and chain to Luke and motioned for him to put it in his backpack and then we escaped with Speed Racer.

We hurried across campus with the kidnapped bicycle in tow. "Go Speed Racer, Go!" I thought as I laughed quietly to myself at the ridiculous caper we had concocted.

When we got back to my garage, Brian was waiting on us and he wasn't alone. Another friend, Jeff, was there too. We called him the guy on the couch, because he always ended up crashing there after a long night of drinking. Brian and Jeff had arranged an arsenal of weapons for Speed Racer's first demolition derby while we were gone. There were a few baseball bats, wooden and metal, some hammers, an axe handle, a hack saw, and a sledge hammer.

"So, this is it huh?" Brian laughed as he squinted through his bloodshot eyes, so red that it made me wonder if they got that way because his eyeballs bulged out like an owl. It was as if the protrusion ruined the aerodynamics of his face and passing air went straight to his eyeballs.

"Yep." Alex said. "So who wants to go first?"

Brian turned to Luke. "Luke, you get first dibs, man. He took more from you than anybody else."

From the row of weapons, Luke chose his trusty baseball bat. It was shorter than a typical bat, black, wooden, and heavy. The grip had been wrapped with duct tape for a better hold. The bike was lying on its side, helpless on the concrete floor. Luke lifted the bat over his head then slammed it down hard against the thin, metal frame. Blow after blow. The body began to distort, bending in all the wrong directions. One by one we all chose a weapon and joined the melee. The five of us took turns as we circled around the bike, smashing it to pieces, relishing in the revelry.

"Everybody step back!" I yelled.

I brought the sledge hammer down. Sparks flew as the wheel rim ground into the concrete. Again and again and again, until the front wheel broke away from the frame. It was as if I was trying to sever every piece of the bike like an embodiment of the friendship that Devon and I shared. The pieces came crashing off, skittering across the floor, and we all cheered.

"Hey, let me try that thing." Brian said, looking overly excited at the sledge hammer.

I handed the oversized mallet to him and watched as he pounded away at Speed Racer's back wheel until it became warped and unrecognizable. Then Luke took the hammer and went to work on the curved red handlebars. When he was finished, they no longer bowed out like Devon's legs, they were completely twisted and mangled. The destruction went on until there was nothing left to destroy. All of us were out of breath when we took a step back to look at the damage we had done.

Devon's bike, Speed Racer, was no more. There was nothing left but tangled metal and rubble spread across the concrete floor.

"What a mess." Luke said as he pushed his blonde hair away from his eyes.

"You know what we should do now?" Brian asked. What? We all wondered, bracing ourselves for an odd response. Without pause, Brian laughed so hard he could hardly speak. "We should go wake Devon up and make his bitch-ass clean it up!"

We all joined in, mostly laughing at Brian as he laughed hysterically. He was right though. It was a mess for Devon to clean up. We loaded Alex and Luke's backpacks with all of the rubble. What had once been spokes or handlebars or reflectors all fit into the backpacks. The mangled wheels we carried separately.

The three of us cut across campus again and made our way to the bike rack. We dumped the scraps from the backpacks onto the empty space where Speed Racer had once proudly stood. The wheels were thrown onto the pile of rubble and Luke wove the lock and chain through what was left of one wheel and wrapped the extra length around the rack. We turned our backs on the mess and walked away.

In only a few hours the sun would rise. Devon would begin the day like any other, assuming he would ride his bike to class, but instead, he would find his bike destroyed, lying in shambles among the other bikes. I wished that I could be there to see his initial reaction. I knew that he would be shocked, appalled, but mostly, he would want revenge.

Chapter 11: The Bar

The lights were off in my room. Noise from the party below rose through the floor board as Claire and I lay on my bed watching a movie. It was the movie where Brad Pitt played a gypsy boxer with an affinity for blue trailers, Jason Statham was his leery manager, and Benicio Del Toro was a diamond thief who robbed a bank dressed as a Hassidic Jew. It was a movie that I had seen more than a dozen times, but never grew tired of. We were watching the movie at nearly full volume to drown out the sounds from the party.

I heard a knock on the door from the bottom of my steps. I ignored it. The knock persisted. I huffed in frustration and looked to Claire who simply shrugged. Fine, I thought, I'll answer it. I stood from the bed and pulled a chain on the ceiling fan. The light nearly blinded me, so I turned a dial and the lights dimmed. The knocking paused briefly only to regain its vigor. "What do you want!?" I yelled down at the door.

"Hey, Chas, are you up there?" a muffled voice responded.

"No, I'm actually downstairs! I'm just really good at throwing my voice!"

"What?"

"Nothing, just open the door and come up!"

The knob turned and the door swung open. Brian closed the door behind him and casually walked up the stairs.

"What's up?" I asked.

He crossed the room and I couldn't help but notice that the circles around his eyes were as dark as ever, hovering there like the opposite of two tiny halos.

"Chas, what are you doing up here?" He asked. "I've been looking all over for you! You're not going to believe this shit I just heard!"

"Okay, try me?"

"You know Devon's roommate? That guy on the soccer team?"

"Yeah, why?"

"He said when he heard about Devon stealing Luke's money and my checks, then about how we fucked up his bike, and all, well, it made him check his own bank account."

"Oh yeah, what happened?"

"He was missing over five-hundred dollars! He recognized Devon's handwriting on two of his checks!"

"Well, what's he going to do about it?"

"It's not what he's going to do; it's what he already *did*. Instead of going to the police, he went to the coach of the soccer team and told him everything!"

"What did the coach do about it?"

"He kicked Devon off the team! He lost his scholarship and everything!"

I was shocked. I had known Devon for years and soccer was his life. With one decision, his soccer career was over, and probably, his academic career too, because he couldn't afford tuition without a scholarship.

"Damn, man, that's pretty harsh." I said softly.

"Yeah, no kidding. His bitch-ass deserves it though."

"I don't know... I don't think he deserved all that."

"Oh well, it's over now." Brian said, laughing. He looked over his shoulder in the direction of his room. "Hey, I'm going to smoke a bowl to celebrate. Do you wanna go? What about you, Claire?"

I looked back to Claire who raised her head from the pillows to politely decline his offer.

"No, man, we're good," I answered. "She's got class in the morning, so we're just taking it easy."

"Alright, suit yourself." He glanced over my shoulder at the television. "What movie are you watching? Oh, never mind, I know this one." Behind me, I could hear the scene where Brad Pitt had been pitted against a behemoth of a man in a bare knuckle boxing match. Brian turned around and walked down the stairs. "Let me know if you change your mind." He said as he walked out and closed the door behind him.

I turned the lights off and walked across the room to my desk where I fumbled around in the flashing glow of the television to find a pad of Post-it notes. I don't know why the idea came to mind, but I felt compelled to write it down. Maybe it was Devon's notes that had inspired me. Or maybe it was the news that Brian had delivered. Either way, I found a pad and scribbled a quote that I had once read. In the dark I wrote:

"Truly generous men are always ready to become sympathetic

when their enemies misfortune surpasses the limit of their hatred."

– Alexander Dumas,

The Count of Monte Cristo

I pulled the note from the pad and stuck it to the desk.

"What are you doing over there?" Claire asked.

"Nothing. I just had to write something down."

I walked to her and crawled into bed. I wrapped my arms around her and pulled her close. I could feel her body heat radiating through me, melting my thoughts away. Her hands touched my face as she kissed me. She closed her eyes, and I touched them with my lips. Her hands moved down my back as I kissed her cheek, her neck, her ear. She pulled my shirt over my head.

Then my phone rang. I paused as my arms and head were tangled in the fabric. I grunted to myself, then let the shirt fall to the floor. "Hold that thought." I pleaded as I reached to the night stand to grab my phone. My mom's number flashed across the caller-I.D. screen. There went the moment, I thought as I answered the call.

"Hello?"

"Charlie?" she asked in a broken voice.

"Mom? Is everything alright? Are you okay?"

"No." She cried, sobbing uncontrollably.

I sat upright in the bed and Claire sat with me. "What's wrong?"

"It's your father... I'm at Oscar's with some of my friends... he showed up...he has his whore with him!... he knew I was here!...they did it on purpose to embarrass me!..."

"It's okay, just calm down and tell me what happened."

I could hear her breathing hard on the other end, trying to reign in her emotions. She began talking again, only slower. "I was here first... so I asked them to leave... then they just laughed at me!... they made me so mad... especially her!..."

"You did the right thing, asking them to leave. So, what happened?"

Her breathing slowed and she began to speak normally. "Your dad was so mad that he started yelling at me. I thought he was going to hit me if some of the other men didn't hold him back."

"What!? Where are you? Do I need to come get you?"

"I don't know. I'm too embarrassed to go back out there. I'm in the bathroom at Oscar's bar right now."

"Just don't go anywhere, I'll be there in five minutes."

"Okay." I heard her say as I ended the call.

I looked at Claire and knew that she had heard it all. "I'm going to pick up my mom. You can wait here if you want."

"No, I'm going with you."

"Okay. We have to hurry though." I jumped out of bed and scrambled into my shirt. I threw on a pair of jeans and stuffed my wallet, keys, and phone into the pockets. From my nightstand I withdrew a knife. I flipped it open to check the blade then closed it back again.

"What are you going to do with that?" Claire asked.

"Hopefully nothing. Come on, let's go."

I slid the knife into my back pocket and watched Claire sling her purse over her shoulder.

"What are you going to do with that?" I joked.

"Hopefully nothing." She replied with playful sarcasm.

"Okay, funny girl, come on."

We walked downstairs and stepped into the party. There were faces that I had never seen and they looked at us as if we had emerged from a room that they had assumed was a closet. I ignored them and went through the front door, ignoring the smokers on the porch. I opened Claire's door on the passenger side of my Jeep, then ran to the driver's side. I jumped in, started the engine, and sped away from the party and steered toward whatever awaited at the end of the drive.

Under ordinary circumstances, Claire would have complained about how fast I was driving. The street lamps and trees were whipping past our windows as we drove on, but Claire didn't seem bothered by my haste. She focused her attention on the road as I did, lost in thought. I wondered how things had gone so far wrong. In less than a year, my family had gone from a seemingly normal family to a never ending episode of the Jerry Springer Show. I was tired of how my family's personal problems had become public fodder for the rumors of Lexington. The myriad of depraved souls who would whisper behind another's back just to avoid their own reflection in the mirror. I was tired of it all, but more than anything, I was tired of how my father perpetuated the rumors with his actions. He wouldn't rest until he had rubbed my mother's face in the mud, and I couldn't rest until he stopped.

As I approached the parking lot of Oscar's, an upscale bar in one of Lexington's oldest neighborhoods, I called my mom and she answered on the first ring.

"Charlie?"

"Yeah, I'm here." I answered.

"Hey, can you wait just a minute? Lisa just told me that your father is about to leave, so I'm going to wait until he's gone."

"Okay, I'll be parked out front, but I'm going to go talk to him when he comes out."

"No! Charlie, please don't do anything crazy! Just let it go. He's caused a big enough scene already as it is."

"I'm just going to go talk to him." I rationalized not sure how true my statement actually was.

I felt Claire tug on my arm and saw her plead with her eyes for me not to go.

"Please, Charlie, just let it go." My mom said again.

"Okay, we'll see. I'll be there when you come out."

I closed my phone as my Jeep crept through the parking lot. I drove past the entrance where groups were gathered at tables on the brick patio. I scanned the faces, but didn't see my dad. I circled around to find a parking spot, then I noticed my dad's SUV parked in the valet section. It was a brand new Hummer H2, jet black in color and monstrous in size. I looked at the expensive eye-catcher and compared it to the darkness of my mom's house and to the lights of her refrigerator as it reflected off of its own emptiness, and I thought, you know what, fuck him and his big truck.

I parked my Jeep and jumped out to the sound of Claire's voice calling after me. I pulled my knife from my back pocket and exposed the blade. I approached the extravagant vehicle and the mammoth tires that it rode in on. I sunk the blade into the rear driver's side tire and slashed it across, ripping the air out. The leviathan groaned like the Titanic as it sank toward the pavement. I removed the blade and moved on to stab the front tire. It popped open with a hiss and I stepped back to admire the sinking ship. With only one side deflated, it looked as if an accidental bump from a car door could overturn the black beast.

It required a conscious effort, but I walked back to my car, sat in the driver's seat, and closed the door. I had desperately wanted to confront my dad. For my mom's benefit though, I decided that now was not the right time. He had already done enough to embarrass and harass her. It was his turn to share in some of the humiliation. I found a space and parked where Claire and I would have front row seats to the show.

I rolled the windows down to hear the quiet of the night as we waited. I felt Claire slip her fingers into my hand.

"Are you okay?" She asked.

"I think so. I'm just really tired of dealing with all of this, Claire."

"I know." She leaned closer to rest her head on my shoulder.

"If I'm tired, then my mom has to be exhausted, I mean look at this, it's unbelievable, she can't even go out and enjoy herself without him ruining everything. And I worry about my brother and sister. I think that's what bothers me the most. His actions now, will affect their future. Blake has started drinking now, and when I'm not around he drinks too much. I worry that he does it as a way to cope with everything. I mean, these are big changes for them, Claire."

"They're big changes for you too."

"I know, but I can handle it. Sydney is just so young though. I mean, she's twelve now, but I just worry that she'll develop some kind of Electra complex without a father in her life." I could feel that I was getting myself worked up again.

Claire kissed my cheek. "She won't. Everything will be okay, I promise."

I smiled and turned to her. "You promise, huh? How can you be so sure?"

"I just am."

"Well, you must know something that I don't" I leaned in to kiss her, but paused, seeing someone exit the bar. "Look, look. There he is." We turned to watch as my dad and his affairee approached the valet attendant. He stood tall as an egoist wearing dress shoes, slacks, and a Hawaiian shirt that implied he had too much money to be concerned about the way he dressed. She wore a black dress with a high slit up the thigh and a low neck line. Her calves were covered by knee high leather boots and her whole ensemble seemed to be suctioned to her body as if she possessed some unseen super-skank power.

The valet hurried away to retrieve his car. As he returned with the H2, it leaned like the hydraulics had broken down in Snoop Dogg's Cadillac. My dad had his back turned talking to someone on the patio as the valet handed him the keys. He slipped the valet a tip, oblivious to the pointing and snickering behind his back. He opened his date's door as if she were a prize to behold. He walked to the driver's side without noticing the tires. He stepped in and began to drive away.

It wasn't only the sight of his lopsided clunker rolling on two tires that I found funny, or the look of the pointing fingers and laughing faces that were aimed at him, it was the sounds too. The high cackle of drunk women and the guffaw of drunk men. The flop, flop, flop of the loose rubber on the pavement. I knew it was cruel to take pleasure in another's misfortune, but some misfortunes are deserved, and those, to me, were hilarious. The most rewarding aspect of the moment, as I listened to him rev the engine in frustration and attempt to speed away from his humiliation, was when I looked at the crowd of laughing and smiling faces and saw my mom. She stood alone in the doorway with tears in her eyes, tears of appreciation for what I had done, and I understood that I had done the wrong thing for the right reasons.

I pulled my car to the entrance and the valet opened the car door for her. She stepped in the car and the door was shut behind her.

She looked at me as I sat in the driver's seat and she smiled through eye-liner streaked tears. "Thank you." She said, and it was more than she had ever needed to say. We drove home and I knew that the problems were far from over. We had merely won a battle among the war. It would only be a matter of time before my dad would find a way to make me pay for what I had done.

Chapter 12: Lake House

The road took a sharp, ninety-degree turn in front of the dorms and my Jeep was parked along the curb. I was in the driver's seat and Luke was riding shotgun. It had been weeks since I had last spoken to Devon. When he was kicked off of the soccer team and lost his scholarship, he seemed to have disappeared. He wasn't showing up for his classes and I had asked around campus, but no one had seen him, or even spoken to him. That was, until he called my cell phone that morning.

When I answered, I was at a loss for words. The last time that we had spoken, I had threatened to break his face and he had warned me that both Luke and I were making a mistake, the biggest mistake of our lives. So when he called, I didn't say much, but I listened to what he needed to say. He asked if we could call a truce, the three of us; him, Luke, and I, and he asked if we could go to my parent's lake house for the weekend. He said that he needed to tell us something important.

My curiosity forced me to agree, but curiosity was only part of the reason. I considered everything that he had gone through and I couldn't allow myself to neglect him during a time of hardship. It was part of my personality to be quick to retaliate and slow to forgive, but I felt that he at least deserved a chance to be forgiven. I decided that I would give him the benefit of the doubt and hear what he had to say. If I was ever down and out, I hoped that a friend would do the same for me.

I spotted Devon, strolling across campus wearing a black and blue UK jogging suit.

"At least he got to keep the clothes." Luke said with a smile.

As he approached my Jeep, I noticed that he was also wearing a black hat with the words, The Rundown in orange lettering above the bill. I assumed that he had stolen it from a movie theater somewhere, or maybe a blockbuster video store. His backpack was slung over one shoulder and he casually stepped toward the door to the backseat. I decided to have some fun with him.

When he reached for the door, I pulled the car forward just enough to make him miss the handle. He slumped his shoulders and looked in at me through the window. He walked forward a few steps and reached out again. I jerked the car forward, beating him to the punch, and Luke and I erupted with laughter. I held the brakes and slipped the drive into reverse. Devon lunged at the door trying to catch me off guard, but I reared the car backwards. He missed the handle, and his hand bumped into the door as we laughed at his expense from inside the car. Even though there was tension between the three of us, old habits just wouldn't die.

Standing in front of the car, Devon let out a visible sigh, but he couldn't stop himself from cracking a small smile.

I changed the gear into drive and rolled down my window. "Okay, okay. I won't do it again. I promise." I stuck my hands out the window. "Look. No hands. See?"

Reluctantly, he made his way to the door and reached for the handle. I pulled away and his grip was empty handed, again. Luke and I were still laughing as I reached into the backseat and opened the door from the inside. Devon dove through the open doorway like a starved fox into a rabbit hole. He reached around my seat and acted like he was going to strangle me.

"God, I hate you guys!" He complained. "It never stops, does it?"

"Of course not." I laughed. Then I hit the gas and we were off.

The drive was slightly over an hour and a half long, and while we rolled down the highway, the previous tensions that had separated us several weeks before seemed to lift like a morning fog. I was amazed how Devon and I had been at each others throats one day, then laughing together the next. It was a testament to the years that we had spent as friends. For me, it was easier to get along with Devon than it was for me to be mad at him. While I drove, Devon handed me a CD. I slid the disc into the receiver and cranked the volume. Hard-hooking, electronic beats vibrated from the speakers. Then the vocals chimed in, and I knew that it could only be the Beastie Boys.

Ohh!!! Steppin to the mic it's your

Man Mike D!........

Mike Who???......

Mike Deez Nuts!!!

And before we finished the CD, we were coasting down the steep driveway that led to my family's lake house. The two-story house was on a golf course, with a neighborhood pool near the top of our driveway. The house was nestled into a clearing of woods that overlooked the lake below. The closest neighbor was on the opposite side of a creek that split the two properties, about a practiced nine iron away.

I parked the car, we stepped out, and we grabbed our backpacks. We had each traveled light. I only brought a change of clothes and a pair of shorts. The swimming pool had already been sealed for the season and the lake was too cold during the fall, but the hot tub on our back porch was open year-round. The front of the house, unlike most houses, had no doors, just windows. Instead, the main entrance was on the side of the house. We walked to the entrance and they waited as I walked to the end of the front porch and pulled the spare key from a hook on the backside of a railing then unlocked the door. We stepped into a large, open room where the kitchen, dining-room, and living-room were all combined to form one great-room. The vaulted ceiling rose up and above the second story loft. A wall of sliding glass doors in the great-room lead out to one of several connecting decks that allowed a view of Lake Cumberland.

"Man… what a view." Devon said with amazement as we dropped our bags on the couch and made our way through the glass doors and onto the back deck that overlooked the water.

The sun was shining and there wasn't a cloud in the sky. Blue, light blue, stretched all the way to the stars. Under the sun, the temperature was mild. We each wore a light, fall jacket and a long pair of pants. It was warm, but not warm enough to take off my pants and jacket. The weather was unseasonably warm for autumn. The trees surrounding the house had already shed most of their leaves. Without their cover, the view across Lake Cumberland was all the more remarkable.

But Devon wasn't satisfied. He wanted the view to surround him. He stood from a deck chair and walked to the railing. "Why don't we go down there?" He pointed to a gentle slope below the deck. Beyond that, the land broke off to a steep hillside of trees, dirt, and rock that angled down to the water.

I knew the land behind the house well. Growing up, my brother and I had fished from the rocks below. Bluegill and the occasional small mouth bass had found themselves on our line. They would gather in the cove where the lake met the mountain creek that snaked its way between our property and our closest neighbor. The creek ended in a twenty foot drop-off to a bed of rocks that slid into the lake. The waterfall sent tranquil sounds up to the house, and we could hear the water trickling down below from where we were on the deck.

I stood by Devon's side at the railing. There was a rock ledge at the brink of the hillside where I had sat many times before. "Yeah, why don't we go hang out down there for a while? Come on, Luke, let's go."

Luke wasn't having it. He was laid back and completely relaxed in his chair and he didn't look like he was ready to go anywhere. "Why would we go sit down there, on the ground, when we have perfectly good chairs right here?" He argued.

"Come on, Luke, the view would be so much better from down there!" Devon said, unable to control the excitement brimming in his voice.

"Luke, come on, man. We might as well humor him." I joked.

"We really don't have anything better to do." Devon added.

Luke let out a deep, annoyed, sigh. "Alright, fine. Let's go." He grumbled to himself and cursed us under his breath as he slowly made his way out of the chair.

Together, we walked down a wooden set of stairs to the lower level deck and out onto the leaf covered ground. We wove through bare trees and small underbrush until we reached our destination, a ledge with a fifteen foot drop-off. Carefully, we each took a seat and let our feet hang free in the air. Looking across the lake, I was thankful for the improved view. There were no trees in the way. We had a clean shot of the lake and the opposite hillside. The water was calm. Gentle waves rippled across the surface. The leaves had fallen from the trees on the opposite hillside and everything seemed peaceful like a Bob Ross painting. I turned to see Devon lost in thought, staring out over the water.

"Wow." He finally managed to say. "This is what life is all about." His tone was far more dramatic than necessary. Luke and I looked at him, confused, not quite on his level of inspiration yet. "No, no, I'm being serious here." He continued. "This is what life is really about. Being with your friends. Enjoying life. Living. Loving every second of it, because there is nowhere else you'd rather be. Do you get what I'm saying?"

For encouragement, I nodded in agreement.

"What if life could always be this way? What if we could live the lives that we've always wanted? What if we never had to worry about money, or work another day for the rest of our lives? What if it could always be like this, and we had the chance to make it happen, would you take it?"

"Yeah, I guess so." I said casually, not sharing the same gravity on the subject as Devon.

He turned and smiled at me with a mischievous grin. "What would you say, if I told you we could make twelve million dollars in one day?" His words didn't make much of an impact on me then, but they were words that I would never forget.

Neither Luke nor I answered his question, at least not with words. We both sat in silence, contemplating his meaning and all that it implied, and we waited for him to go on, because our unconscious answer was yes, tell us more.

Devon took a deep breath and leaned back, carefully planning his next words. His eyes were loosely focused across the water, and he knew that he had our attention.

"I really don't know how to tell you boys this." He said. "So, I guess I'll just come out and say it. About a month ago, I came across the opportunity of a life time. But, I know I can't do it on my own."

"Do what? Just spit it out, man. What are you talking about?" Luke asked, tired of the roundabout word game.

"Okay." Devon laughed. "I guess I should just start from the beginning. Earlier this year, when school started, they gave Ethan a tour of Transy's Special Collections Museum. Most people don't get to go in there, but I guess he did because he's in the school's art program. This place is where they keep all of their valuable paintings and books and stuff like that. Ethan said they've got stuff in there worth millions."

"Like what?" Luke asked, skeptically.

"I had to do some research, but it turns out, they've got this really rare set of books. Each book is filled with original paintings by John James Audubon. Like, have you guys ever heard of that bird watchers group, the Audubon Society?"

"Yeah." I answered.

"Well, they named themselves after this guy. Back in the early 1800's, this guy explored all across this country and painted the animals he saw, but he was mostly known for his paintings of birds. What's so crazy though, is that somehow, this collection of his original artwork has ended up at Transy! How crazy is that?"

"Yeah, man, that's crazy and everything, but what the hell does that have to do with us?" Luke asked.

Devon held up a finger. "Hold on, I'll get to that in a minute. I've already done most of the groundwork for all this. I went through a few of Ethan's connections in the art world. They were some people that had sold some of his work before. It took some digging, but I went through a connection of a connection and found what I was looking for. I found an art dealer in Amsterdam that wanted to buy the collection. So I flew over there."

"You flew over there. Over where? Amsterdam?" I asked.

"Yeah, I met with a few different buyers, but I think I found the right one. You should have seen these guys, these black market guys. They looked like something straight out of a movie. European underground all the way – ponytails, suits, bodyguards, and everything."

"So, what happened?"

"I cut a deal with the highest bidder. He agreed to buy the collection, and you won't believe the price that he agreed to pay."

"Twelve million dollars!" Devon's voice rose in excitement. "What do you think about that, boys!? TWELVE... MILLION... DOLLARS!.." Devon yelled, elated at the number, his voice echoing from the trees that surrounded us and from the lake down below.

I had always known that Devon was a little off center, maybe even slightly crazy, but at the moment, I realized that he had lost his mind. I thought the emotions and the stress from losing his spot on the soccer team and from facing the fact that he could no longer afford college without a scholarship were making him desperate. He had pulled off hundreds of petty crimes in the past, maybe a few checks here and there, filching from a wallet or a purse from time to time, or shop-lifting instead of shopping, but never anything of the magnitude and scope of a multi-million dollar heist. The idea seemed insane. Everything that he had said seemed outlandish. There were multiple questions running through my mind, but I started with the most outrageous statement that he made. Devon, broke-ass Devon, flying to Cleveland seemed improbable – let alone Amsterdam.

"Hey, man." I said to get his attention. "How the hell did you fly to Amsterdam?"

"In an airplane."

"Okay, smartass. I meant, how did you get the money to fly over there? The plane ticket alone had to be at least a grand."

The question seemed to catch him off guard. He suddenly looked uneasy. "I knew this would come up again eventually." He said. "I should have told you two about this before." He paused, gathering his words. "I had to have the money to pay for those plane tickets. So, I used Luke's money from your dresser."

"What!?" Luke yelled.

"I know, I fucked up, Luke. I should have told you, but I didn't have time to explain it. I couldn't risk you saying no. I knew that you both had plenty of money anyways, and for all of this to work out I had to use some.

And when you told me about the casino, I knew that you two would be perfect for this job."

I gave Luke a harsh glare. I knew that he shouldn't have told Devon anything about the money or the casino. But Luke had already realized his mistake without need of any further prompting from me. He was already fuming with righteous fury.

"You piece of shit!" Luke yelled. "When I told you about that, I trusted you! Then you went behind my back and robbed me for some fucked-up idea! What the hell is wrong with you?!!"

"Luke, it's not fucked-up, man! And, I didn't rob you, I just borrowed the money! Think about it, Luke, we're all going to be rich soon. Twelve million dollars! That's three million for each of us! Me, you, Chas, and Ethan. That three grand was nothing. It was chicken-shit compared to what we're going to have soon!"

"It was thirty-five hundred." Luke stated flatly, still breathing hard and looking as if he was tempted to shove Devon over the cliff.

"Whatever. Still, it's not that big of a deal. All we have to do now is get these paintings, these books I was telling you about, and we're set. For life. But, while were talking about it, it's not like you two aren't guilty too. I saw the security tapes from the dorms. Even though you were covered up, I know the way you walk. I know that it was you two, and some other guy, that destroyed my bike. *And*, I know you told my roommate about the checks."

"Yeah, that was us that wrecked your bike. We did it to teach you a lesson." I admitted. "What can I say, payback's a bitch—but we never said anything to your roommate. He found out on his own." I said to clarify the point. "He found out after my roommate told him. But yes, I was the one who told *my* roommate that you stole his checks. I warned you, months ago, that if anything came up missing in my house, I would hold you responsible. You're just lucky that I convinced him not to go to the cops about it. He was satisfied enough by what we did to your bike. The whole thing with your roommate though, that was collateral damage, man. And honestly, I'm sorry that all of that happened with the soccer team and everything."

Devon suddenly grew solemn. "I lost everything. I lost my scholarship, my dorm room, my soccer career is over, and my mom won't even speak to me. I even lost my girlfriend, Amy, over all of this."

I knew they had been together for four years and on top of everything else, her loss had to be a tough blow. I knew how much he loved her. Claire and I had gone on double dates with them throughout the years and it was hard to imagine that she would just leave him like that. I felt that he deserved some of what he got, but most of the consequences were too harsh.

"But, listen." Devon said, as he regained his vigor. "I don't care about all that. All of that is in the past. I don't care about the bike, the money, school, soccer – all of it." I noticed that he failed to mention his mom, or Amy. He still loved her. "All that matters is what we do from here, now. So, how about it, boys? What do you say? Are we all in this together?"

When no one responded, he looked to Luke. "Can you forgive me? I did what I had to do. I'm sorry."

Luke softened his glare. "Yeah, man, we're cool. But, next time, just ask me for the money."

Devon laughed. "Yeah, I know. I shouldn't have taken it. I just knew this was the opportunity of a lifetime and I couldn't let it pass me by. So, Luke, what do you say? Are you in?"

"I'm going to have to see what we're working with, but yeah, for now, you can count me in."

"Alright! That's what I'm talking about!" Devon opened his hand and gave Luke a one shouldered hug that sealed the deal.

"Chas, what about you? Can we call it even?" I didn't know it at the time, but things were far from even between us. He had already set a vengeful chain of events in motion, but I didn't think he was capable of such malice.

"Yeah." I responded. "I would say it's probably about as even as it's going to get." Not knowing how far my words were from the truth.

"So, can we count you in?"

I had to admit that I was curious. I wanted to know more, but my first instinct was to say no. I had been lucky at my first attempt at crime, but I didn't want to push my luck. I already had enough money, legal and some not so legal, but it was enough for my family and I to get by. And there was always the rental properties that my dad and I still owned together. The money was untouchable then, but it was there. I didn't need to get wrapped up in one of Devon's schemes, I reminded myself, but I didn't want to prematurely turn down the offer too soon. What if it actually worked? What if it wasn't too far fetched? What if we really could make twelve million dollars in one day? I decided to stay undecided. I would wait and see how things developed.

"The best I can do for now is maybe." I finally answered.

"That's okay." Devon responded. "You still have plenty of time to decide."

I allowed my thoughts to relax and I focused on the sights that surrounded me. There were so many colors from the fallen leaves, reds and yellows, oranges and browns. The water seemed greener and filled with more life than ever before. The sky was a beaming, brilliant ball of blue. It was like I was looking through a kaleidoscope, seeing the ordinary world in a new, engaging, compelling, awe-inspiring way. The change occurred not only in my eyes. My ears were tickled by the soft sounds of the trickling stream. My nose was keenly aware of the rich woodsy aroma of the trees, and more than anything, I felt alive. I know now that such moments were just a small, cheap glimpse into the true, beautiful nature of the world and of life itself.

Chapter 13: Into the Pit

Our view from the ledge wasn't enough, we wanted more. We wanted to seize the day, or carpe diem, as they say. We wanted to explore and embrace the world around us, and we wanted an adventure. We just didn't realize the kind of adventure that the world had prepared for us.

We decided to hike down to the water and we discovered, too late to turn back, the hike wasn't easy. We zigzagged down the hillside, clinging to trees for support as loose layers of leaves gave out beneath us. But somehow, we managed to climb down to the water.

The cove was wide at its mouth and narrowed back to meet the waterfall in a roughly defined point. The shoreline was stacked with rocks like a staggered staircase. Clumsily, we made our way toward the waterfall.

"What are we doing down here? Why don't we just go back to the house? This was a stupid idea." Luke complained.

I felt like that was all I ever heard, him complaining about something. I stopped to pick up a skipping stone. "Just chill out and try to enjoy yourself for once. We'll go back to the house in a little while." I tossed the stone and watched it bounce across the calm water.

Devon walked across the trickling stream at the base of the waterfall and crossed to the other side. I picked up a large rock and threw it into the lake beside him. A booming splash erupted from the water and a few stray drops landed on him.

"Bollocks! Watch where you're throwing those things!"

Near where I threw the rock, I noticed there was something floating in the water. It was big, brown, and looked like it could be alive.

"Hey." I pointed toward whatever it was, floating near the shore. "What the hell is that?"

Devon took a few steps back. "It looks like a small bear or something."

"Then get away from it, dumbass." Luke chided.

"It's not alive. It wouldn't be floating like that. Here watch this." Devon tossed a small stone at the floating mass of wet and matted fur. The stone bounced off, unnoticed by the ball of floating fur.

Encouraged by his first throw, Devon picked up a rock with two hands. He heaved the heavy rock down and it struck the carcass with a solid thud. The brown blob bobbed up and down from the impact. Whatever it was, it wasn't alive, not anymore.

"If that thing is actually a dead bear, does that mean there may be more *live* bears in these woods?" Luke asked.

The realization hit each of us quietly, and we each recognized the potential danger that we were in. We were more than a thirty minute climb away from the house and unarmed. We didn't stand a chance against a territorial bear. Each of our heads were turned toward the woods as we silently searched for any sign of a roaming bear. We hoped to find it, before it found us.

Luke was the first to spot something. Further up the shoreline, he pointed to a figure in the brush. The three of us gathered from a distance and tried to decipher what it was. I could barely make out a set of beady eyes.

"Maybe it's a weasel." I suggested.

Devon picked up a rock. "I don't know, but I'm about to find out." Without a second thought, he flung the rock toward the unsuspecting set of eyes. He missed, by several feet, and the eyes never so much as blinked. They simply stared in our direction.

Devon bent to grab another rock and Luke attempted to stop him. "What the fuck are you doing? Just leave it alone!"

Devon being Devon, he didn't listen. He threw the rock anyway. It bounced just short and the eyes lifted from the ground to reveal a wide, thin face. Devon quickly reloaded and I had seen enough.

"You're going to piss that thing off! We don't even know what we're messing with here, so just leave it alone!" I took a few steps back and made sure that Devon was between me and his target. I was in no mood to be mauled by a rabid weasel.

Devon turned his head back toward me while his body and the rock remained squared toward his target. "He's just a little guy. What's he going to do?"

"I don't know, man. I just know you shouldn't mess with wild animals like that."

And he let the rock fly. I couldn't believe it, but the rock smashed into the animal's face. It was a direct hit. The animal reared its head back and unleashed a wild hiss. Quickly, it vanished into the brush, but we could hear it moving. It was coming toward us.

The animal's head and beady eyes emerged on top of a fallen tree. To my astonishment, and horror, I saw the body behind the head. It was terrifyingly big, nearly as long as I was tall, the head was the size of my hand, and the body was as thick as my forearm. It was by far the biggest snake that I had ever seen in the wild and it was racing toward us. Its colors flashed vividly across the rocks. Pale greens and browns covered its entire length like army camouflage.

I was terrified of snakes and it was only an instant before I found myself running in the opposite direction. I ran past the point of the cove, past the waterfall, and lunged for the nearest ledge hoping to climb out of harms way. I scrambled up the rocks and pulled my head above the ledge, and there, three feet from my face, an identical snake stared back at me. Huge, green and brown with beady, unblinking eyes that stared coldly at me as it sat coiled, ready to strike.

"Whoa!" I yelled as I threw myself away from the ledge. My body hit the rocks in an awkward roll as I attempted to regain my balance. Wide eyed, Devon and Luke had caught up and were wondering what I saw. "There's another one!" I shouted.

"Another what!?" Luke asked.

"Another snake!"

"What!? Oh, man, this is bad. I told you guys we should have gone back to the house!"

I wanted to tell him to shut up and stop complaining, but I was too scared to think of anything other than the two snakes that were watching us.

We started walking, hurriedly, along the cove. We had a long way to go, maybe seventy or eighty yards to get to the climbable trail that would lead us back to the house. There were no other feasible routes, because everywhere else, the wooded terrain was steep, wild, overgrown and nearly impossible to climb.

I was pulled away from my thoughts when I almost stepped on something along the rocks. Maybe two feet long, solid black, and wrapped within itself, another snake waited at my feet.

"Back up!" I shouted and the three of us bumped into each other as we shuffled backwards.

"Whoa! Stop! Stop!" Luke yelled.

"What?"

"Don't move!"

I looked back at Luke, frustrated, then I saw the problem. A small black head had craned its neck out of the water and onto the rock, inches from Luke's foot.

"Where in the hell are these things coming from?" I asked, directing the question to no one in particular.

"I don't know! Let's just get out of here before this thing bites me!"

Slowly, we started moving and we each timidly stepped over the black snake in front of us. We walked in a line, 1-2-3, back to front, back to front. I lead the way and when I looked ahead and looked at the rocks all around us, I froze. From every crack and crevice, I could see beady eyes staring back at me.

It was like waking up to realize that I was still trapped within a nightmare. I couldn't comprehend where they had come from or why we hadn't noticed them until then. It was improbable beyond all reasoning, but somehow, we had stumbled into a snake pit. The sun was beginning to set and we could do nothing but watch as dozens of snakes emerged from their crevices in a slow, slithering slide to rest on the surface of the sun-warmed stones. They seemed to be basking in the fading sun-light. The variety of species and the sheer volume of snakes that surrounded us was mind-blowing. They were small and wiry and black, fat, bloated and brown, red with black and yellow bands, and black with thin red stripes. They were tan and they were patterned with a blend of tan and brown. They were huge with camouflage spots of green and brown, and in the water, swimming silently along the shoreline, they were long and lean and black with heads like a fist.

I was unarmed, unprotected, and a long climb away from safety. To say that I was scared would be a vast understatement. I had never been in a life-threatening situation of such magnitude before. I didn't know much about snakes or their habits then, but I knew that if I, or one of my friends, was bitten by a snake that happened to be poisonous, then we would face serious injury or even death. If I wanted to live to see the following day, then I would need to focus, push my fears to the side, and try to survive.

Together, we gathered our courage and tried to make our way to the trail, jumping over and dodging snakes and their snapping fangs along the way, but the trail was too far down the shoreline and there were too many snakes. Over and over, we could do nothing but watch as new waves of snakes swam from across the rippling water and crawled onto the rocky shore. Some slithered up and disappeared into the woods, others found holes within the rocks to hide, and still others remained near the waterline and all around our feet. As the sun dipped below the hillside horizon, casting the last few sunlit rays across the sky, we were overwhelmed.

Each and every minute seemed to crawl by like an ant marching the length of a football field, but somehow, the minutes crept into hours. The full moon sat high in the starless sky like a shy, pale-faced bride, who at the moment, was hiding behind a veil of clouds. We found ourselves back where we had started, near the ledge where I had fallen, and a stones throw from the waterfall. We were huddled together like beggars around a fire. Our eyes watched the ground near our feet and we looked over one another's shoulders for the dangers at our backs. We had each been bitten several times, but due to our long pants and shoes none of the bites had punctured our skin. Through hours of trial and error, we had adapted to a system of stillness and silence in an attempt to blend in to our surroundings like three stone statues. One trifling movement or a noise too loud could potentially elicit a violent reaction from any of the dozen or so snakes that rested within striking distance.

"Hey, guys." I whispered softly, fearing I would startle the snakes. "Look around. See if you can find some sort of stick or something."

"Why?" Luke asked, barely audible.

"If I don't get these things away from my feet, I'm going to go crazy." Silently, I scanned the slope of rocks.

Behind a brown snake with a fat, heavy body I found a tree limb. It looked to be about three feet long and was perfect for what I had in mind. Very carefully, and very slowly, I reached out to grab the limb. The snake began to grow restless. My hand was above its head as I reached across its body. The snake slowly tensed and flexed preparing to strike. I grabbed a hold of the limb and lifted it with deliberate surgical precision up and over the snakes head and held it close to my body. I flexed the limb in my hands. It felt sturdy. I noticed that Devon had also found a piece of old driftwood.

"Devon, let's get rid of some of these things." I whispered. "Just take that stick and throw them in the water."

"Okay, but if we're going to do this, we need to be quick about it."

I tentatively lowered the limb to the unsuspecting snake at my feet. "Ready?" I asked, not sure if I was truly ready myself.

"Yeah. Ready."

"Go!"

I lifted the snake with the tip of the limb and flung it as far into the lake as I possibly could. I found another and threw it out into the open water, and then another. By my side, Devon was also frantically flipping snakes into the lake. I lunged for another, but it slithered away from the limb and coiled itself around Luke's shoe.

"What are you doing!" He panicked. "Get it off my foot! It's wrapped around my shoe!"

He shook his foot, trying to knock it down, but the snake held on tight. I used the tip of the limb to scrape it from his shoe and the snake landed on the rocks and tried to slither away, but I caught it and launched it toward the moon. For an instant, I looked toward the sky and the snake flew across the face of the moon, like the alien in the movie E.T., only without a bicycle.

I searched the ground for more snakes at our feet, but for the moment, our immediate area was clear. I took a breath of thankful relief for the first time that night.

As I looked behind me though, something caught my attention. About knee level, four feet away, something was juxtaposed against the rocks. It was the darkest black I had ever seen, and it was enormous. It was so dark that it seemed to consume any and all light around it. With my eyes, I followed the trail that wound up the rocky slope, over the ledge, and appeared to connect to a tree.

"Hey." I whispered, so quietly that I was nearly miming the words. "Do you guys see that?"

Their eyes traced from the rocks to the tree and back again.

"What the hell is that?" Luke asked.

"Whatever it is, it's huge." Devon answered, but he wasn't alone in his confusion, we were all baffled. The sheer size was preposterous.

"Guys, if that's a snake, we have to kill it." I said in a flat monotone.

"What? Are you out of your fucking mind!?" Luke complained.

Devon seemed to be sizing it up. "Chas, if we both bash it with these sticks, I think we can kill it."

"We have to! Look how close it is! It's right behind me!"

"Let's do it then!" Devon agreed. He gripped the log like he was holding a Louisville Slugger.

I held my own limb high above my head, ready to strike down with as much force as I could possibly manage.

"Stop!" Luke yelled, grabbing us both by the arms, and we all stopped moving as his voice echoed from the hills. The sudden noise caused the snakes that surrounded us to grow restless once again. We didn't move and we hardly dared to breathe as we waited to see how they would respond. Some repositioned themselves and a few of them inched closer to where we stood.

When he was sure that the snakes would move no further, Luke continued in a whisper. "Think about what you two are about to do."

"Luke, we have to do something! It's too close!" I argued.

"We don't even know if it's a snake. If you two swing at that thing and it turns out to just be an ordinary tree root, then we'll have to deal with all of these other snakes. And what are you going to do if the ones up there come down?" He gestured toward the ledge where three camouflage-colored snakes sat perched, watching our every move. When the light from the moon caught their unblinking eyes, their eyes glowed against the darkness like six floating orbs of eerie green light. Their presence on the ledge was a constant terror, and I was always aware of the possibility that they would slither down the slope. I had no idea how we would deal with them if they did. I decided that I would compromise with Luke.

"Guys." I whispered. "Hold on a second. I'm going to take a closer look at this thing. Don't move."

I bent down, slowly, quietly, and inched my face closer. Inch by agonizing inch, the dark figure became more clear. There was a knot where the darkness met the rock, like a diamond shaped club. It trailed up the slope like an unbreakable line of rope. I moved closer until my face was six inches away. After close inspection, I decided that it was only a dead, lifeless root.

I turned my head to whisper to Devon and Luke who were anxiously waiting for the verdict. "False alarm, guys. No big deal. It's just a root."

Responding to the sound of my voice, I heard a gut-wrenching hiss, mere centimeters from my ear. I could almost feel the cold-blooded breath on the side of my face as a chill of fear ran through my body. I could hardly react. By instinct, I turned my head and followed the noise. I stared, face-to-face, at the largest snake that I had ever seen, and it stared back at me with two glossy black eyes like stones of smooth onyx. I watched as its jaw stretched open. Wide, wide enough to fit a head, a face, my face, but I couldn't move. Its mouth was the pale color of soft flesh. The hissing grew louder, more violent, but I couldn't move. I was frozen in the face of death. The jaws unhinged, stretching, reaching. There were black pits in the lining of flesh and the throat was a dark circle that was quickly increasing in size, like a black-hole in deep space. I could feel something touching my shoulders, wrapping around them and gripping tight.

"Chas, get away from it!" Luke yelled. His voice woke me as if from a dream and I realized that he was pulling me back, away from the snakes open jaws.

"Whoa....whoa!" I stammered "Holy shit, it's a snake! That fucking thing's a snake!"

"We've got to kill it!" Devon yelled, raising the driftwood log above his head.

"No! Don't do it Devon! Just leave it alone!" I begged, knowing that we would be no match against such raw power. We could only hope that the monstrous snake would calm down.

"I can't take this shit anymore! We've got to kill it! We've got to kill all these things!"

The root shifted, hissing, and slid closer, positioning itself within three feet from my pant-covered legs. It was preparing to strike. All around us, the snakes were in a frenzy and they all seemed to be following the root's lead. They were all crawling closer.

"Shhh!" I whispered, furiously. I grabbed Devon by the shoulders. "Shhh."

We watched in agonizing silence and waited for the snakes to settle themselves again. Their every move was a potential strike. It was a slow, exhausting torture and I couldn't take my eyes away from the root.

If it came any closer, I told myself that I would have to dive head-first into the water and take my chances with the swarm of snakes that were swimming the shoreline. The grueling seconds drug on, and somehow they turned to minutes, but the minutes wouldn't end.

"We have to get out of here! We have to do something!" Devon panicked.

"Like what? What the hell can we do, Devon?" Luke said, sarcastically.

"I don't know! I don't care! Let's swim! Let's do something!"

"Shhh!" I urged, frantically looking from snake to snake, and back to the root again. I watched as it hissed a final warning of danger, then closed its massive jaws. It seemed to have calmed itself, and finally, I felt that I could look away. I turned toward Devon and his face was paler than the moon. His eyes seemed as big and round as two golf balls.

"What?" I asked. "What's wrong?"

"Don't move!"

"What? Shhh, calm down."

"Don't move!" He screamed. "It's right behind you!"

I imagined the root directly behind my heels, mouth open, preparing to strike. I couldn't look and I couldn't move. I braced myself for the pain.

"Where? What are you talking about?" Luke asked.

"There! It's right there! Behind his head! Don't you see the eyes!?"

The eyes, the glowing green eyes. How could they be so close? The ledge was at least five feet away, but it was my fear that reacted first. I hunched my shoulders and slowly ducked my head.

"Yeah, I see it." Luke said. "But you need to chill out, Devon. It's not right behind him."

"Yes it is! Oh my God! It's going to bite him!"

I braced myself for the pain again. "Luke, where is it?" I asked with a tiny voice.

"It's behind you, but it's not as close as this jackass keeps screaming."

"How close?"

"Four, maybe five feet."

"Am I okay to turn around and look?"

"Yeah, you're fine."

"Oh my God! Don't do it Chas! It's going to bite you!"

"Devon! Shut up!" Luke forcefully closed Devon's mouth.

I mustered what little courage that remained within me and turned to face the green eyes. Glowing in the moonlight with haunting nocturnal luminescence, the eyes stared back at me. The snake's carnivorous head hung over the ledge by a foot as its forked tongue probed the air, lustfully savoring the scent of fear. Thankfully, I knew the snake wouldn't be able to reach me across the short distance without sliding further down the rocky slope.

"Devon, what's your problem, man? You scared the shit out of me."

He shook Luke's hand lose from his mouth. "Stop moving! It's right—"

Luke grabbed his mouth and covered it again by force. "If you don't shut up, I'm going to throw you in the goddamn water! I'm serious! Don't make me do it!"

Devon couldn't be still. His body trembled with fear and his eyes were wide, staring directly behind me. Each of us were unraveling at the seams. It had been a long, miserable night and our overworked nerves were in tatters. We couldn't survive in such conditions much longer. We had to do something that could save us all. It had become a situation of survival of the fittest and it was time to adapt and try a different approach. Luke and I made eye contact and I knew that we were both thinking the same thing.

"He has to go." I said.

"If he doesn't, he's going to get us killed." Luke agreed. "Devon, I'm going to let go of your mouth now, but you have to promise me you'll stay calm. Okay?"

Devon nodded and Luke dropped his hand.

"Listen, Devon." I said. "You're freaking out, man. If you stay, we're not going to make it."

"What!? What are you saying?"

"I'm saying you have to go."

"No. Where can I go? I can't go alone!"

"Shhh."

"We can't all go." Luke added. "Someone has to run up the hill and get back to the house to call 9-1-1."

"We can all go!"

"No we can't." I insisted. "You have to go. It's the only way."

"No! I can't do it!"

"Yes you can, Devon." Luke urged. "Only one person can make it. If all three of us run up together, we won't make it. After the first person runs past them, they'll be biting anything that moves. The next two people wouldn't stand a chance. And if any one is going, it has to be you."

"No! Someone else can do it! I can't do this!" Devon's fear was breaking him down. His voice had become a soft plea of disbelief.

I tried to refocus his attention. "Devon, listen to me. You can do this. You're the only one who can. I wouldn't make it three feet. I would lock up. You can scramble up this hill. You can do this. You're our only hope."

"Devon, all you have to do is get to the house and call 9-1-1. You can make it."

Devon's breath began to match the speed of his racing heart. He grunted in frustration at the understanding of what had to be done as if a battle of life and death was being fought within his thoughts that reached the very core of his soul.

"Okay! Okay! I'll go!" Devon finally decided, and when he did, a long silence followed. The emotions running through him were so clear that I could almost feel them myself. He was scared, yet understanding of the possibility that he may not live to see the next day.

He would be running through a gauntlet of snakes. Poisonous, or not poisonous, he would be taking his chances like a game of Russian Roulette. Spin the chamber. Pull the trigger. He accepted that he was going to be struck and bitten, without a doubt. But, he had to go. It was our only hope to survive. Survival of the fittest.

As I watched his tall, thin, shivering figure, I had an idea. Without moving my legs, I slowly unzipped and pulled off my jacket. "Here, take this, Devon. Put it on over your jacket. That way you'll have a little more protection." He took the jacket and zipped it over his own with a genuine nod of appreciation. "Luke, give him yours too." I suggested and Luke willingly handed his jacket to Devon, who tied it around his waist to cover the backs of his legs.

Devon looked back and forth between each of us. His usual jovial and joking demeanor was solemn. He looked more defeated than I had ever seen him before.

"This is it, boys. I don't even know what to say. I just never thought it would end like this. If I don't make it—"

"You're going to make it, don't talk like that." Luke interrupted.

"No. Just hear me out on this one, boys." He pleaded.

His eyes were filling with tears. His tears tugged at my heart and my vision blurred with moisture. I looked at him and realized that I may never see my friend again.

"If I don't make it—" He stammered. "I just want you both to know that I love you. And I swear. I swear that I'm going to do whatever I can to make that call. I'm going to get you out of here. But, if I don't, and somehow, you make it, please, promise me you'll tell my family that I love them. Tell Amy, and my brother, that I tried. Tell them I'm sorry and I love them."

"Devon, don't worry, you're going to make it." I insisted, trying to make myself believe my words. Something wet touched my check and I realized that a tear had fallen from my eye.

"Just tell them, please."

"Of course, man, you know I will."

Devon wrapped his arms around both of us, and I hugged him for what I knew could be the last time. Devon let go and wiped his tears. "Well." He said in a funny western accent. "I guess it's time for me to hit the old, dusty trail." True to form, he clung to his sense of humor through thick and thin like a drowning man to a life-vest. Even in the face of death, Devon found reason to laugh.

Devon began to prepare himself for the most difficult task that he had ever been asked to do. If he was alone, he wouldn't attempt such a risky escape, but he wasn't. He was with his friends and he was willing risk his life to save us all. If I had ever had a negative thought about the friendship that Devon and I shared, in that moment, I forgot and forgave them all.

The staggered incline of rocks where Devon was about to run was layered with snakes of all shapes and sizes. Above the ledge that Devon would climb, there was a gap between two bushes. Three snakes of camouflage color and glowing green eyes were coiled under a bush to the right side of the gap. Beyond the gap, he would still have to make an extremely dangerous climb up the steep, jagged hillside that was slick with dead and decaying foliage. I looked into the impending woods and saw nothing but complete darkness within the trees. He would make the climb blind, and honestly, I didn't believe it could be done.

"You can do this, Devon!" Luke encouraged.

"Just stay to the left. Those three are on the right." I reminded him and patted him on the shoulder as he continued to take deep, furious breaths. "You've got this!"

Devon's entire body was tensed in an upright, sprinter's stance. Tears of frustration clouded the fear in his eyes. He tilted the brim of his black hat down to protect his face, and across his forehead it read, The Rundown. An inside joke, a line from Family Guy, were Devon's last words.

"That's my mama!" He yelled.

And he was gone. He took off in a dead sprint. Two steps, three steps, he was trampling over the unsuspecting bodies. The sound of hissing snakes filled the air. Devon's bowed legs pushed forward, dodging bite after bite that barely missed his ankles. He was moving fast and his legs were pumping hard. He reached the ledge and frantically scrambled up, but he lost his footing. He slid back, he slid down, nearly falling from the ledge.

"Keep going, Devon! Don't stop! You're our only hope!" I yelled, awkwardly, unable to think clearly as my hopes and fears were tied to Devon and his slipping foothold.

He managed to regain his balance and he kept moving upward. He climbed wildly on all fours like a mangy dog. He was on track, shooting the gap between the two bushes and he avoided the glowing green eyes that lurked at his side. He was almost out. He was almost into the woods. He stretched for a hand-hold to pull himself away from danger. He frantically searched for a rock, a root, a tree, solid earth, anything. His hand hooked under a root from a young sapling and he pulled himself upward.

But he didn't get far. The root snapped and an awful pop resounded in my ears like the sound of shattered hopes. Devon fell backward in a freefall until he landed flat on his back. His fall was partially broken by a bush and by the bodies of three gargantuan snakes who had seen him coming through luminescent green eyes. And instantly, all bodies were moving. Limbs and bodies and heads thrashed through the bush. The sound of violent hissing rang in the air like buzzing electricity as Luke and I stood powerless to help our friend. We could do nothing but watch as the massive heads rose from the ground and pelted Devon with bite after bite. Each attack landed with the forceful sound of bone on flesh.

"Go, Devon!" Luke screamed.

He was disoriented. His arms and legs were flailing in every direction as he tried to fend off the attack and regain his footing. He grabbed a hand hold against something sturdy, then it moved. It pulled back and he discovered that he was holding a snake by the throat. With raw, natural power, the snake lunged toward Devon's face. The open jaws struck the bill of his hat with the force of a prizefighter. Devon swayed but didn't fall. Somehow, he scrambled to his feet. He climbed furiously on all fours, crawling upward as fast as his body would take him. The snakes refused to let him get away. The sounds wouldn't stop. Bone on flesh. Bone on flesh. He couldn't get away fast enough. And then he was gone.

Chapter 14: Alone With Two

I felt the touch of something cold and wet against my skin. I turned my palms toward the sky and felt the touch again, and again. I lifted my head in disbelief and silently asked myself, why? Why, when I thought that our situation couldn't possibly get worse, why did it have to rain?

There were black clouds covering the sky like a wool blanket and the moon was bundled somewhere beneath them. The falling raindrops increased their speed and increased their fury. They hissed as they hit the rocks and hissed as they blew across the open water. Luke and I had given our jackets to Devon, and without them, we had nothing more than the t-shirts on our backs to protect us from the brutal onslaught of icy rain. There was nothing that I could do but let the rain soak through my clothes, and stand there, and bear it.

My breath came and went in short bursts like little puffs of smoke that fought against the cool air. In an attempt to stay warm, I tucked my arms within my damp t-shirt and hugged myself, but still, I shivered beyond control. I wasn't sure how much longer I could last. It was adrenaline, the fear of death, and my will to survive that had held me upright through the endless hours within the snake pit. But the fight within me was fading as the inevitable enemy of exhaustion took hold. The thought of sleep had become the most beautiful thought in the world. If I could have sat down to rest for two minutes it would have seemed like a lifetime of peace.

"Hey, did you hear that?" Luke whispered through chattering teeth, stirring me from dreams of sleep.

"No, what was it?"

"I don't know. I thought I heard Devon."

I looked into the dark forest of trees and listened, but all I could hear was the soft sound of falling rain.

"I can't hear anything. Do you think he could have made it to the house yet?" I asked, already knowing the answer.

"No. I think he's lost. It sounded like he fell, but I can't hear him anymore."

"I can't either. I haven't heard him for almost an hour."

Luke didn't respond. I wasn't sure whether he had actually heard anything, but I hoped that he had. We both drifted into one of the long spells of silence that we had become accustomed to. The rain was slowing down to a drizzle and the moon was peeking out at us from behind a patch of clouds. I held a shivering palm up to the sky and felt a few drops, but then I didn't feel anymore.

"I think it stopped." I said as if speaking to no one.

"Hey, Chas?"

"Yeah?"

"Do you think Devon's dead?"

"Yeah."

The wind that had brought the rain, left with the rain. I glanced down to our feet and looked into the eyes of the snakes that had hidden themselves within nearby crevices to shelter themselves from the rain.

"Stay." I commanded them as if they had become obedient pets. I peeled my wet t-shirt from my body and wrung the water from it. While the water splashed against the rocks, the night air clamped down on my exposed skin like a giant, icy hand. I didn't want to do it, but I put the wrung-out, damp shirt back on my body, hoping that it would eventually dry and provide some small amount of warmth.

"Devon!" Luke suddenly screamed, and Devon's name echoed over and over from the surrounding hills.

"Devon!" He called again, but the silent sentinels of the forest offered no response.

"Hey, Devon!" I yelled, and I yelled again until my lungs felt like they would burst, but I only heard my own voice bouncing in desperation from place to place, searching in vain for the friend we had lost.

"Devon —" Luke began to scream, but stopped and violently shook his leg. "No! No! Stop! Don't do that!"

"What? What's wrong?"

"A snake's on my leg!"

I looked down at his leg, but I couldn't see anything. "Where? I don't see it."

"It's crawling up my goddamn pants! Do something!"

"Like what!?"

"I don't know!"

I searched the ground by his feet and I could see the end of a dark tail poking out from the leg of his jeans. I leaned down and lunged for the tail. My fingertips grazed against slippery scales as the snake slid away and disappeared within Luke's pant leg. Luke grunted and cursed and teetered on the verge of hysterics. I leaned back and I could see the snake wrapping itself higher and higher up Luke's leg.

"Hey, Luke?"

"What?" He growled through clenched teeth.

"Is that a snake in your pants, or are you just happy to see me?'

"Damn it, Chas! It's not funny!"

"I know, I know. My bad." I knew it was no time for jokes, but for some reason, a slaphappy delirium had crept into my mood and I couldn't seem to control it.

"Oh, no! No, don't do that!" Luke tensed reflexively and clasped his hands over his groin.

"What? What's it doing?"

"It's going for my balls, man!"

I cringed, imagining myself trapped in Luke's situation. I had never felt more sorry for him than I did in that moment. All I could think to do for him was to try to comfort him. I patted him on the shoulder for support. "Hang in there, man."

"*Hang in there*? ...How the hell am I supposed to *hang in there*!?

I've got a goddamn snake in my pants! *Do* something, man!"

"What do you want *me* to do about it?"

"Okay here's what we can do. I'm going to unzip my pants and you can reach down real quick and pull it out."

"Whoa! No way, man! I'm not reaching down there! You've got to be crazy!"

"It's gonna bite my balls, man! Come on!"

"I'm sorry, but you're on your own on this one. I don't want to reach down there and grab the wrong snake."

"I'm not joking right now, Chas. This is serious! This thing's going to bite me if I don't get it out!"

"Then reach down your own pants and pull it out."

"Fine! I'll do it myself!"

He removed one hand from the protective grip that covered his groin and unfastened his belt buckle then unzipped his fly. He held his hand above the waistline of his pants as he prepared to make the grab, but he hesitated. He changed his mind.

"The damn thing's looking right at me." He whispered. "It's like it knows what I'm about to do."

"Just do it quick then."

"No, I'm just going to have to wait until it turns around." He re-zipped his fly, refastened his belt-buckle and resumed the two handed grip on his groin.

The moon came out of hiding and illuminated our rocky, snake-infested world. Our last glimmer of hope had died with Devon in the woods and we had given up on our attempts to fight back and clear the snakes away. We knew that they would only come crawling back or be replaced by others. We resigned ourselves to our fate and let nature take its course.

While the moon was out, I used the opportunity to take inventory of our surroundings. There were a few brave snakes that had crawled out of their crevices and continued their vigil upon the rocks, mere inches from our feet. Their cold-blooded bodies seemed to be drawn to what little heat remained within ours. I glanced behind my feet and found the root lying motionless in the same position as I had last seen it. There were two sets of green reptilian eyes that glared down at me from the ledge. They had moved from one bush to the other, but I wasn't sure where the third set of eyes was hiding.

I noticed something moving, sliding down the slope. I looked for the distinct green eyes, but the eyes held no color. The snake was smaller and sleeker than those on the ledge. It flowed with the contours of the rocks like water. It slipped stealthily between crevices in a winding, but decisive path. And the path lead directly to me and Luke. I nudged Luke and motioned to the moving figure.

"You've got to be kidding me." Luke whispered in disbelief.

I didn't move and I didn't speak. The snake slid down and down and then it paused. A flat, triangular head dangled over the edge of a rock and I recognized the hourglass pattern that ran down the length of its rusty-brown scales. It was one of the most poisonous snakes in the world, a copperhead, and it had positioned itself within four inches from both of our knees. It flicked its tongue, probing the air, sensing us, and one of the tongue's forks nearly brushed against my jeans. Instinctively, I began to back away. The snake stiffened its neck, hissed, and opened its jaws, exposing two needle-sharp fangs that curled inward like two cruel daggers, and I stopped moving.

I held my breath and waited for the pain to come, but it wasn't me who felt the pain. It was Luke.

"Shit!" He growled. "It bit me!"

I had watched the copperhead closely but hadn't seen it move. "Where did it bite you?"

"Somewhere on my thigh. It's moving down though."

I realized that it was the snake in Luke's pants that had bitten him. I checked the copperhead and its eyes gleamed like black scarlet as it aimed its strike for whichever knee that happened to move first. I was determined to not let my knee be the first to flinch, but I also hoped that Luke could hold steady. I stood as still as my weary legs would allow and I chanced a look down to Luke's leg. The leg that was furthest from the copperhead seemed to be moving. The snake was crawling down his thigh and wrapping its way down his calf. I watched as a black head, slightly larger than my thumb, peeked out from the bottom of Luke's jeans. It slithered onto the rocks and a long, slender body followed. It dipped its head into the water, and thankfully, it swam away.

I had hoped for a moment of silence, but I heard something shift along the shore. Rocks broke away like shale and tumbled down to the water. I searched for the source, but couldn't see what was causing the commotion.

"Oh, shit." Luke whispered, and I immediately understood what was happening. I felt my heart flood with fear and I scanned the rocks for the body that I knew was sliding down. Two green eyes flashed behind a wide, pale face. Its body landed heavily onto each crumbling rock and it was unconcerned for anything in its path. It slowed its descent then suddenly stopped. A few loose rocks continued to tumble into the water, but when the last few trickled down and the water calmed, we were left in silence.

Neither Luke nor I dared to breath. I glanced over Luke's shoulder to see the green eyes looking up at us, less than two feet from Luke's ankle. For the second time of the night, I had never felt sorrier for him than I did in that moment.

We were completely boxed in and any movement by either one of us meant an attack. Our situation was so bad that I didn't even bother to watch, because there was nothing that I could possibly do to save myself, or Luke. We were at the mercy of nature and it was our own fault. We had unknowingly stumbled into the wrong place at the wrong time of year. The cove, Lily Creek Cove, was the breeding ground where snakes gathered from miles around throughout the autumn season, but we were forced to learn the lesson the hard way, and as lessons always come, we learned it too late.

I looked into the sky and looked into the face of the moon. I was beginning to think that I wouldn't survive to see the sun rise. I missed my family and I missed Claire. I wondered whether I would ever see them again.

It was hard for me to fathom the conclusion of my life. I told myself that I was too young to die, but I knew that was a lie. I knew that life was fragile, but I wanted to believe that it wasn't. I wanted to believe, as most teenagers do, that I was invincible, and sometimes I did believe it. But as death seemed like the only plausible end in sight, I knew the truth. Death has no favorites. It comes for us all, young and old, whether we are ready for it, or not.

I held my gaze at the moon and I understood that I may be seeing its pale face for the last time, and it had never looked so beautiful as it did in that moment. The silver-white glow seemed to shine from its surface and I could see the grey outlines of craters, millions of miles away. I was thankful for the sight of earth's majestic crown and I didn't want it to be my last, but we rarely get what we want. Sometimes though, as it has been said, we get what we need.

I heard a strange noise drifting through the air. It sounded as though it was somewhere far away, off in the distance. I pricked my ears and followed the sound as it grew louder, and slowly seemed to get closer. In the still of the night, the noise cut through the air like a rusty chainsaw. It grew louder and louder until the noise seemed to vibrate the very hills that surrounded us. Then I saw it. A boat swung into the open channel.

"Luke." I whispered.

"I know." Was all he said in response. There was nothing more that needed to be said.

A searchlight panned from side to side, flashing up and down the rocky shore. The light found us and I had to squint to see through the sudden brightness. I waved my arms in welcome to the rescue boat that raced across the water, but I didn't move my legs, still wary of the copperhead, the root, the glowing green eyes, and any others that lay at our feet.

I looked down at the copperhead, only to find it gone. The snakes at our feet were slipping into the water, disappearing, one by one.

"Where are they going?" I asked.

"I don't know."

I had to assume that the vibrations and the noise from the motor, along with the bright searchlight, had scared them. Snakes all around us were creeping back into nearby crevices and into the water. Even the snake with the glowing green eyes was lumbering its massive green and brown camouflaged body back to its perch on the ledge. I turned and looked behind me, expecting to see the root gone. But in the bright white light it looked more terrifying than ever. Its eyes gleamed like black glass and each scale looked like a pebble of slick onyx. Its huge head remained motionless and the way its jaws were angled it looked like a sinister smile stretched across its face. I rubbed my eyes and looked away, trying to forget the image, but it was an image that I could never forget.

The boat slowed and prepared to tie onto shore. Without a word, both Luke and I dove into the boat.

"Go! Go!" I yelled, before I had even seen who our rescuers were.

The boat spun around and we sped away. As the shoreline grew smaller and smaller, the searchlight continued to pan along the rocks.

"I can't see no snakes." A voice called out.

I saw a man wearing a worn-down pair of overalls and a jean jacket standing behind the light.

"I don't care." I responded. "Just get us out of here."

"Don't worry, boys. We're going to get you home." The man operating the manually steered motor at the rear of the boat said. He wore a Carhartt jacket and a Bass Pro Shops hat.

"Thank you." Was all that I could manage to say. I wish I would have said more to the men who saved our lives, but as the thought of home set in, and the realization that I was safe, and that I had survived, I was profoundly exhausted.

"Where's Devon?" Luke asked.

"Who?" The driver answered.

"Our friend, Devon."

"Oh, you mean the other boy. He's up at the house. He called about an emergency, then the sheriff called me to come get ya'll."

Devon did it. I don't know how he climbed up the steep wooded hillside in the dead of night without any light to guide him, but he did it. And the three of us survived.

We all made a pact that night, when we were all safely back within the house. We all agreed that if we were ever to retell the story, we would never repeat the words that Devon shared about his trip to Amsterdam, the buyers, and the rare books at Transylvania. But like so many other promises that the three of us made over the years, our pact was bound to be broken.

Chapter 15: Trick or Treat

Throughout the days and weeks that followed our rescue from the snake pit, I tried to readjust back into my regular lifestyle, but something had changed. It was like my survival had opened my eyes to a broader view of life. I began thinking about my life as a whole and dwelling on ideas like right and wrong. I started asking myself questions like, why should I do anything other than enjoy life while it lasts? And while I searched to find the answers, going to class didn't seem important anymore. On the days that I did go, I would stare blankly at the professors and watch their mouths move up and down, but I couldn't pay attention to anything they said. I instead of going to class, I began sleeping through the days, throwing parties, and drinking through the nights.

Some mornings Claire would bring a box of chocolate doughnuts and a bottle of orange juice from my favorite bakery to entice me out of bed. Those were the mornings when I would rise before the crack of noon. I was enjoying my new schedule, but Claire couldn't stand it. I hated to admit it, but I knew that Claire and I were slowly growing apart. It seemed like every day brought a new fight. She wanted me to change back to the way that I had always been, but I didn't know how. It became another question that I needed to answer.

Halloween came along and I threw a costume party to celebrate. I was dressed in a full-body spandex suit as a yellow ninja. The outfit was intended as a joke. It was barely big enough to cover my body, but I thought the outrageously small size only added to the humor. Luke was dressed as a blue ninja and together we were Scorpion and Sub-Zero, two characters from Mortal Kombat. The costumes came with plastic swords and colored face cloths that hid everything other than our eyes. The colorful ninja garb fit us like shrink-wrap, but skin tight was the over-the-top, outrageous look that we were going for.

"Hey, girls." I watched as Claire walked into the party dressed as a French Maid, and Rachel walked in beside her dressed as a go-go dancer. "Get over here!" I yelled, staying in character with my costume.

I couldn't help but look as Claire sauntered toward me through the crowd. She wore a short black dress with white frills of lace that showed the lithe contours of her long legs. Her long black hair was styled in a flattering French-braid.

"Look at you." I said as I hugged Claire and gave her a quick kiss that she almost turned away from. "You look great."

"Thanks." She said as she dropped her eyes to my costume. "So you're a ninja, huh?"

"Yeah." I laughed. I flexed my arms, trying to rip through the tiny costume. "What do you think?"

"Great." She flashed a phony smile and two thumbs up.

I ignored the slight, and gave Rachel a hug, trying to change the subject. "Did you girls bring anything to drink?"

"No." Rachel answered. "We pre-drank at my house. We've already had a few shots."

"What have you girls been drinking? I've had a few shots of Jaeger myself."

"Whiskey." Claire responded. "We'll take some of that if you've got it."

"Yeah, I've probably got some in the freezer. Let's go check."

I didn't think about it at the time, but whiskey and Jagermeister was a dangerous combination for two quarreling lovers.

The three of us walked together through the crowd of friends. There were all sorts of different costumes in the crowd. There were guys and girls wearing togas, pimps with suits, hats, and canes, hoes in skanky dresses, rock stars, groupies, fairies and angels with wings, devils with capes, she devils with red horns and tails, even two guys wearing trash bags, sunglasses, and white gloves who claimed to be dressed as California Raisins.

We stepped into the kitchen and I opened the freezer. I pulled out a one-gallon, glass handle of Jim Beam.

"Here." I said, as I handed the jug to Claire. "Do you think that will be enough?"

She looked at the bottle wide-eyed. "I think this is more than enough…"

"There's shot glasses over there." I pointed to the alcohol splattered counter that surrounded half of the small kitchen in an L-shape. From the bottom of the freezer, I pulled out my bottle of Jagermeister. "Hey, Luke!" I yelled into the beer pong room. "Devon! Come on! It's time for another shot!"

After the lake house incident, the three of us were closer than ever. We had shared a close encounter with death and the experience caused us to share an uncommon bond. In our eyes, we were survivors. We started to believe that since we had escaped death, we were untouchable, something close to invincible, but that was the hubris of youth showing through.

Luke walked into the kitchen.

"Get over here!" I mimicked scorpion's move for the hundredth time of the night.

Devon was dressed as a crack-head, a character from the Chapelle Show named, Tyrone Biggums. Devon wore a cheap sweatsuit with a red toboggan and he had white powder caked around his mouth and nose to complete the costume.

"Are you guys ready? It's shot-thirty." I tapped my wrist to indicate the time.

"Yeah, why not? Pour us another!" Luke answered.

Devon scratched his neck and twitched as if he was suffering from drug induced DT's. When he noticed the bottle of black liquor he did a little dance and mimicked Tyrone's voice. "Why…I'd love some akahol."

"Okay, Tyrone. Here you go." As I poured out three separate shots, Deuce stepped into the conversation. He was dressed as himself, wearing khaki pants, a long-sleeved Polo shirt, and Ray-Bans on top of his head. He believed a costume would cramp his impeccable sense of style.

"Hey, Chas." Deuce said as he fidgeted with his hands. "I bet you can't take all three of those."

"What? The shots?"

"Yeah."

"Of course I can."

He chewed ravenously on a piece of gum as if he were trying to ensure that it wasn't alive. "No, I'm saying like all three in a row. Like back to back to back. Without stopping. Like, without a breath."

"I'll bet you I could do five." I shot back. Deuce and I were in the habit of betting on anything and everything. It was mostly Deuce who was willing to go to extreme lengths to win bets. I had seen someone bet him five dollars that he wouldn't let someone throw a dart at him. In front of a room full of people, he dropped his pants and said, "Just aim for my ass." Needless to say, he won the five dollars.

We had played poker together for years and we had bet against one another for even longer. When he challenged me to drink the shots, in poker talk, a language we both spoke, I called his bet and raised the pot. I raised it so he would think I was bluffing and he called my supposed bluff.

"I bet you a hundred dollars you can't do five!" He challenged, taking the bait that I had set for him, hook, line, and sinker.

"Alright, show me the money and I'll do it."

He put a one hundred dollar bill on the sticky, liquor-splattered counter. I grabbed two more shot glasses from a nearby cabinet and filled them to the rim. I lined all five glasses in a row and prepared myself to take the shots. Then I felt a tap on my shoulder. I turned around to see Claire glaring at me like a woman scorned.

"What do you think you're doing?" She asked.

"What does it look like I'm doing? I'm about to take these shots and win a hundred dollars."

"What, are you an alcoholic now? Don't you think you should just slow down?"

I turned back to Deuce, Luke, and Devon, who were watching and I shrugged. "Oh, well. I guess she's got money riding against me!" I joked. We all laughed and I immediately regretted being so rude to Claire. She only had my best interests at heart, but I couldn't seem to realize it. I was vaguely aware of her turning away and walking into the beer-pong room as I looked down at the five shot glasses of black alcohol that awaited my assault.

"Alright! This one's for my homies!" I joked.

"I bet he spits it out on the fourth one!" Deuce yelled. "Any takers? Anybody else want to bet?" He looked around the room, but didn't find any gamblers.

I pulled my ninja mask out of the way. I took a deep breath and I grabbed shot number one. I opened the hatch and threw it back. I moved on to number two and slammed it down. I reached for the third shot and it went straight to my stomach. Number four followed with ease and I grabbed number five. It sloshed like liquorish syrup in my mouth, but I tilted my head back, forced it down, and swallowed.

"Wooo!" I yelled as I shook my head with alcohol shivers.

"Damn it! Double or nothing!" Deuce protested.

I laughed, still feeling the burn like candy flavored fire in my throat. "Maybe another time, Deuce. On top of everything I already had, I think five more was enough for tonight." I grabbed my hundred dollar bill, patted Deuce on the shoulder, and walked out of the kitchen. I followed after Claire into the beer-pong room and left Luke and Devon to pour their own shots.

I noticed that Claire and Rachel had already found their way into a beer-pong game.

"Hey, who's got next game!?" I yelled, but no one voiced a claim. "Alright, me and Luke have next!"

I watched Claire play as she made a conscious effort to ignore me. She and Rachel were winning and I was impressed by how well they played. After a few more well placed tosses, they won. They high-fived each other and refilled their cups nonchalantly as if the win hadn't challenged their prowess.

"Hey, Luke, we're up!" I yelled into the kitchen.

Luke squeezed into the small room and we stepped to one side of the table and remade the triangle of cups, filling each halfway with beer. Luke nudged me with his elbow. "Let's show 'em how beer-pong is really supposed to be played."

I looked across the table. "I'm sorry to have to do this to you ladies, but we're still the undefeated champs."

"Whatever." Claire shot back. "You're not going to be undefeated forever. We've been practicing."

I smiled. "Oh yeah...I can tell. You girls look good, but I don't know if it will be enough to beat us."

"Yeah, Claire made us practice with cups of water because she wanted to beat you guys so bad." Rachel said.

"Ha!" Luke nudged me again. "Cups of water! They've been practicing with cups of water!"

"Whatever! Screw you guys, you're not going to be laughing when you get beat by two girls!" Claire fired back. She was ready to play and I could tell that she was determined to win.

As gentlemen, we let the girls have the first turn. They started and when Rachel sank their first shot, I almost wished we had taken the first turn. Luke pulled the ball from the cup and chugged the beer. He pulled the cup away from the table quickly, because one of our house rules was the death cup. If two balls landed in the same cup, then the game was over instantly. The rule kept the games going faster and kept the people who weren't paying attention off the table. When Luke and I looked across and saw the fire in Claire's eyes, we both knew that we needed to stay on our toes.

Claire took her turn and sank the ball into another one of our cups. With both shots made, they got a roll back, which gave them each another shot.

Out of their two extra shots, they made one and missed one, and I was worried our undefeated streak may come to an end.

"Shit!" Luke said as we made eye contact.

We knew we were in for a tough game. We had been in the same situation before and we had always come back to win. We had ice in our veins, or more likely, an extremely high amount of alcohol.

We were down by three cups and the first to make all ten won. We did our best to rally back. We made shots, the girls made shots, and we all chugged beers. The lead went back and forth and we had attracted a large crowd. People had packed in around the table to see if Luke and I would break our streak, and adding insult to injury, lose to my girlfriend.

It came down to a tied game. Both teams had only one cup left and only one shot was needed to win. The way the rules of the game worked, on the final cup, if one team made the shot, the other team would get one last round of shots to try to send the game into overtime.

Rachel had the ball. She aimed carefully, threw, but missed long. Claire stepped into the center of the table and lined up her shot as I nervously awaited her throw. She looked so determined that I could almost feel our streak breaking before she even threw the ball. She aimed and let the ball fly. It splashed into the center of our final cup.

"Yes!" She screamed. "I told you! I knew we would beat you!" She pointed at us across the table and she flashed one of my favorite smiles, but it wasn't meant for me. It was meant only for herself, because she was proud and excited and happy, all at the same time, and it was there because she had proved her point and had beaten me.

The room went wild, cheering for the excited girls, but the game wasn't officially over. We still had our chance to tie the game and send it into overtime. A part of me was happy for Claire and knew that if I had to lose, I would want to lose to her so that she could win. But my pride played a bigger part in my actions that night.

I stood at the center line of the table and I lined the little white ball up like I was throwing darts.

"Hey." I said as I reached the ball over to a blonde girl in a she-devil costume. "Blow on this for good luck."

She smiled and blew with pursed lips as I smiled across the table at Claire and winked. She looked back at me in disgust.

I refocused my attention, aimed one last time, and let the ball fly. It rattled around the rim of the cup, then fell in. I did it. I tied the game and guaranteed our chance to survive. The room erupted with both cheers and jeers. The noise in the room was so loud that no one could understand what anyone was saying. People shouted over one another and during all of the commotion, the girls weren't paying attention. They forgot about the ball that was still floating in the cup. I almost warned Claire that she needed to pull the cup away from the table, but again, my pride acted rather than my heart. I stayed quiet as Luke saw the opportunity and took it. He took his shot. It landed right next to the other ball, inside the cup. He landed the dreaded death cup. The game instantly ended. There was no over-time and no tie breaker. They lost by way of the death cup, and we won.

"What!?" Claire yelled when she realized what had happened. "No! You can't do that! We weren't looking!"

The crowd was a jumbled mass of hysteria and no one could seem to believe what had happened.

"I'm sorry, Claire!" I yelled, trying to shout over the voices but she couldn't hear me.

"No! That doesn't count! We weren't looking!"

"Those are the house rules. The death cup breaks the tie." Luke answered. "But it's okay, Claire, you can try again some other time!" Luke threw up his hand for me to high-five. I gave him a high-five and went down a row of people giving high-fives along the way to the kitchen. I went to the refrigerator to grab a few more beers. Out of the corner of my eye I saw Claire as she stormed through the kitchen, ignoring me.

"Hey, Claire!" I yelled as I hurried to catch her. I put my hand on her shoulder. "Whoa, Claire, slow down. Where are you going?"

She spun around to face me. "Don't touch me!"

"What's wrong with you?" I asked, not fully believing her anger to be real. After all, it was just a game, wasn't it?

"You're what's wrong with me!"

"Are you seriously mad about the beer-pong game?" I asked.

"No, I'm mad because you're a jerk!"

"You know what, Claire? I'm sorry. But, look at it this way; at least you got one consolation."

"Oh yeah, and what's that?"

"At least you're dating the greatest beer-pong player in the world!" I joked. I playfully laughed, hoping she would join in, but she didn't.

"Screw you, Chas! You're an asshole!"

"Whoa! Easy, where did that come from? Here. Come here. I know what you need. You need a hug."

I opened my arms and leaned in to give her a hug, trying to apologize, but I couldn't seem to give her the earnest and warm apology that I truly wanted to give her. She was angry and embarrassed and I felt like I could have somehow prevented her pain.

She jerked herself away from my arms. "Don't touch me!"

She raised her right hand and slapped me. My face stung and my jaw hung open in disbelief. She had never slapped me before and my heart stung far worse than my face.

"What the hell was that for?" I asked.

Without hesitation, she slapped me again. I didn't think about what I was doing, or why, and I reached up and slapped her back. It was a light touch, but still, I couldn't believe what I had done. I couldn't believe how far from my values I had gone. I was instantly sorry and I instantly regretted what I had done. I wanted to apologize, but upon my touch she exploded like a live grenade in a fit of rage. She reached up to smack me again, but I caught her hand. She threw the other hand at me and I caught it and held her in both of my arms. She tried to kick me with her feet and break away from my grasp.

"Let go of me!" She screamed. "I can't believe you hit me, you piece of shit! Let me go!"

We had drawn a crowd and people were staring, watching the show as if it were live reality TV, but I didn't care. She was the only person in the room that I truly cared for.

I held her arms and I tried to look into her eyes. I tried to make her see me. I tried to apologize with my eyes and let her know how sorry I was and how much I loved her, but it was too little, too late.

"Let me go!"

"Claire, I'm going to let go, but just calm down."

She called me every curse word imaginable and flailed her body wildly to get away from my embrace. I felt like if I let her go, I would lose her, but I couldn't stand to see her upset, so I let her go.

She burst into tears, pushed me away, and ran upstairs to my room.

I hated to see her cry. After my dad left, I had seen my mom and sister cry too many times. A soft spot had grown in my heart for girls and tears, and I felt compelled to do whatever I could to dry their eyes. I followed Claire upstairs. I didn't fully understand why she was crying, but I wanted to fix whatever it was that was hurting her. I didn't realize, until later, that the only thing hurting her was me.

I stood at the top of the stairs and saw Claire from across the room. She threw a change of clothes and her purse into an over night bag. She was leaving. She turned and noticed me.

"Get away from me!" She screamed. "I hate you!" Her words pushed through her tears and turned her sadness into anger.

There was only one thing that I should have said, but I couldn't seem to find the words.

"Claire, just calm down! Talk to me! What's wrong?"

"You're an asshole!" She eyed my collection of DVD's that were stacked among three tall racks of several hundred movies. She grabbed the racks and flung them to the floor.

"Claire, stop it! Just stop!"

She saw picture frames that she had given me. There were pictures of the two of us, pictures of friends, and pictures of my family throughout my room. She grabbed several pictures of us and slung them across the room. I cringed as the glass frames smashed against the wall.

My own anger was beginning to rise and the right words that I had sought were lost. "There you go!" I antagonized her. "Break them! Does that feel better!?"

"Yes! You and I are over! We're done! I'm getting rid of every one of these pictures!"

She finished off the pictures of us, the us that didn't exist anymore, then moved on to other pictures. She grabbed a picture of my family and flung it to the floor. For a split second, she realized what she had done. She wanted to push my buttons and pull the emotions out of me. The broken image of my family sparked my anger.

I stepped toward her. "Don't you dare touch another picture of my family!"

"What family!?" She jabbed back. "You call that a family!? You're all screwed up! That's what you are! All of you! Your dad is a lying, adulterous piece of shit. Your mom cries all the time and complains about money, but she won't even get a job! Your little brother is turning into an alcoholic and your little sister doesn't even have a father in her life! She's probably going to end up like your dad's secretary, a home-wrecker that only looks for older men to fill the hole in her life!"

A rage burned inside of me that I couldn't control. She had taken my own worries and fears that I had confided in her and spat them back at me to cause me pain.

With nothing but hateful words, she had torn down everything I loved and held close to my heart, including her.

"And you!" She screamed. "You're the worst! You're a piece of shit just like your dad! I knew I shouldn't have stayed with you after he cheated on your mom! I thought you were different, but you've changed. I don't even know who you are anymore. You're just like your dad!"

That was the worst insult that someone could say to me. My dad had single handedly destroyed my family and crushed the hearts of those who loved him. Her words had cut deep. They struck a nerve and dug into my very core. Sometimes though, to avoid pain, you can't run from it, you have to run toward it. I ran toward it and masked the pain with anger.

"Go ahead, Claire! Do it!" I shouted. "I don't care anymore! Do you want to hurt me!? Is that what you want!? You're ripping my fucking heart out! But, if you want to hurt me, then do it! Hurt me! Go ahead, do it! Hit me!"

She cocked her right hand back and threw her fist as hard as she could. The punch landed on my left cheek, but didn't have much effect.

"There you go!" I yelled. "Now you're hurting me! Does that feel better!?"

She responded with more punches. I held my face out as any easy target, but her punches weren't having the effect she wanted. She wanted me to bleed. She wanted to see blood, my blood. She grabbed my face and dug her nails deep under my left eye and screamed with primitive fury. She dug until skin tore away and she had what she wanted. She made me bleed. I could feel warm blood trickling down my face.

Someone grabbed Claire and pulled her away and I realized that it was Rachel. She had watched the whole scene unfold from across the room. Claire noticed it was Rachel who held her and she snapped out of her rage and her anger returned to sobbing tears.

Rachel put her arms around Claire's shoulders and led her toward the stairs. "Come on, let's get you home." Rachel looked back at me sadly and shrugged.

I touched my face, then looked at my hands. They were spotted with blood. I watched the two of them walk away. They walked down the stairs and Claire was gone. She was gone.

I was alone.

I walked to a mirror and looked at my beaten and battered face. It was covered with red blotches and under my left eye there were streaks of blood. It looked as though my tears had turned to crimson.

The gash from her nail would eventually grow into a scar. It was a scar that I would carry for the rest of my days. Every time that I looked into a mirror, I would see the scar. For a long time, the scar served as a reminder of how deep someone that I trust could dig. On the night of violent, clashing emotions, I built a wall around my heart and lost faith in everyone around me. If I couldn't trust the girl I loved, and had loved faithfully for years, then who could I trust?

Chapter 16: Christmas

I woke up in my old room in the basement of my mom's house as someone called my name through the darkness.

"Chas! Chas! Wake up!" In my sleep-filled fog, I recognized my sister's voice. "Chas! Hurry up! Come see!"

"Okay, okay." I grumbled as I rolled around in bed, not wanting to leave its comfort.

"Hurry up!"

"Why the rush, Syd?"

"Santa Clause came!" Her voice couldn't contain her excitement.

I smiled, happy that she was happy. I got out of bed, threw some sweatpants on, and found her waiting for me at the bottom of the stairs. When she saw me, she ran up the staircase as fast as her twelve year old legs would carry her. "Hurry up! Come see! Santa Clause brought us *everything*!"

It was Christmas morning and it was our first Christmas as a broken family. My mom had begged my dad to put the negotiations of the divorce aside and help her with money to buy Christmas presents, but he refused. She couldn't get any help from him unless the court ordered him to, and even then, he drug the court orders out as long as possible so that she would break down and agree to his terms. But, she wouldn't sign his offer. They were in a stalemate and the people most affected by their inability to agree were the kids, my little brother and sister, and I didn't realize it at the time, but that also included me.

I believed that Christmas was one of the highlights of a childhood. I couldn't stand the thought that the difficultly of Blake's and Sydney's first Christmas as a broken family would be exacerbated by our father's selfishness as he attempted to force us to experience Christmas without him and without gifts to unwrap. To stifle his efforts, I had given my mom several thousand dollars and told her to buy them everything and anything they wanted. I wanted her to spoil them. I wanted them to understand that no matter what life could throw at us, what remained of our family would be fine. We would get through it, together.

I stood at the top of the stairs and Sydney grabbed my hand. She pulled me through the living room, through the kitchen, through the dining room, and into the family room. The Christmas tree was lit and colors sparkled with dazzling brilliance across the room. There were boxes and bags and piles and there was one pile of non-wrapped presents intended for each of us. Each pile was as big, or bigger, than it had always been, every pile except for one. In the place where my mother's presents should have been, there was only an empty red stocking with her name written in glitter on the white cuff. Tears welled along the lids of my eyes as I looked at the empty stocking. We had made them by hand and decorated them ourselves, years before as a family. But now there was nothing underneath it. There were no gifts near it. When I saw what lay across the stocking I nearly cried. Three candy canes had been placed with care atop the crushed red velvet. I realized the three candy canes were all that she had allowed herself. She had spent every penny of the money I had given her on us and had neglected to buy anything for herself. It was her first Christmas in twenty years without her husband. It had to be a difficult day for her, but she hadn't even thought of herself. She had only thought of her kids.

Luckily though, I had thought of her. I had taken Blake and Sydney shopping and we had bought her as many presents as we could find.

Blake, Sydney, and I were looking through our gifts as my mom walked into the family room wearing silk pajamas. "Merry Christmas!" She said with a soft smile.

"Merry Christmas, Mom." I walked across the room and gave her a knowing hug.

"It's time to open presents now!" Sydney insisted.

We all took a seat as Sydney passed the boxes out to each of us from under the tree. It was a tradition that we would go around the room, opening and unwrapping presents, one at a time. Blake went first and I watched with pride as he opened a huge, square box. He tore through the wrapping paper like a rabid dog in his haste to discover what was hidden inside. The paper fell by his side as he looked at the unwrapped box.

"Wow!" He said, amazed. His eyes looked as bright as the lights on the Christmas tree.

"What is it Blake?" I asked, feigning surprise.

"It's a surround sound system and a DVD player!"

"Do you like it?"

"Like it? I love it! This thing is awesome!"

"Okay, I'm next!" Sydney said with enthusiasm only a child on Christmas can muster. She tore through the wrapping paper of an average-sized box and found a digital camera inside. "Whoa, cool! I can take pictures now!"

She held her prize high above her head in excitement for us all to see.

I was expected to go next, so Sydney handed me a present from my mom. I had told her that I didn't need anything, but still, she had already given me a pile of non-wrapped presents with movies, games, and clothes, and she was giving me more. I undid the wrapping paper and opened a long, wide box. Inside I found a cashmere sweater and a pair of dress pants.

"Ohh, nice!" I held the sweater up to my chest. "Here, Syd. Feel this." I handed it to her.

"Eww, it's so soft"

I looked across the room to the person who had picked it out. "Thank you, Mom. It's really nice."

"Is it the right size?"

I checked the tag. "Of course, you always get the right size."

"Okay, Mom, it's your turn!" Sydney insisted.

I could tell by the look on her face as she unwrapped the box that she hadn't expected any gifts. She opened the box and she saw a new black purse from Coach.

"How did you know!?" She looked around at our smiling faces, expecting an answer. "I've been wanting to buy this purse!"

I knew that she had been waiting until she had the money, but I didn't want her to wait anymore. I felt that if I couldn't use money to make life better for the people I loved, then money had no purpose.

"We just took a guess." I said with a wide grin.

Sydney passed out more presents and we went around and around the room opening them all. I watched the expression on my mom's face as she looked around the room at the gifts and the joy and the love that we all shared. She seemed like she was amazed that we had actually pulled it off. Even though we may have been a broken family, the moment, and our hearts, seemed whole. I caught her eye, and smiled. She smiled back, then began to cry.

Sydney sat beside her and put her arm around her shoulders. "What's wrong, Mom? Are you sad because Santa Clause only gave you some candy canes?"

My mom laughed. "No, honey, these are happy tears." She looked back and forth between Blake and I, as tears ran down her face. We walked over to her and wrapped our arms around both of them and we squeezed them tight. We held each other in a big, group hug. Then, for no apparent reason, we all started laughing.

People have said that money can't buy happiness. On that Christmas morning, I believed it could.

Chapter 17: Hit the road

Winter turned to spring, and as the weather changed, new life bloomed in the Bluegrass. It was time for my seasonal lawncare service to resume where we had left off in the fall. I was in the process of trying to expand my small business and I reached out to take on new partners. It was Luke who decided that a lawn care service would be a good way to invest some of his money that was slowly dwindling away. For five thousand dollars, I sold him twenty five percent of the business and we became partners. Another twenty five percent, I gave to my brother, Blake. I retained fifty percent, and together we incorporated under the name, Lawncare of the Bluegrass, and we were open for business.

I learned a valuable lesson as the business grew. I learned that friends should never be hired as employees. Partnerships could work, but an employer, employee relationship between friends could lead to problems. And the spring season was filled with problems.

I was at Keeneland, Lexington's historic horse track, betting on the races and trying to enjoy a beautiful, sunny day as a maiden claiming race was in progress. I was vaguely aware of the horses careening around the final turn, because rather than enjoying the race, I was screaming into my cell phone. I was in the center of a crowd of people within the grandstand clubhouse seats who were dressed to the hilt. Girls and women wore spring dresses of green, pink, teal, cream, yellow, and white, and together they formed a pastel collage around me like gorgeous May flowers. Guys, including me, wore sports coats and ties. It seemed like all of Lexington, the thoroughbred capital of the world, seemed to be watching the race. Everyone including Brian, my roommate, friend, and recently acquired employee. He was somewhere, hiding in the crowd.

"Do you hear me, Brian? You're costing me money!"

"It's cool, man, I'm going to get it done." He said, referring to a job that he had scheduled and cancelled and rescheduled several times, assuming that as his friend, I would let him have some extra slack.

"It's not *cool*, Brian! I told you it had to be done today!"

"I'll get it done tomorrow. I already talked to the rest of the guys and we're going to do it in the morning."

"You said the same thing yesterday, and the day before that! You know what? Don't even worry about it!"

"No, wait—"

I hung up the phone. I looked to Luke who stood next to me, wondering what I had been yelling about. The thunderous sound of hoof beats stormed by us as silk uniformed jockeys whipped their charge toward the finish line, spurred on by the roaring applause of the crowd.

"That was Brian." I said, dismissively.

"What happened? He not show up today?"

I laughed. "Not only did he not show up, he's here."

"What do you mean he's here?"

"Yeah, he decided to take the day off and come to the races."

"Again? So he didn't get that job done?"

"Nope. You know what that means don't you?"

The horses crossed the finish line and I glanced at the ticket in my hand. I usually bet exotics like exactas and tri-fectas, but to begin the day I had bet across the board on the favorite to win, place, and show. She finished fourth, one place off the money. I looked back to Luke and I could see the disappointment in his face. "But we just got here. It's only the third race." He protested.

"I know. But we have to get this done if Brian can't."

Luke and I said a few goodbyes as we walked through the crowd and made our way to the parking lot.

"Hey, that was quick!" An older man with a scruffy mustache said as he walked toward me. He was a parking attendant who walked with a slight limp, but he seemed to get around well enough. Every time I was at Keeneland I made a point to find him and he made a point to look for me. The parking lot stretched in rows for a square mile, but he always found a spot for me near the door.

"Yeah, I just wasn't feeling it today, maybe my luck will be better tomorrow." I said as I shook his hand and slipped him a twenty dollar bill. It was amazing what a difference a little green piece of paper could make. Opportunities would come knocking and doors would open.

"They say Alibaba is gonna run away with it in the eighth, tomorrow. But you didn't hear that from me." The old man winked and when he smiled he ruffled his mustache.

"Alright, thanks for the tip. I'll check it out."

I found my Jeep the way I had left it, the doors were unlocked and my keys had been left in the floorboard. I drove through the expansive parking lot and wound down the roads that led to the highway. The thought that I had to cancel my plans for the day to do a job that should have been finished a week before, festered in my mind. Every minute I grew more and more agitated, especially at Brian and his carefree work ethic. I tried to let it go, but for some reason, I couldn't.

Luke and I stopped by my house to change out of our dress clothes and into work clothes. Luke had moved out of his apartment and I was renting him a room. He turned the beer-pong room, the sun room at the back of my house, into his bedroom. The beer-pong table had been moved into the garage, which Luke and I had remodeled into a wall-to-wall party room. As partying was high on our list of priorities, we spared no expenses on our remodeling project. We dry-walled the ceiling, painted the walls, and laid carpet within the detached two-car garage. We built a bar, complete with stools, neon beer signs, and a TV, we added a full-size refrigerator that we equipped to cool a keg, a pool table, which was mostly used for beer-pong, a foosball table, and couches to line the walls. We packed the room with speakers and a CD player, and it was ready for a party. But partying would have to wait for the time being, because we had work to do.

Luke and I each came back to my Jeep in different clothes. We drove to the warehouse where our equipment was stored. We hooked a trailer to the tow hitch that hauled our heavy machinery and we threw the tools that we would need in the back of the Jeep.

We arrived at the job-site and we worked for hours, spreading piles of mulch, digging holes, planting flowers and bushes, and sowing grass-seed throughout the front and back lawn of a property that belonged to an elderly woman. She had been patient and understanding as she scheduled and rescheduled repeatedly for the same service. While Luke and I worked, she insisted that we take breaks from time to time and she brought us tall glasses of lemonade to cool us down. It took us every available hour of sunlight, but we finished the job and drove away a few dollars richer than when the day began.

When we arrived home it was dark. I was dirty, tired, and hungry. I wanted to go inside, get something to eat, shower, and relax. I walked through the door expecting to do nothing less and nothing more. I went into the kitchen and grabbed a box of cereal and a gallon of milk. I opened the cabinet to grab a bowl, but the cabinet was empty. I looked across the counter and saw a pile of dirty, disgusting, unwashed dishes. Every dish in the entire house was filthy and piled within the sink or along the counter. Every roommate in the house had a chore and the dishes happened to be the chore that Brian had chosen. Seeing the dishes piled in the sink like a small mountain of filth, and knowing that Brian's laziness was the cause, was more than I could bear. Something within me snapped like a dry twig. All of the stress and frustration that had boiled within me earlier in the day rose to the surface. I lost control and erupted in a fit of anger.

I slammed the cabinet door shut so hard that one of the hinges broke loose. "Goddamn it, Brian!" I shouted and waited for a response. I listened but I didn't hear an answer. "Brian! Why are these dishes dirty!?" It seemed as if I was only yelling to myself.

"You worthless piece of shit! Where are you!?" I stormed out of the room in search of the cause of my wrath. I knew he was somewhere around the house. I had seen his car parked in the driveway. I flung the door to Alex's room open and there he was.

"What the hell are you doing!?" I demanded.

"What, man!? What does it look like I'm doing!?"

He sat comfortably in a chair and Alex lounged on his bed, and it looked and smelled as if they had recently smoked a fresh bowl of weed.

"Nothing! You're not doing a goddamn thing, and *that's* the problem!"

"Why is *that* a problem?" He asked, sarcastically.

He stared at me with bloodshot, bug eyes. His sarcasm only pushed me further toward the ledge of violence where I was already teetering.

"It's a problem because you're a lazy piece of shit who sits around smoking pot all day and I'm sick and tired of it!" I yelled back.

"Screw you, man!" Brian complained as he sat back in his chair.

From where I stood in the doorway, I found a can of Mountain Dew that was unopened and hard as a rock. I grabbed it and threw it in Brian's face like a Nolan Ryan fastball. The can hit him between the eyes with a loud pop and an eruption of soda spewed in every direction, soaking Brian and the furniture within Alex's room. I waited for Brian to stand and fight me, but he didn't move. He stared at me as his forehead and nose grew red from the can's outline and his face dripped with yellow, sugary liquid.

"What the hell, man!?" He asked as he shook the soda from his wet hands and wiped his face.

"Do something about it then!" I demanded, trying to convince him to fight.

Alex stood instead. "This is bullshit, Chas! This is my room and you just sprayed shit all over the place!"

"*Not now*, Alex!" I pointed at him with an evil glare in my eyes. "I'll deal with that later! This is between me and Brian." I stared at Brian and waited for him to stand. I didn't believe it was fair to fight someone who was sitting down, so I waited and I taunted him.

"Get up, *bitch*!" I yelled trying to provoke him, but he didn't move. I scoffed and walked out of the room, taunting him as I walked away. "That's what I thought. You're nothing but a little *bitch*." I thought the argument was over, so I went into the kitchen and grabbed a beer from the refrigerator. I opened the can of beer casually and took a seat at the living room table.

My taunts must have had the effect that I desired, because he finally responded.

"What did you say to me!?" He yelled from the other room.

"You heard me! Why don't you come in here if you want to talk back to me!?"

He walked into the living room and stood over me as I sat in one of the wooden chairs and sipped my beer. He was around six feet tall, my height, but outweighed me by at least thirty pounds. He leaned over and spoke into my ear. "I'm here now you son of a bitch! What do you want to do?"

I set my beer down slowly and stood from the chair. "I want you to get in my face--one more time." I warned

Brian stepped in front of me and spoke into my face. "Here I am you son of a —"

Before he could finish his sentence, I grabbed the back of his head and slammed my forehead into his nose. He staggered backward and I saw blood. Blood gushed from the bridge of his nose and ran down his face. He came toward me and threw a punch. He was quicker than I expected. My head snapped back to avoid the blow, but the punch caught me in the mouth.

I punched back. I threw a right, a left, a right, but he protected his face with his hands. My punches grazed against the side of his head. I threw punch after punch until he was backed against a door. He used the door as leverage to grab me. I held his arms and we crashed to the red oriental rug that covered the floor.

We rolled under the living room table, flipping it on its side and knocking over the chairs. The fight became a wrestling match. We were in a small area and didn't have much room to move. We scrambled viciously, fighting for position.

Brian ended on top of me at an awkward angle. His body was sprawled across my stomach and my arms were free. I held his head down with my left hand. My right arm didn't have much space to swing, but his shirt was pulled up and left an open target at his kidneys and ribs. I punched him over and over in his exposed side. I wanted it to hurt. I wanted him to feel as much pain as I could possibly inflict, but my punches weren't enough. I wanted to unleash every ounce of anger that had been bottled within me from my parents' divorce, from the day when Claire left, and for every bit of pain that I carried each day, but would never admit. I unleashed it all and it was Brian who happened to be there when it boiled over.

I sunk my teeth into his side. I bit down as hard as my jaws could clench and I felt the crunch of his skin as it tore away from his body. I ripped a patch of flesh from his side and spit it out as blood dripped from my mouth.

Brian screamed in pain and fear like a child in the clutches of the monster within the closet, the creature under the bed, and the boogeyman, all at the same time. I almost lunged for another chomp, but his body writhed in pain and I let him loose. We both stood from the red oriental rug and I was ready to fight again, but Alex jumped between us. I saw the shock in both of their eyes.

"That's enough!" Alex yelled. "This is over!"

I took a deep breath and tried to calm my racing heart as I assessed the damage around me. I saw the blood stains seeping into my oriental rug. The table was pushed across the room and turned on its side. My beer was soaking into the hardwood floor. The chairs were knocked over. Brian's nose was still trickling with blood like a faucet. And Brian had a glistening red hole in his side that was oozing fresh blood and a chunk of his flesh the size of an ear lay on the rug--far away from it's owner.

"He fucking *bit* me!" Brian yelled in disbelief.

I knew that there was nothing left between Brian and I.

"Hey, Brian." I said, trying to catch my breath. "Don't worry about working for me anymore."

"Don't worry, I'm not."

"And another thing. You've got till tomorrow to get all your shit out of my house or I'm throwing it on the curb."

His mouth nearly dropped to the floor where the remainder of his side lay. "How am I supposed to do that by tomorrow?"

"I don't care. Just figure it out, or I'll do it for you."

"Fine, asshole." He walked away bleeding, toward what had been his room only moments ago.

I knew I had fired an employee. I knew that I had kicked a roommate to the curb. I even knew that I had lost a friend. What I didn't know was why. I wondered, briefly, as I stood there in the wake of my own destruction, did the situation really need to be taken so far? I tried to think back and remember a time when I wouldn't have lashed out in violence, but my thoughts were clouded by the rusty taste of blood in my mouth. What I did realize though, was that I needed to find new roommates.

Chapter 18: Goodwill for All

Devon pointed to a wooden workbench beside the furnace in my unfinished basement. "Over here, I'm going to turn that into a bar. And over here." He pointed to a square space between wooden support beams and the concrete-block wall. "This is going to be my bedroom."

He was giving me the grand tour of his soon-to-be, deluxe flat. He had visions of grandeur that he could turn the empty, concrete space into his own suite. As long as he was willing to pay me fifty dollars a month rent and split the utilities, I didn't care what he did. It was cheap, but at the time, he had no where else to go. His parents were in the middle of a divorce and living with either of them presented problems. He couldn't afford to rent Brian's old room, a proper room upstairs, but he was happy to pay what little he could afford and live in the basement. And I was happy that I could help him.

He was doing his best to get his life back on track, but he was still struggling. His scholarship had been dropped at the university and without the finances to pay for tuition, he was no longer enrolled. The I.D. business that had once been lucrative eventually floundered and he had picked up a part-time job as a cook in a neighborhood diner and he was trying to save his paychecks, but they only seemed to be enough to make ends meet. I wished there could have been more that I could do to help him. I offered him lawn care jobs from time to time and usually paid him more than the usual hourly rate, but somehow, his money always seemed to disappear.

"This spot over here." He continued. We turned to look at a long, open area that connected to his imaginary bedroom. Most of the floor was covered with an old, light green carpet that I had found in storage. The rest was covered with Astroturf that Devon had stolen from a hardware store. "This is the spot where all the magic is going to happen."

I laughed. "What are you talking about?"

"You might laugh now, but very soon, this is going to be the new spot to chill." He kicked off his sandals and felt the Astroturf on his feet. "Now that's nice. Take your shoes off and dig your toes into this."

"I'll take your word for it."

"You're missing out, my friend. But anyways, this is where it's going to go down. I'm going to put some furniture right here, maybe even a coffee table. Yeah, I think a coffee table would pull it all together. I could kick back right here and watch TV." We glanced across the room to where the TV sat on another wooden work bench in the corner. "Yeah." He said, as if he could envision it all playing out in his mind. He may not have had much in terms of possessions, but whatever he may have lacked in possessions, he more than compensated for with his vivid imagination. "As soon as I put some furniture in, there'll be copious amounts of marijuana smoked right here."

"So this is where all the magic will happen, huh?" I asked, mockingly.

The sound of footsteps turned my attention toward the rickety set of stairs that lead to Devon's new room. I noticed a pair of multi-colored Nike's, green, red, yellow, orange, and black, as Ethan stepped into the room. He wore khaki pants and a neon yellow t-shirt. Even for an art student, Devon's childhood friend had a unique style about him. He was short, maybe five foot six on a good day, with thick, shaggy brown hair.

"Hey." Was all he said as he entered the room.

I knew that by letting Devon have a place to stay, it meant that Ethan would also be spending a lot of time at my house. I was okay with that. Ethan never seemed to bother anyone. He was quiet and usually kept his thoughts to himself. He lived in a dorm room at Transy, so a house where he could crash was a vast improvement.

"Hey, Devon, are you ready?" Ethan asked.

"Did you get a truck?"

"Yeah, I'm borrowing one, so we should probably get going." Ethan seemed anxious to leave, but I didn't think much of his antsy demeanor, because as long as I had known him, he never cared for social situations.

"Alright, let's go then."

"Where are you guys going?" I asked.

"We're going to get some furniture from Goodwill."

"Goodwill? The place that sells clothes for the homeless."

"They sell furniture too. Do you wanna come with us? I'm going to find some new stuff for my room."

I laughed, thinking Devon was ridiculous. "No, I'm good, man. I'll be here when you guys get back."

Devon and Ethan left the house and climbed into a green compact truck. They drove casually through downtown Lexington. They pulled into the parking lot of a Goodwill store within a shopping center of a run-down neighborhood.

"Where should I park?" Ethan asked.

"Just pull up right in front of the door. We're only going to be a minute."

"But it's a no parking zone."

"Who cares!? I don't think they'll arrest us for a parking violation."

Ethan parked the truck along the curb in front of the store. They walked through the front entrance and browsed the merchandise. There were rows and racks of used clothing, most of which, were shabby and dull. There was a woman with a small child in her arms, arguing at the check-out counter. She seemed to be haggling over the price of the items that she had selected. Laid across the counter were baby clothes that, most likely, she wouldn't have been able to afford anywhere other than Goodwill.

Devon looked through the furniture section of the store. There were worn couches and chairs and tacky glass tables and wooden nightstands that had been donated after years of heavy use.

"Look at those. Those are perfect!" Ever the optimist, Devon found a matching pair of cloth chairs that were a faded tangerine-orange color.

"I like this one." Ethan admitted as he lounged in a yellow easy chair.

"Alright, we'll take that one too!"

"Excuse me." A middle-aged man wearing a Goodwill uniform and a smile walked toward them. "Can I help you boys?"

"Yes." Devon said, returning the man's smile. "We've decided to get these three chairs, but we could really use some help carrying them to our truck."

"Okay, that's no problem. I can help you carry them. The two orange chairs are ten dollars a piece, or fifteen dollars for the pair. The yellow chair is ten dollars. Is there anything else that you're looking for?"

"Yeah, actually there is. Do you have any coffee tables?"

"Yes, right over here." He led them across the room. "We have a real nice wooden one for fifteen dollars. Should I go ahead and ring it up?"

"Actually, you know what? I still need a few more pieces. So, let's go ahead and try to load these into the truck and see if there's still any room left over for me to keep shopping. Do you mind giving us a hand?"

"No, sure. I don't mind."

The three of them each carried one of the light weight, cheaply made chairs out of the store and loaded them into the bed of the pick-up truck. Devon and the Goodwill employee walked back into the store through the automatic sliding-glass door and each of them grabbed an end of the wooden coffee table. They carried it out and handed it to Ethan who made sure it was secure in the truck bed.

"See that! We still have plenty of room for a few more chairs!" Devon said, excitedly. "I'll be right back." Devon gave Ethan a sharp glance. Devon turned back to the employee. "I'm going to pick out a few more chairs if you'll help me carry them out again."

"Sure."

The man had pegged Devon as a college student who was branching out from home, looking for cheap, college-house furniture. He saw them often, and Devon's khakis, sandals, polo shirt and over sized aviator sunglasses were a dead give away.

"We still have some nice chairs left. I'm sure we can find something else you might like. The best part about these items is that all of the proceeds go to help the homeless." The man stated proudly.

"Oh, that's great! What if I'm homeless? Can you help me?"

The man laughed awkwardly, not knowing how to respond.

"Okay." Devon said, answering his own question as he walked through the automatic door. "Let's see what else we can find."

The man followed closely behind him as they walked to the back of the store and into the furniture section. Devon looked around. There were only a few people absent-mindedly browsing through the aisle. There was a woman scanning price tags at the cash register. And everywhere he looked, there were no cameras.

"How about this couch over here? How much does that cost?"

"That couch is one of our nicest. It's a little more expensive because it's pleather, but it looks like real leather. It costs thirty-five dollars."

"Oh, okay how about that over there?" Devon pointed behind the man, who turned around following Devon's finger, and as he looked away, Devon sprinted toward the door.

"Hey! Where are you going!? Get back here!"

The automatic door slid open. Devon flew through the open doorway with the man chasing after him. Devon dove into the open passenger side of the truck and Ethan peeled out, leaving the man yelling and running after them in the parking lot.

As they drove back to the house, they drove back laughing. They weren't worried about the police, or about being chased. Their biggest concern was how the furniture should be arranged in Devon's room.

Within the living-room, I watched as each of them carried an orange chair through the front door.

"Orange?" I asked simply.

"Yeah, there's a yellow one in the truck too if you want to give us a hand."

I went to the truck and hefted the yellow easy chair out of the truck-bed and carried it down to Devon's new room. Luke had seen the furniture carried through the house, so he went to the truck and grabbed one end of the coffee table as Devon grabbed the other. They carried it down the feeble set of stairs that wobbled and threatened to collapse under each step. Devon placed the two tangerine chairs side by side, while the easy chair sat caddy-corner to them both.

"There." Devon said, as he placed the coffee table in the center of the chairs. "Perfect. Well, almost perfect." He noticed that the three seats were already taken by me, Ethan, and Luke. Ethan had been quick to claim the yellow chair as Luke and I had each claimed one from the orange pair. "We're going to need one more chair."

"You need another chair?" I asked.

"Yeah, we need one more seat."

"I've got an old, chaise lounge up in my room if you want to use it. It's just taking up space right now."

"That blue one, with the patterns all over it?"

"Yeah, you want to use it?"

"Sure, but we can get it later though. I just need somewhere to sit for right now." Devon walked to the other side of the furnace and wheeled an old, leather computer-chair around to where we sat. There were slits where the black fabric had been torn and holes where it had been worn through. But it completed the circle that surrounded the coffee table. Devon turned the TV on and changed the channel to the news and sat Indian-style within his seat.

"You boys wouldn't believe how we got these chairs!"

"They look like shit." Luke was quick to complain. "Where did you find these things? On the side of the road?"

"What!? These chairs are great! And the coffee table, look at that, it's perfect!"

Luke and I looked at each other and laughed. "So how much did you pay for these things?" I asked, to humor Devon and his new acquisition.

"That's what I'm trying to tell you! I didn't pay anything! We just stole them!"

"You stole them from Goodwill...the charity store!?"

"Yeah, we just ran in there and ran out!" Devon turned to Ethan and pointed to a water bong that was on the shelf. "Hey, will you hand me that?"

Ethan passed the bong to Devon, and he set it down on the coffee table. The bong was almost a foot tall and made of red glass with swirls of gold. Devon had named it the Red Dragon. He pulled a baggie from his pocket and packed a bowl.

"Devon, what the fuck, man? You just robbed Goodwill? The place that gives stuff to homeless people?" Luke asked.

Devon passed the bong to Luke. Luke lit the bowl and took a hit.

"Yes! What's so hard to believe about that? Look at it this way. You say they help homeless people, right?"

Luke exhaled in response and the room filled with smoke. He passed the bong to me. I wasn't much of a smoker, but I thought, why not? I held the bong while the cherry was still burning. I took a long pull, held my breath, then took another inhale. I passed the bong to Ethan as I exhaled.

"If they supposedly help homeless people," Devon continued, "then why do they give them furniture? They're homeless!? They don't need chairs! They don't even have a house to put them in! Are homeless people supposed to be on the street-corner sitting in recliners!?"

I couldn't help but laugh. "You've got a point." I admitted. "*But*, it still makes you a horrible person."

He was used to my casual reminders against his character. Devon only laughed in response and coughed as he tried to hold two lungs full of smoke, but couldn't, because his laugh overpowered his efforts.

"You know what you lack, Devon?"

"I don't know, but I'm sure you're going to tell me."

"Yeah, I am. You lack common decency. And hold on, hear me out on this one. You might be thinking that I don't have room to talk, since you're not the only one in the room who has ever stolen anything. But there's a difference. You stole from a *charity*! A *charity*, Devon!"

"And what was that casino, your own personal charity?" He fired back.

"No. What I did was wrong too. But what I'm trying to say, is that what you did is a different kind of wrong. Almost like there are different degrees of wrong. Like if you could rank it from zero to ten, with ten being the worst, stealing from a charity is definitely somewhere on the high end of the scale."

Devon shook his head and paused to take another hit from the bong. He exhaled and passed it on again. "No, I don't see it that way. To me, wrong is wrong. But today wasn't like that. I needed some furniture, I didn't have enough money to pay for it, so it was like Goodwill just helped me instead of helping some random person. And what's wrong with that?"

"Everything!"

"Hey, hey!" Luke interrupted. "Turn it up, quick!"

"Turn what up?"

"The TV! Hurry up!"

Devon hustled to the television set and raised the volume so that we could all hear a breaking story that was on the news. There was an anchor woman with brown hair reading from the teleprompter.

"And in local news, a charity did not only receive donations today, but was forced to give them as well. A local Goodwill was robbed in broad daylight, by what was described as two young men in a green pick-up truck."

The news cut to an on the scene reporter who was interviewing a middle-aged man wearing a Goodwill uniform. "Sure, I saw them. They came in the store and they were all nice and polite. I even helped them load the truck, but never in a million years did I think they would just run off like that."

The bong moved around the coffee table and I took another hit. I passed it around to Ethan and turned my attention back to the television. The camera cut back to the news room. One of the co-anchors, a man with grey hair, asked the woman what she thought of the story.

"It's a sad realization," she said, "that no matter how much charity a society is given, there are always people out there who want more."

My eyes turned toward Devon, carrying as much accusation as I could muster. He ignored my reproachful glares and took the bong as it was passed to him in turn. He looked down at the bowl and I saw disappointment cloud his face. There was nothing left in the bowl but ashes.

"The bowl's cashed." He announced. "You boys want to pack another one?"

And I remember thinking that the anchor woman's words could not have been more true.

Chapter 19: Say Goodnight to the Bad Guy

It was late in the evening as I watched a movie in my bedroom, a Brain De Palma film titled, "Scarface". Al Pacino played a Cuban refugee who assumed the name, Tony Montana when he washed up on the shores of Miami in search of the American Dream. Poverty didn't suit him, so with nothing more than will and determination, he took huge risks and quickly rose in wealth and power to become an international drug lord. But with the money and the power, also came more problems.

On the screen, Tony Montana was dining in an expensive restaurant with a table of his closest friends and rag-tag followers. His girlfriend, Elvira, a papier-mâché woman with a blonde pageboy and a drug habit that the American pharmaceutical industry would have trouble supplying, complained about the way Tony chose to live his life and conduct his business. Tony stood from the table, causing quiet murmurs from the high-class onlookers within the restaurant, and proceeded to vehemently profess his beliefs about what it meant to be the bad guy. He claimed that everyone within the restaurant secretly did bad things within their lives. They lied, they stole, they cheated on their taxes and cheated on their wives, but he was the only one in the room with the courage to admit his faults. If the world needed to point an accusatory finger at someone to prevent their own misdeeds from coming to light, then he would gladly take the blame. As he walked through the exit doors he told everyone, "You'll never see another bad guy like me! So, say goodnight to the bad guy!"

For some reason, even when I was a kid, growing up I had always wanted the bad guy to win. Not the bad guys like serial-killers and rapists, but the bad guys who operated outside the law, and sometimes even above the law, to get ahead in life, not because they had to but because they could. It was like rooting for the underdog, because naturally, society rooted against them. Maybe most people wanted the bad guys to lose so they could ease their fears or justify their loathing, but not me. I admired their fight against the odds. I knew that they were only characters in fictional movies, but it was the roles they played that I idolized. It was Robert Deniro's character in "Heat" and Matt Damon in "Rounders". It was Pierce Brosnan in "The Thomas Crown Affair", Nicholas Cage and Sam Rockwell in "Matchstick Men", Brad Pitt in "Snatch", and George Clooney in "Ocean's Eleven". The characters, and many others like them, were thieves, gamblers, drug dealers, con-artists, and crooks, but those were the characters who I looked up to. And those were the characters that I rooted for, every time.

Through the vulgarity and volume of Tony Montana's voice, I heard the door to my bedroom open, then close. A familiar set of keys jingled as someone walked up the staircase. I turned the volume down and looked across the room to see the last person I could have expected to see, and the only person I wanted to see. It was Claire, standing at the top of the stairs.

"Hey." I said, surprised.

"Hey." She answered.

I wasn't sure why she was there, but within the time that it took us to say two words, I had already begun to hope that she was there to try to make things right between us. But rather than showing how much I had missed her, I told myself to wait until I knew why she had come, because I didn't want to get my hopes up, only to have them come crashing down again.

"Are you busy?" She asked.

"No, I'm just watching a movie. Why?"

"I was kind of hoping we could talk."

"Sure. Come on in."

I paused the movie and pressed a button on the remote to turn on the overhead lights. In the light, I looked around my bedroom and was embarrassed by how trashed the room had become during the months while we had been apart.

"Sorry about the mess. It's probably about time for me to clean up a little bit."

"Yeah…" She said as she walked gingerly through piles of dirty clothes and clutter to cross the room. When I was sure that she had made it across unscathed, I dimmed the lights in an attempt to hide the mess that surrounded us.

"So, what's up?" I stacked a few pillows against the bed's headboard and sat back against them. I patted the open space next to me and invited her to take a seat. She looked at the bed, almost cautiously, then shrugged. She dropped the purse from her shoulders, stepped out of her tennis-shoes, and climbed onto the wide, Tempurpedic mattress. She leaned back against a stack of pillows and slowly sank into place beside me.

We sat in silence for a few moments, but it was a comfortable silence. We both looked toward the frozen image of Al Pacino, as he sat behind a desk with a mountain of white powder like the Swiss Alps on the desktop in front of him, which was paused on the television screen. Eventually Claire took a deep breath, and sighed.

"I don't know what to do anymore." She stated flatly.

I shook my head. "Me neither."

"I just don't like this, whatever this is between us."

She paused, and I had a hundred things that I could have said, and wanted to say, but I didn't respond. I listened intently and waited for her to continue.

"I think things got way too out of control when we got in that fight. I mean, I was drinking and you were drinking..." She paused again, letting me hang there in the balance, and I couldn't wait any longer. I had to agree.

"I know. We never should have let things get so out of hand."

"And, I know I said some things about your family that I shouldn't have. I didn't even mean anything I was saying. I'm sorry, I was just so mad..." She turned her head and looked away, and I slid closer to where she sat.

When she looked at me again, I reached my hand to her face and lightly touched her cheek and under her jaw line. She let my hand rest there as I spoke. "It's okay, Claire. I know you didn't mean it. But that night wasn't only your fault. It was my fault too. I don't know why you ever slapped me in the first place, but I never should have slapped you back."

She let my hand fall and looked away again. Her dark hair hid her face like a curtain of silk. I positioned myself in front of her and tried to look into her eyes, but she wouldn't come out from behind the curtain. I slid my hand across her forehead and tucked her hair behind her ear, revealing her vibrant, blue-green eyes like a magic trick worthy of applause.

"I'm sorry." I said softly but fervently as I looked into her eyes.

"I can't take back what I did, but I promise you, I never meant to hurt you, and I never will, because I love you."

And love her, I did. Even through the time while we were apart, I had never stopped loving Claire. Once you open your heart and truly love someone that love goes on forever, even if you come to hate the one you love, because love comes from the part of us that never dies. My love for Claire was the same as it had always been, but I knew that my heart had changed. It was somehow more constricted, less innocent, and I knew there were locked doors that I wouldn't open for anyone, even her.

"I love you too." She answered, almost sadly. She looked into my eyes and touched my face with each of her hands as her thumb traced the scar underneath my left eye. It had healed in the previous months, but the indention from her nail would always be there.

"Is that from me?"

I nodded my head as it rested in her hands.

"I'm sorry." She leaned forward and gently kissed the scar-tissue with her lips. "There. Is that better?"

I smiled. "A little bit. I think it needs a little more though."

She kissed the scar again and leaned back. "How about now?"

"Yeah, it's getting there. Maybe just a little more."

She leaned forward to kiss the scar again, but I intercepted her lips with my own, and we kissed. After the months that we had been apart, the moment felt like our very first kiss, all over again. I parted my lips, just enough to talk, and smiled.

"There. That did it. It's all better now."

She smiled and it was my favorite of all her smiles. It was the one smile that only said I love you.

That night, we forgave each other for the past and I was glad to have Claire back in my life. I knew that things between us would be different, but we were together and that was all that seemed to matter. When we fell asleep, we fell asleep in each other's arms. My conscious mind may have been at peace for the moment, but as I slept, the unconscious took control.

I dreamed that Claire and I sat on a park bench during a dark night where no stars sparkled in the sky. Tall trees surrounded us like a wall of darkness. There was a swing set with three empty seats, swinging back and forth, but the air was still.

When I looked toward Claire, she kissed me. I kissed her back and she tasted and smelled of ginger. I pulled away and I noticed a faint sound, somewhere in the distance.

"Did you hear that?" I asked.

But for some reason, Claire wouldn't answer me. She only looked at me with eyes like the quiet depths of the sea. We stood from the bench together and I led her toward the sound. We walked along a narrow footpath, hand in hand, and the sound grew louder. I looked back at the swing set, but the three seats were no longer swinging. I began to recognize the sound. I knew that it was something familiar, but I couldn't quite place what it was. The trees around us began to move and sway as if the wind was violently gusting, but I felt no wind.

I began to wonder where we were. The sound grew louder and something rolled and bounced toward us like a wave on the ocean. A swarm of frogs bounced and hopped by us and we watched them curiously as we continued to move forward along the path. On the distant horizon, a tower rose up before us and I immediately understood that the tower was our destination.

I looked down and the path turned into a staircase. If we were ever going to make it to the tower, I wondered why the stairs led down, rather than up. I ignored the thought and held Claire's hand tighter as I led her down the stairs. I noticed the sound again. It clattered in my ears like a cheap maraca. And I realized that was exactly what the sound was. It was a rattle. But something was wrong. It wasn't a baby's rattle that I was hearing. It was a snake's rattle.

I looked down again and noticed that the stairs were moving. Long, round bodies slithered under my feet, and Claire and I began to run. Each step landed on the back of a monstrous snake, and the snakes began to notice our presence. The rattling was replaced by a sea of hisses and the snakes began to strike. I ran as fast as my legs would carry me, but I missed a step, and I fell. I reached out for Claire's hand, but she was too far away. I landed among the snakes. I tried to fight my way to my feet and I tried to fight my way back to Claire, but I couldn't. The snakes began to coil around me. The snakes wrapped themselves around and around and tightened their grip until I could no longer move.

Then I woke up. I was breathing hard and my heart was racing as if I had run a marathon in my sleep. I opened my dry, sleep-filled eyes and looked across the darkness of my bedroom. My vision was blurry, but I could see two glowing green eyes staring back at me from the floor. For an instant, I was frozen with fear. I rubbed my eyes and tried to clear my vision, but the sight wouldn't go away. It didn't make sense. I couldn't understand how a snake could have found its way into my bedroom. My hands fumbled across the nightstand to find the remote. I pressed a button and the overhead lights illuminated the room, but the two glowing eyes were still there, staring back at me.

I blinked my eyes wildly and my vision slowly cleared. There was a black box that surrounded the green eyes, and I understood what it was that I was looking at. I was looking at the green lights on my computer, and I felt ridiculous.

"What are you doing?" Claire's sleepy voice asked.

"Nothing. I think I just had a nightmare."

I turned the lights off and laid down again. Claire rolled over and rested her head on my chest. I could feel my heartbeat racing and I tried to slow the pace of my breathing to match hers.

"It's okay." She whispered sweetly. "It was just a dream."

I wanted to believe her, I really did, but I couldn't. Fragments from the nightmare replayed across my thoughts as I tried to fall asleep again, but a terrible feeling kept me awake. There was something very real about the nightmare that I couldn't ignore. I laid awake for hours through the night, and I waited for morning to come.

Chapter 20: Ronald McDonald and the Gang

The sun shined within the endless blue expanse of the sky and the air was crisp and warm as I walked Claire to her car. It was a short walk down the street to where she had parked the night before. Quaint, brick homes and the occasional tree, grown tall through generations past, lined the relatively calm and empty neighborhood street. When we reached her car, a factory-new red Jeep that her parents had recently bought for her, I opened the driver-side door for her, gave her a quick kiss, then closed the door behind her. I briefly watched her drive away before I walked down the empty road and back to the house.

"Hey, Chas?" Devon called from the porch. He was rocking back and forth on an old, wicker porch-swing. "You mind giving me a lift?"

"Where to?" I walked up the porch steps and took a seat on the brick and stone, masonry railing.

"I need to stop by the restaurant."

"You working today?"

"No, the bastards fired me."

"Why? What happened? I thought the job was going good."

"Yeah, I thought so too. I showed up late a few times. But that was it! That's the only reason that I could think of!"

"How many times is a few?"

"I don't know, it's hard enough having to borrow Luke's bike and make it across downtown anyways. What do these people expect!?"

I laughed. "They probably expect their cooks to show up for work on time."

He stopped rocking and eyed me with a cold glare. "So, are you going to take me, or not?"

"Yeah, I'll take you. Just give me a minute."

I went to my room and got dressed. I put on a pair of khaki shorts, a black polo shirt, and slipped into a pair of brown leather sandals. I grabbed my keys, my wallet, and my sunglasses from the nightstand. As I walked down the stairs, I slid the sunglasses over my eyes. Any time that I could wear sunglasses, day or night, without seeming ridiculous, I would, because I thought the golden-brown tint of the lenses made the world around me seem more vivid.

I walked onto the porch and noticed that both Devon and Luke were waiting beside my Jeep. I pressed the button to unlock the doors and climbed into the driver's seat. Luke sat in the passenger seat and Devon sat in the back.

I started the engine and turned to Luke. "Where am I taking you?"

"Nowhere." He chuckled. "I'm just along for the ride. I wouldn't miss this for the world."

I backed out of the driveway and drove toward the restaurant where Devon had worked. It was early in the afternoon and the downtown streets were only sparsely scattered with traffic. We turned around a corner and the restaurant came into view.

"Do you want me to just drop you off at the door?"

"Yeah. This will only take a second. You don't even need to park. Just pull down the street and wait by the curb."

I stopped in front of the entrance and Devon smiled. "Boys, if I'm not back in five minutes, send in the reinforcements!"

"What reinforcements?"

"He's just being stupid." Luke answered. "You'll see what he's talking about."

Devon wore blue jeans and a black, hooded sweatshirt. He pulled something from his pocket and I realized that it was a clear, plastic mask. He strapped the mask around the back of his head and the clear plastic distorted the features of his face. To complete the disguise, he pulled the black hood of his sweatshirt over his head and slipped a pair of gloves onto his hands.

He opened the door and stepped out of the Jeep. "Well, that's my mama!"

I understood what he was doing, or I thought I did. I considered driving away and leaving him there for catching me off guard, but I didn't. He was my friend and I couldn't leave him stranded, even though I knew that he was about to do something illegal.

I drove a few car lengths further and pulled alongside the curb. I watched the entrance in my rearview mirror as I waited for Devon to return.

"What the hell is he doing?" I asked Luke.

"You'll see. Just get ready to drive."

A black, hooded figure came into sight in my rearview mirror as Devon busted through the restaurant's doors and out onto the sidewalk. His gloved hands were filled with three, huge, paper bags the nearly blocked his view. He sprinted full tilt toward the safety of my Jeep as some of the contents within the bags toppled out and landed at his feet. I didn't see anyone chasing after him, so I decided to have some fun with him and give him a hard time for not warning me about his true reason for needing a ride to the restaurant. When he was within a few feet of the Jeep, I released the brake and slowly pressed down on the gas. The Jeep rolled ahead and Devon wildly ran alongside us and desperately lunged for the door handle, but I kept driving faster, keeping the door just out of Devon's reach like the rabbit that leads the dogs.

"Hey!" He screamed. "Come on, boys! This isn't funny!"

Luke and I laughed as he ran and scrambled to carry the bags and reach for the door. I rolled down my window. "Come on! Stop messing around and get in the car!

Devon made a full sprint toward the door and I revved the engine and left him running behind us again. I checked my rearview mirror and the restaurant was no longer in sight. I slowed the Jeep to a crawl and reached into the backseat and opened the door. Devon jumped into the open seat like a hobo diving into the last boxcar on the express train. The paper bags that he carried and their contents crashed onto the seat with him. I sped away as Devon closed the door behind him. I made a few quick turns and we disappeared within the myriad of side streets and back roads of Lexington's downtown.

I glanced into the backseat as Devon took his mask off and panted heavily for air. "It never fails, does it?" He asked, then started to laugh.

"What?"

"That joke just never gets old for you boys, does it?"

"What joke?" Luke asked. "The one where we make you run down the street looking like an idiot?"

"Yep. That's the one."

We all laughed and I reached into the floorboard where the paper bags had fallen. I reached into one of the bags and felt several large, individually wrapped packages. They were cold.

"What is this?"

Devon pulled a few packages out and read the handwritten label on the side of the white paper packaging. "Let's see. Here we have three and a half pounds of sirloin steak. Some barbeque ribs. Looks like we have some veal and a few pounds of rib-eye. And I know we have a bunch of hamburger patties in here somewhere..."

I burst out laughing. "Are you serious? That was what that was all about? Some frozen meat!? That's the most ridiculous thing I ever heard! You robbed those people for some hamburger patties!?

"Yeah..."

"Who the hell are you, the Hamburglar!?"

Luke laughed and Devon joined in too. He knew what he had done was absurd and he had no trouble laughing about it.

"When I first walked in there, everyone got really nervous, but they didn't know what to do when I walked right past the bar and right past the cash register. I walked straight into the back, went through the kitchen, and went straight to the freezer. No one even cared! I ran out of there with my hands full and everybody just stared at me."

"I can see it now." I chided. "The headlines tomorrow will read: Cheeseburger Lovers Beware! Hamburglar Strikes Again!"

Devon laughed again, then suddenly grew serious, or as serious as his good-humored nature would allow. "I wasn't going to work that shitty job and get fired for nothing. I had to get something out of the deal. And now, you boys can't complain about me not pitching in for food around the house. All this should hold us over for a few months."

"It's a nice gesture." Luke chuckled. "But you didn't have to do all that. You could have just stopped drinking the milk straight out of the carton and I would've been happy enough."

We laughed the rest of the way home and after a few more turns, I drove onto our street. The house that we lived in was the third house from the corner on Beaumont Avenue. I parked the Jeep in the driveway and the three of us stepped out and walked into the house. Our other two roommates were sitting on the couch watching TV as we each carried a bag of stolen meat through the front door as if we had come home from the grocery.

"What's all that?" Skip asked. He was the guy who I had chosen to replace Brian in the house. And honestly, he was a terrible choice. He was a big, fat slob who had a natural stink that three showers each day couldn't cure. His funk seemed to permeate through the entire house like an invisible fog. Aside from how terrible he smelled, I liked Skip. I had met him through the Fraternity that I had joined. SAE, or Sigma Alpha Epsilon, was the biggest and best fraternity on the UK campus, so I joined during my first semester. My fraternity affiliation was short lived though. I preferred my parties to theirs, so I dropped out, but I remained friends with a lot of the guys who were still active SAE's.

"It's dinner." Devon announced proudly. "You boys can call me the bread-winner of the house now, because I officially brought home *the bacon* today."

"There's bacon in there too?" Luke asked.

"I don't know. I was just talking metaphorically, but there might *actually* be some bacon in here." They both set the bags down on the glass coffee table of the living room and sorted through the contents.

Skip raised his massive body from the couch to glance into the paper bags. "Where did all that come from?"

"Whoa! Slow down there, big guy." I answered playfully. "You're asking *way* too many questions. There's only one question that you should be asking yourself right now, and that is, are you ready to eat?"

He grinned from ear to ear. "Look at me. I'm always ready to eat."

"Good. Fire up the grill out back and let's get to it." I handed the bag that I was carrying to Skip's eager hands. "What do you guys think about having a cookout tonight?"

"Like a party, or just us?" Jeff, the roommate who had replaced Alex, asked. Jeff was short and stocky with short blonde hair. He had lived on the living room couch nearly every weekend throughout our first semester, and when Alex moved out, Jeff wanted to rent a proper room.

"A party."

"Sounds good to me."

"Either way, you know I'm up for whatever." Devon agreed. "But this food's not for everyone. I just want it to be for us, you know, everyone in the house."

"Yeah, of course. The cookout's for us. If anyone else wants to eat, they can bring their own food."

Everyone either nodded or shrugged their approval and Skip began to rummage through the bag that he was holding. "What does everyone want? I'm going to go ahead and start cooking."

"Are there any filets in there? If not, I'll just have a sirloin." I answered.

Everyone placed their orders with Skip and Jeff offered to stock the remaining meat in the freezer. Luke and I took to the task of calling people to let them know that we were having a party. My first call was to Claire. Her phone rang several times before she answered.

"Hey." She said as she picked up the phone.

"Hey, we're having some people over tonight, so call around and let your friends know."

"Okay. What time?"

"Whenever. It doesn't matter. Call as many people as you want. Call your sorority sisters, oh, and make sure you call Rachel." Luke turned and looked at me at the mention of her name. I winked at him conspiratorially. "I'm sure Luke would like that."

Claire laughed. "Okay, I'll see what I can do."

"Alright, I'll see you later. I love you."

"I love you too."

I ended the call and continued to make quick calls to friends as Devon, Luke, and I walked downstairs into the basement. Bed sheets of a wide variety of colors and patterns were nailed to the exposed rafters and hung loosely down to the Astroturf covered concrete floor, partitioning Devon's room from the rest of the unfinished basement. Devon pulled a pink sheet to the side and we stepped into his room. Luke and I each took our usual seats in the tangerine chairs and Devon stepped behind the bar. He had converted an old workbench near the furnace into a makeshift bar by adding wooden panels to the front and sides and by covering the wooden countertop with a sheet of glass.

Since Devon had moved in, I had to admit that he had turned the cold, stone space of the unfinished basement into a nice, comfortable, and cozy living area. Devon had made many additions to the room, but my favorite addition may have also been the most random. Within a cheap, wooden frame, there was an old movie-poster that Devon had hung over the only window in his room. The movie-poster portrayed an old man in shabby clothes, running with outstretched arms toward his granddaughter, and they were both beaming with joy. Written in large gold letters, the words Life is Beautiful stretched from one side of the frame to the other. Sometimes I would stare at the poster, as the sunlight streamed in behind it, for long spans of time. I felt like there was a deeper meaning within the seemingly ordinary picture and the three golden words, but the meaning was beyond me at the time.

"Who's thirsty?" Devon asked as he set a bottle of Goldschlagger on the bar. I could see the flakes of golden-foil floating in the clear, cinnamon flavored liquor from where I sat.

"What time is it?" Luke asked.

I stepped over to the bar and chose the cleanest-looking shot glass that I could find. "It's shot thirty." I grabbed two more glasses and poured three shots. "Come on, Luke, here, I've already got you a glass." When everyone was positioned around the bar, I raised my shot-glass. "This is a rare occasion tonight. Dinner *and* drinks are on Devon for a change, so let's enjoy it! Clinkies!"

We all touched glasses and took our first shot of the night. We followed the first with several more before we let the bottle rest. After we had our fill, Luke and I resumed our seats in the tangerine chairs and Devon remained behind the bar. He pulled a plastic bag from his pocket and spread a small handful of white pills across the counter top.

"Oh, great." Luke groaned. "What's the druggie got his hands on now?"

I shrugged. "Who knows?"

"Xany Bars!" Devon yelled as he laughed wildly. He was never more excited than when he was preparing to do drugs. Xany Bars, or Xanex, were one of Devon's drugs of choice. With a razor blade, he broke down several of the white bars and chopped them into a fine powder. "Does anyone have a dollar?"

I pulled a one dollar bill from my wallet and handed it to him. "Here. You know, Devon, we've been through this before but, they make those things in pill form for a reason."

"I know. I just like the way it burns."

He rolled the dollar into a straw and snorted two lines. "Wooo! That's what I'm talking about! Shit Fire… That burns! Let me get some more of that!" He lowered the straw again and snorted two more lines.

The rickety set of basement stairs rumbled as someone walked down and I turned to see who it was. The pink sheet was pulled aside and Ethan stepped into the room.

"What's up." He said in a flat monotone as he sat down in the yellow lounge chair. I noticed that his hair had grown long since the last time I had noticed and he was growing a mustache that Burt Reynolds would have regarded proudly. As with all of his choices in style, I assumed that it was normal for an artist to dress and act the way he did.

"Xany Bars! Who's next!?"

Ethan shrugged. "Sure. I'll take one."

"Fuck it, it's a party right?" Luke said as he stepped to the bar.

"What about you, Chas?" Devon waved one of the while pills in the air. "Xany Bars..."

"I'm good. You go ahead. I'll take another shot though."

Devon poured four shots. Luke and Ethan each swallowed a pill and chased them down with a shot of cinnamon flavored liquor as Devon and I each followed with another shot.

"How many pills did you break up, Devon?"

"Three, why?"

"And you already snorted all three?"

"Yeah, so?"

"So that's a lot, don't you think?"

I was tired of trying to reign in Devon's excesses and he was tired of listening to me try. It was a subtle dance between conservative and liberal views, but very rarely did we step on each others toes. He only laughed, then changed the subject.

"Hey, Ethan, did you close the door behind you?" Devon asked.

"Yeah."

"Okay, good. While we're all here we should go over those plans."

"What plans?" I asked.

Devon walked across the Astroturf covered floor to his sheet-enclosed bedroom. He came back and laid a piece of paper on the stolen coffee table, and we all took our seats. "These plans."

I leaned forward to see what he was referring to. It was a hand-drawn sketch of the layout within Transylvania's library. Judging by the crisp lines and accurate dimensions, I assumed that Ethan had drawn it. There were four X's, each of a different color, at various points on the layout. Each X started in a large, open room, walked to a circular staircase that rose to a secluded, second-floor room, where all four X's ended.

"All four of us will go through the front door, right here." Devon said as he touched his forefinger to the paper. "We are going to walk together until we get to the staircase. From there, two will go up and get inside the room. There should only be one librarian in the room, but at most, there may be a security guard in the back. Here." He indicated the location on the sketch. "We need to time it so it's only the librarian though. When we get to the top of the stairs, the librarian will have to type in the security code on the door to let the first two in, then when the door's open, the other two will come up. When we get in there, we have to take her down, hard and fast and then we—"

I interrupted him. "Who do you have to take down?" I didn't think any of the conversation applied to me, because I had told them to exclude me from their plans, but still, Devon had put four X's on the paper, so I went along with the discussion out of interest.

"The librarian. When we get in there, we have to take her down, quick."

"She? Please don't tell me that you're going to tackle an old lady?"

"No, I wouldn't say old, middle-aged maybe. Trust me, I don't like the idea anymore than you do, but we have to do what we have to do. "

"Tell him what her name is." Ethan prompted.

"Oh, you won't believe what this poor woman's name is. Her name is Anita Bonner!"

"So?"

"So!? So say it slowly. A-need-a Bon-ner."

"I-need-a-Bone-er?

"Yes!" Devon said through a fit of laughter that overwhelmed his features like a mad clown. When he finally calmed himself, he continued to explain the details of his strategy. "Alright, where was I? Okay, here we go. So we take, I Need A Boner down, hard and fast. We tie her up with something. Maybe duct tape or zip ties, I don't know yet, but we can figure that out later. We grab the books. As many as we can get. We need to get the whole set of the big books, Birds of America. Those are the Audubon books. There's four of them and they're heavy. I mean real heavy. So, we throw them on bed sheets and each of us can carry a corner. We will all have backpacks too, so we can grab some of the other books and paintings while we're in there.

Bed sheets, I thought. That was Devon's answer for everything.

"When we get all the loot, we can get out of the Special Collections room, one of two ways. We can get out through the door where we came in, but if it closes behind us, then we'll be locked in. It's solid glass and rigged to a security system. If we break the glass, the alarm goes off. But don't worry. There's one other exit." Devon pointed his finger to a small box on the paper. "There's an elevator. From the special collections room, the elevator only works with a key. I Need A Boner, has that key. So, we get the key from her, we take the elevator down, and we run out to the G.T.A.V., the get-to-and-away-vehicle, we drive away, we sell the loot, and we're twelve million dollars richer!"

Devon seemed pleased by the simplicity of his plan. He looked around at each of us to see if anyone else shared his enthusiasm. Both Luke and Ethan seemed moderately pleased by the plan, but I was far from convinced.

"Hey, Devon? Can I make a suggestion?" I asked.

"Of course."

"I think you should lay off the drugs for a while. After all this time, I think you've finally done it. You've actually smoked yourself retarded!" I couldn't help but laugh. I laughed in Devon's face and I watched his expression of a job well done disappear.

Through my laughter, I grabbed the piece of paper that held Devon's plan. I turned the paper over to the blank white backside. "See this? This, is a normal brain!" I pointed to the clean white paper. I flipped the paper over again to reveal the plan. "This! This is Devon's brain on drugs!"

Devon snatched the paper from my hands. "You think this is funny!?"

"Yes!" I said, gasping for air. I noticed that Luke and Ethan were also laughing.

"Tell me then, smart-ass, what's so funny about it?"

"You really want me to!?"

"Yeah, here. Go ahead." He handed me the plan.

"The whole thing is ridiculous! It's like you've been brain-storming with Danny Ocean, or something. You should just stick to what you do best. You're the *Hamburgular*! No one steals hamburger patties like you do, and you can be proud of that!"

"Fuck you, Chas! Do you have anything to say about the plan, or not?"

"I'm not even a part of your stupid plan, but yeah, I've got a few comments. For starters, you have all four people going into the room. You don't even have a lookout or a driver waiting outside. Second, you act like you're just going to be able to walk right in there, get the books and run out. Run out where? Through the front door? You're fucking crazy! Everyone in the whole library will see you!"

"No they won't!" Devon insisted. "Yeah, they'll see some people running out, but they won't see us!"

"Oh yeah, how's that?" I asked skeptically.

Devon's face regained its typical arrogant smirk. "Because. We're going to be in disguises. That's how. I haven't decided what they should be yet, but I've already come up with our code names."

"Code names? Why the *hell* do you need code names." I looked to Luke and Ethan, but they seemed as though they had already heard Devon's code name idea.

Devon pointed to one of the X's on the paper. "You see that yellow X there? That's me. My code name is Mr. Yellow. Over here—"

Ethan interrupted. "I don't understand why I can't be Mr. Yellow."

"Because, I'm Mr. Yellow." Devon brushed the comment aside and moved on. "This, right here, is Ethan, and like it or not, Ethan is Mr. Green. Over here is Luke. Luke is Mr. Black." I turned toward Luke to see that he wore a satisfied grin upon the mention of his code name. I knew that he liked being the darkest color. "And you, you're right here." I saw the X that was intended to signify me as Devon looked at me with a toothy smile. "You're Mr. Pink." Luke and Ethan found the mention of my supposed code-name hilarious and erupted with laughter. I assumed that my code-name was an inside joke that the three of them had been waiting to reveal.

I was caught off guard and I lashed out defensively. "I'm not even a part of this stupid shit! But if I was, I wouldn't be called Mr. Pink! I can tell you that right now!"

And my anger only made them laugh harder.

"What's wrong, man?" Luke asked. "You don't like Pink?"

"All of the other colors were already taken." Devon smiled. "So, you have to be Mr. Pink."

I wanted to press the issue and insist on another color, pointing out how their own colors weren't even used in the movie where the concept of coded names had originally come from, but they would have enjoyed that. I thought about the movie. I thought about how each character's situation played out, and I decided that I liked Mr. Pink. Steve Buschemi's character was always overlooked and underestimated, but when the chips fell and everyone turned against each other, he stayed alive and walked away with the briefcase full of diamonds.

"You know what? Even though I'm not a part of this, you can call me Mr. Pink. But I have to warn you. When the movie ends, he's the one who comes out on top."

They looked at me and none of them were laughing anymore.

"Okay." Devon said uncomfortably to break the awkward silence that had consumed the conversation like a bad joke within a funeral procession. His eyes silently scanned each of us around the coffee table. "It's settled then. Mr. Pink. Mr. Black. Mr. Green. And Mr. Yellow. We have a job to do."

"Whoa! Not so fast. You mean, *you guys* have a job to do."

"Whatever, same difference. I still think you'll change your mind."

"No, I doubt that." The lawn-care season was in full-swing, and between Luke, Blake and I, we were making good money. It had been a while since I had last worked for my dad's auction house, but I was still appraising houses on the side and I still had money leftover from Bullfrog's casino. And if all else failed, a large amount of equity continued to grow within the rental properties that I co-owned with my dad. I didn't need to take anymore risks.

"Hey! Dinner's ready!" Skip's voice boomed down from the top of the stairs. "Come get it before it's gone."

"We'll continue this later." Devon said quickly as he snatched the plans from the coffee table. He stood from the old, leather computer-chair, stumbled and fell face first onto the coffee table like a wayward drunk. As he regained his balance, he laughed at his own expense. We all laughed at his expense. The three of us stood from our chairs and I watched Devon stagger back to his bedroom. I couldn't resist the opportunity to taunt him.

"I told you three was too many."

"Too many!?" He scoffed as if the notion were absurd. "You can never have too many!"

He vanished into his bed sheet enclosed bedroom and reemerged like a triumphant zealot with a white pill in his hand. "This is what I say to your too many!" He dropped the pill into his mouth, poured himself a shot at the bar, and drank the shot to wash down his fourth Xanex of the night, and at least twice as many shots.

I laughed and shook my head in disbelief. "Yep. That should do it." I turned toward Luke. "My money's on Frazier going down in the fourth."

"Ahh, he can handle it. He's in his element right now. Look at him. He's floatin' like a butterfly and it's going to sting when he pees."

I laughed. "Yeah, you might be right. His druggie body *needs* those drugs to feel normal."

Luke and I each shrugged to one another and I pulled a pink bed sheet to the side and we walked up the rickety set of stairs. A plate with a sirloin steak was waiting for me in the kitchen. I glanced out of the kitchen window and noticed that the sun was beginning to set. I knew that the house would fill with people soon. I tried to eat quickly, but by normal standards, I ate slowly even when I tried to eat fast. When I finished my steak, a group of people had already gathered in the living room. I left my plate in the sink and walked to the bathroom to take a shower.

I undressed, stepped into the shower, and turned on the water. Through the bathroom door, I could hear the sound of voices within the house growing louder each minute. The stereo was turned on and through the trickle of water I could hear the base from the music rumbling through the walls.

Someone knocked on the bathroom door. I didn't respond and another few knocks followed the first. I thought I could hear the sound of girls giggling on the other side of the door. I turned the water off and dried myself with a white towel from the closet. I dropped my clothes into a nearby hamper and tucked the towel around my waist to cover my lower body.

There was another knock at the door, so I unhooked the latch and swung open the door. The loud roar of hip-hop music filled my ears as the door opened and two girls, Stephanie and Rebecca, stood in the doorway. Stephanie, the taller of the two, had long brown hair that was tied back in a thick pony-tail and Rebecca had short blond hair with short bangs that framed her face. They both wore spaghetti strap tops that hugged their figures and high-cut skirts with higher cut heels. The duo was known around campus for their promiscuity and as they stood there, blocking the doorway, I realized that I was only wearing a towel.

"Can we come in?" Stephanie asked.

"Yeah, I'm done. It's all yours." I stepped toward the doorway, but they didn't move.

Rebecca giggled. "No, silly. We mean with you."

I looked at them and they looked at me. I knew what they had in mind. They were both attractive in their own, unique way, but I was dating Claire again and although I may have been a lot of things that I wished I wasn't, I wasn't disloyal.

"Sorry, girls. I've got to go get dressed."

Stephanie rolled her eyes and Rebecca scoffed as she threw her hands on her hips. Any attractiveness that their features once held turned ugly with undignified reprisal. They acted as if by declining their offer I had spoken the rudest comment their ears had ever heard. I highly doubted the possibility. I squeezed past the two of them and their akimbo limbs, and stepped into the short, narrow hallway where three guys, who I had never seen before, leaned idly against the wall, pretending like they hadn't been eavesdropping on our conversation. I eyed each of them and shook my head as I walked by.

Water from the shower dripped onto the hardwood floor as I held the towel at my waist and weaved through the bustling crowd that had overwhelmed the living room. Voices throughout the house were competing with one another to be heard and the music washed over all the voices except for the fragments of conversations that I could hear as I walked by. I opened the door to my bedroom and slipped into the stairway, closing the door and instantly muffling the sounds behind me. As I walked up the stairs, the sounds grew quieter with each step. When I reached the top of the stairs, I looked across the room to see Claire sitting in the office-chair at my desk. She was wearing a pink blouse with a white skirt, an outfit that she knew I loved to see her wear.

"Hey." I said as I walked toward her.

She swiveled the chair around to face me. "What took you so long?"

"Nothing, I just got out of the shower." I said, omitting the short delay that occurred outside of the shower. I dressed myself, wearing khaki shorts, a red polo-shirt, and a black hat, each item sharing the same alligator logo. I was selective about the clothing that I would wear. Everything that I owned was name-brand. I had closets and dressers filled with expensive clothing, but I never paused to realize how fortunate I was. I slipped into a pair of leather, thong sandals that had molded to the shape of my feet and slid my favorite pair of Maui-Jim sunglasses over my eyes. Everything around me became tinted with a polarized golden-brown shade.

A golden-brown version of Claire walked toward me and playfully reached for my sunglasses. "Not the sunglasses again…" She teased.

I dodged her hand each time she reached for my eyes. "Why not?"

"Because it's dark outside."

"So?"

"So, it's stupid."

I laughed and dodged her hand again. "You think so?" I playfully wrestled her to the bed and pinned her hands down. My face was only inches above her face, my lips nearly brushing against her lips. "How about now? Do they still look stupid?"

"Yes!" She burst into laughter and I couldn't help but laugh along with her.

"Okay. I'll meet you halfway." I lifted the glasses from my eyes and placed them above the bill of my hat. "How's that?"

"That's better."

"Good. Come on, let's go down to the party. I helped her from the bed and she smoothed her skirt and checked her hair as we walked together toward the stairs. The noise from the party grew louder with each step down and hit us like a wave when I opened the door. We stepped into the party and acknowledged the people we each knew as we made our way to the kitchen.

Before I could even get to the refrigerator to find a beer for Claire and I, Luke approached me.

"Hey, do you have an extra key to my room?" Luke asked.

The door to his room was in the back corner of the kitchen. I looked over Luke's shoulder and noticed that Rachel was waiting beside the door. I smiled mischievously at Luke.

"Sure, I've got one. How did it get locked from the inside though?"

"I thought I saw Devon go in there earlier, but I knocked on the door and no one answered. Maybe he accidently locked it on the way out."

"Maybe…" I answered tentatively.

I began to worry that Devon may have stolen from Luke again, as he had during the fall semester. I pulled my keychain from my pocket and flipped through a dozen keys before I found the key to Luke's door. I knocked on the door and listened to no avail. I turned the key in the lock and the deadbolt slid open.

I stepped into Luke's dark, tiled bedroom, followed by Luke, Rachel, and Claire. The shades were drawn on all six windows and I could barely make out the wood-paneled walls. My eyes began to adjust to the darkness and I thought I could see someone lying under the blankets of Luke's bed.

"Is that who I think it is?" I whispered.

"Devon!" Luke yelled, loud enough to wake him from his drug-induced coma.

Devon rolled lazily beneath the blankets of Luke's bed and squinted at each of us with a profound look of confusion.

"Devon, what the *fuck* are you *doing*?"

"Unggh…" Devon groaned in response and covered his face with a pillow.

"Devon! I'm serious! Get out of my bed!" Luke forcefully removed the blankets from the bed and immediately realized that he had made a mistake.

Rachel gasped at the unexpected sight. "Oh my God, he's naked!" She yelled.

Devon's bare, white ass glowed in the darkness like the bright side of the moon. Each of us who beheld the shocking sight of Devon's exposed back-side erupted with laughter.

Luke pulled the pillow away from Devon's face and hit him with it. "Get up you, bum! Get your naked ass out of my bed!"

"Unggh... alright. Stop hitting me." Devon slurred as he crawled to the edge of the bed and sat with his feet flat on the tile floor. He pulled a pair of socks onto his feet, then slipped into his tennis-shoes and laced them tight.

"Devon, where are your clothes?" Claire asked as she and Rachel searched along the floor of the dark room.

"Pssht!" Devon scoffed, waving their question away as if the thought of clothes was a pesky fly buzzing about his head. He stood from the bed, wearing nothing more than the socks and shoes on his feet, then stepped out of Luke's bedroom and into the party.

I shook my head and Luke shrugged in response. It was only a few seconds later when I heard the first scream. The high-pitched squeal sounded as if some unsuspecting girl had seen a ghost, but I knew that Devon's pale-white, nakedness was the only cause for her terror. He swayed drunkenly through the kitchen like a mummy risen from the tomb. The first scream was followed by several more and followed by a stream of excited yells and laughter.

"He's naked!" Someone shouted.

"Why's he so hairy!?" A girl wondered out loud.

"Look! Look at him! Look!" Someone else shouted.

When hysteria struck a crowd, cleverness was thrown by the wayside and people resorted to the most basic forms of communication. The four of us who were in Luke's bedroom followed after Devon as he walked through the frenzied crowd of onlookers. His balance was questionable, but he walked with his usual proud, pigeon-toed strut and seemed completely at ease with his nakedness. He casually strolled through the taunts and through the laughter as if he were the only person in the room. He opened the front door and walked out onto the front porch.

I followed after him to see where he was going. He stepped in front of a small group of smokers, three girls and one guy, who were lounging on the stone porch-railing. With wide eyes, they looked up and down at the nude intruder.

"Can I bum a cigarette?" Devon asked.

They laughed and the girl nearest to him dug through her purse until she found what he asked for.

"Here."

"Thanks." Devon put the cigarette in his mouth and it balanced precariously on the edge of his bottom lip as he spoke. "You got a light?"

"Sure." She handed him a neon-pink lighter.

Devon carefully lit his cigarette, guarding the flame with his opposite hand until the fire took hold. The girl held her hand out to retrieve her lighter, but in a flash of neon-pink, Devon flung the lighter from the porch.

"Hey! Whadya do that for!?"

Devon ignored her as he inhaled a drag from the cigarette and enjoyed the burn. When he exhaled he blew smoke into the girl's face and into the small gathering of smokers.

"Oops!" He said sarcastically and laughed at his own joke, and standing by his side, I laughed too.

I put my arm around Devon's shoulder and tried to steer him toward his room. "Come on, man, I'd say you've had enough fun for one night."

He didn't move from his staggering position. He took another puff from the cigarette and laughed as he blew smoke toward the crowd. "No, I'm good. I'm going to stay." He mumbled through an uncontrollable fit of laughter.

"Alright, suit yourself."

As I turned to walk back inside the house, I saw Devon brace himself against one of the pillars that supported the porch. He leaned against the pillar and casually smoked his cigarette as if he were James Dean in "Rebel Without a Cause", only instead of the leather jacket and jeans, he preferred socks and tennis-shoes, and nothing else.

After the initial shock of Devon's nudity wore off, the party continued on into the night, and no one seemed to care that he was naked. He was just another guy at the party who happened to not be wearing any clothes. When exposed to even the most bizarre situations for a long enough time, human nature was bound to adapt, and what was once bizarre became normal. And for the life of me, I couldn't remember what normal was supposed to be.

Chapter 21: Consequences

It was early in the evening when I pulled into a parking space outside of the apartment complex that housed Bullfrog's casino. It had been months since I had been there last. I had continued to play cards there for several weeks after the robbery, only to displace any suspicions that Bullfrog may or may not have had about me. When the weeks drug by uneventfully, I assured myself that I was in the clear and slowly phased myself out of the casino. But through the idle hours each night, as I lay in bed trying to fall asleep, my conscience would weigh heavily on my thoughts. I would reason with myself that I only did what I had to do, but my conscience would never be satisfied with my excuses. My conscience would respond by using my doubts and my unfounded fears against me. I would often wonder, what if Bullfrog knows? What if I made a mistake? And if I did, I worried my fate would be the same as Val Kilmer's character in "Wonderland" – Intruders crashing through my door in the dead of the night to bash my head in with lead pipes. As I lay in bed contemplating the possibilities, I wondered what I would do if he ever sent someone to watch my house, threaten me, rob me, or even attack me? I honestly didn't know, but such thoughts replayed on a loop each night like reruns of Home Improvement on TBS.

It wasn't my conscience that caused me to step out of my Jeep and walk toward the casino again, it was my curiosity. I needed to reassure myself, one last time, that my worries and my fears were only a byproduct of my guilty conscience. I entered the criss-cross maze of sidewalks within the apartment complex and glimpses from the night of the robbery played across my mind. I remembered looking through the eye-holes of a black ski-mask as a black hood hung low over my head, further shrouding my face in darkness. I remembered how the wind was blowing between the tall, silent buildings that surrounded Luke and I. And as I walked past the maintenance room again, I remembered the feeling of anxiety that gripped me like a vice as I searched from window to window while Luke went to work on the door. As I approached the unassuming door that led to the casino, I reminded myself that that was another night, and today, was a new day.

I opened the door and entered a small corridor where there was a door to my left, a door to my right, and a staircase to the second floor. Cameras mounted to the walls watched me as I climbed the staircase and stopped in front of a heavy, reinforced door. Before I could even knock, the electronic lock clicked and I opened the door. I stepped inside and the door closed and locked behind me. Everything within the room looked the same as it had months before. A lively game of poker was in progress under the dim lights that hung above the table and billows of cigar and cigarette smoke drifted through the air like fog. I chanced a quick glance toward Bullfrog and he only eyed me with a glazed look of indifference. I nodded cordially and walked toward the blackjack table in the back room. As I walked through a narrow hallway, a wave of relief rushed over me like a cool zephyr on a humid afternoon in July. I smiled inwardly with personal satisfaction and felt foolish for ever doubting myself.

On my left, in a room that adjoined the hallway, I noticed Slim lounging in an uncomfortable-looking wooden chair as he took a drag from a cigarette. I passed him by and stepped into the back room. The room was as plain and as unfurnished as I had always known it to be. Every stool at the blackjack table was empty. The last few rays of sun were shining through the closed window and I noticed that the latch above the window had been locked into place. I took an empty stool at the center of the table and it was only several seconds later when Slim walked through the doorway. Without a word, he stepped behind the table and began to shuffle through six decks of cards.

"How's it going, Slim?" I asked, attempting to make small-talk.

He shrugged and spoke as if his voice were powered by a respirator machine. "Same ol' same ol'…"

I rested my elbows on the plush green felt as I listened to the sounds of casino chips clacking and voices chattering while money exchanged hands across the poker table in the other room. The only sound in the blackjack room was the rhythmic shuffling of cards as Slim prepared the decks. One by one, Slim spread a deck of upturned cards before me for my inspection, then continued shuffling. I pulled my wallet from my pocket, removed five one hundred dollar bills, and laid them on the table.

At the end of the shuffling process, Slim stacked all six decks into the shoe and slid a plastic card across the table. As always, I placed the card near the end of the shoe to cut the house thin.

"Changing five hundred." Slim announced as he collected the money from the table and exchanged the five bills for five short stacks of twenty five dollar chips.

I laid a chip into the betting-circle and waited for the cards to be dealt. Slim pulled four cards from the shoe. I was dealt a nine and an eight for seventeen, and Slim was showing a king. I waved my hand over the cards to indicate that I would stand at seventeen. Slim overturned his second card to reveal another king.

"Dealer wins with twenty over your seventeen." Slim swiped the chip from the betting circle and I replaced it with another.

A hard seventeen with no face cards against a solid, two-king twenty was a bad way to start the day. Several more hands followed and the shoe only grew colder. My luck seemed to have abandoned me. The count that I tracked sank lower and lower into the negative numbers and my stacks of chips were dwindling away, hand by hand. Like a stubborn mule, I continued to play because I believed my luck would change. When it did, it only changed for the worst.

I slid another chip into the circle and sat back in the stool. I listened for the sounds of voices and clacking chips in the other room, but my ears were met with the sound of deafening silence. And sometimes silence could scream louder than any other noise. My intuition told me that it was time to walk away, but it was already too late.

Bullfrog stepped through the doorway with a shotgun slung over his shoulder, and paused, eyes ablaze. His massive, slumped form filled the frame of the only escape, and I felt my heart skip a beat. I swallowed and tried to ignore the sudden icy grip of fear, but my heart began to pound on the wall of my chest like a battering ram. I instinctively stood from the stool and prepared to run. I didn't know where I hoped to go. I only knew that I needed to get out of the room, somehow, someway.

"Sit down!" Bullfrog yelled. His voice sounded like the low, slow rumble of a locomotive. He lowered the shotgun and aimed it at my face. His eyes were red and swimming with a mixture of alcohol and rage. His bulbous face was swollen and blotchy from many years of long nights and stiff drinks.

As I looked into the barrel of the shotgun my instinct to run ran away without me and I was left only with the instinct to survive. I sat down slowly, and as I did, I remember thinking that I was about to die. In a flash, I thought back to the day when I had first been introduced to the casino. The day when Deuce had escorted me through the heavy, reinforced door and vouched for me. Years later, as I stared into the black cylinder of a loaded shotgun, I wished I had never stepped through the door.

"Take it easy, Frog...Just put the gun down..."

With violent efficiency, Bullfrog pumped the action and re-aimed the shotgun, staring into my eyes as he looked down the barrel. He breathed hard through flaring nostrils as he approached me, step by step.

"You must think I'm stupid? Don't ya, kid?" His voice rumbled and crawled like the start of a rock slide.

"No, Frog... I don't know what you're talking about... Just put the gun down..."

He stepped several feet in front of me and when I looked toward Slim, I realized that he was no longer behind the blackjack table. He was standing behind me. My fingertips found the Saint Christopher medallion that hung from my neck and I touched it through the fabric of my shirt.

"Did ya really think I wouldn't find out?"

"Find out what, Frog... I don't know what you're talking about..."

"Don't lie to me!" He yelled and beads of saliva shot from his mouth. The corners of his chapped lips were webbed with dry white spittle.

"I'm not lying to you... I really don't know what you're talking about..."

For a man of his size, Bullfrog moved quicker than I could have anticipated. In one fluid motion, he took a step forward and smashed the hard, wooden stock of the gun into my forehead. My head lashed back like I had been struck with a baseball bat. I jumped to my feet and attempted to take a swing at Bullfrog, but Slim caught my arms and held me back. I tried to struggle free from his grasp but his hands held me fast like a straight-jacket.

"How's *that*, kid! Ring any fuckin' bells yet, ya thievin' piece of shit!? Huh!?" Bullfrog shouted, spittle flying at my face.

I was so angry and so scared in the same instant that I didn't feel like I had any control over my actions. My body shook as the flush of emotions ran through me and I stared into Bullfrog's enraged eyes. I could feel the hot flow of blood as it began to run down my nose and over my mouth. I licked my lips and tasted the rusty, metallic flavor of my own blood.

"Did ya really think I wouldn't find out!? Huh!? Answer me!"

"I don't know what you're talking –"

Before I could even finish my sentence, the stock of the gun was slammed into my stomach while Slim continued to restrain my arms. The air was forced from my lungs and I couldn't breathe. I gasped for air and I could feel my eyes welling with tears as my emotions ran unchecked.

"*I know it was you! And if ya fuckin' say I don't know, one more time, I'm gonna fuckin' kill ya right he*re! Ya understand me!?"

I clenched my teeth and stared at him with every ounce of hate in my body to fight back the feeling of fear, and I nodded my head in agreement.

"Now we're gettin' somewhere. Now, I'm not sure how much ya got me for, but I know how much ya owe me. Ya understand? Are you still with me? Nod your head if ya understand what the fuck I'm sayin' to ya." He squinted and looked over the tip of his nose at my face like a surgeon examining his work.

Blood ran in streams over my lips and when I exhaled, droplets of blood blew into the air, falling just short of where Bullfrog stood. I hated to do as he asked, but I nodded my head.

"Between you and your friend, the guy who helped ya rob me—"

My eyes grew wide at the mention of a second person.

"Oh, look at that. Ya really do think I'm stupid, don't ya? *Don't ya!?*" He screamed as his anger flared again.

I shook my head in disagreement, because I didn't trust my mouth to say anything other than the foul words of hatred that ran like hot blood through my thoughts.

"Ya didn't think I knew about your partner, did ya? All I know about the guy is his name is Luke Little. I don't know who he is and I don't care to know, as long as me and you can get along, got it?"

I nodded my head fervently in agreement. I couldn't understand how he knew so much. I must have made a mistake that I didn't anticipate. I didn't know how it could have happened, but I didn't have time to contemplate my failure under the circumstances.

"I like ya, kid, I really do. I don't want this to get out of hand anymore than you do, but this is my business and ya stole from me. Now, you're gonna pay me back. Understand?"

I nodded again.

"I figure ya stole about seventy or eighty grand from me, am I right?" He had overestimated the number by more than ten thousand dollars, but I didn't respond. I only stared back at him. "So, between you and your friend, ya owe me a hundred grand."

"*What!?*"

"Yeah, I tacked on some interest. That's for makin' me wait all these months before ya came back around. I thought about payin' ya a visit, but I knew ya'd come back."

"How the hell am I supposed to come up with that kind of money!?"

"Don't play stupid, kid. I know your type. Your family's got money. I'm sure your friend's family's got money too. I don't care how ya get it, just make sure ya get it."

"And what if I don't?"

"There's lots of ways we can handle this, but like I said, I don't want this to get ugly. But if ya wanna go down that road, go ahead."

"What if I go to the police?"

Bullfrog burst into a rasping guffaw and Slim chuckled behind me. Their raucous laughter stung me like a slap across the face.

"What are ya gonna tell 'em, kid? That ya broke into my apartment and robbed me? If anyone can go to the cops in this situation, it's me."

"What if I tell them you're running an illegal gambling operation."

"Ya really do think I'm stupid. How do ya think I've been doin' this for over twenty years now? Go ahead, take a guess."

I sighed defeated. "They let you."

He looked over my shoulder to Slim. "Look at that! And they say a college education's not what it used to be!" He turned his attention back to me and pressed the barrel of the shotgun into my chest. "You're a smart kid. Maybe too damn smart for your own good. But ya act like you're the only one with a brain around here. I hope I'm not the first one to tell ya, but you're not."

I simply stared at him as he tapped my chest with the barrel of the shotgun.

"Like, ya probably think I didn't know you've been back here countin' my cards all this time. I just couldn't prove it, but I knew ya were because ya win too much. Nobody's that lucky, only cheaters and cardsharps. But even their luck runs out eventually, because like they say in Vegas, the house always wins." He smiled a broad, ugly smile that had been stained yellow through the years.

"So here's how this is gonna work. I'm gonna let ya walk outta here today, and you're gonna start workin' on gettin' my money. Ya understand?"

"Yeah."

"Now, I think you're too smart to try anything stupid. I know where ya live. I know where your family lives. I'd really hate to get them mixed up in this too."

The thought of Bullfrog coming anywhere near my family infuriated me, but under the circumstances, I could only agree.

"Ya don't gotta get all the money right away. But you're gonna check in with me every now and then, and when ya do, ya better not come empty handed."

"Fine."

He raised the gun away from my chest and slung it over his shoulder. I shrugged out of Slim's grip and he let my arms fall free.

"Now, go on, get outta here."

Bullfrog stepped aside and I walked out of the room on shaky legs. I walked down the hallway and into the large room where the abandoned poker table waited patiently under the dim lights. Both Bullfrog and Slim followed me into the room as I stood by the door, anxious to leave. Bullfrog pressed a button at his desk and the lock clicked open. Without so much as a glance over my shoulder, I swung the door open and stepped into the corridor. I hurried down the stairs, taking two steps at a time, and I heard the heavy door close behind me like the door to a tomb I had narrowly escaped. I opened one last door, and thankfully, I stepped out of Bullfrog's building and slipped out into the night

I walked quickly through the maze of sidewalks and hopelessly looked up to the starry black void of infinity that stretched above me. I noticed one small star that flickered futilely against the endless expanse of darkness that fought to extinguish its glow. It had fought bravely against the odds, but how long could it truly hope to last.

I sighed and continued to the parking lot where my Jeep awaited my return. I tried to fathom how my life had gone so far off track at such a young age. I was nineteen years old and I owed one hundred thousand dollars to an illegal gambling operation.

I didn't know how I was ever going to come up with such a large amount of money. I had nearly twenty thousand dollars in cash, still leftover from the robbery, and I had almost fifteen thousand in personal savings and stocks. There was value in my lawn care company, but it wasn't much, at most another ten or fifteen thousand. It had taken years to build my small net worth and I felt like it would take several more years to come up with the rest of the money and pay off the debt I owed.

I considered whether I should tell my parents and plead to them for help, but I was too ashamed of what I had done. My situation was no one's fault but my own. I had chosen to steal the money from Bullfrog's desk and it was my responsibility to pay him back. I didn't even see any reason to include Luke in the responsibility. His share of the robbery was all but gone and his only income was through his ownership in the lawn care company. And although Luke's parents were financially stable, I didn't see how he, or they, could be of any help.

I realized that I was on my own. As I walked to my Jeep and climbed inside, I felt completely and utterly alone. I flipped down the vanity mirror and inspected my face. Dried blood was caked in streaks that ran down my face and onto my white, button-down shirt. There was a deep, but small laceration in the center of my forehead that was still slowly oozing blood. The wound wasn't going to close on its own, I needed stitches. I shook my head in disbelief of the reality that I had created for myself, and closed the mirror.

My emotions simmered within me like an unstable pot of soup left untended for too long. I put the key into the ignition and started the engine. I sank down into my chair, deflated, all will and motivation had left my body, and I leaned forward to rest my face on the wood-grain steering wheel. I took a few short breaths of self pity and self loathing before any life within me returned. My emotions turned to anger. I sat up straight in the seat and took my frustration out on the interior of my Jeep. I punched and beat the steering wheel and dashboard in a wild rage until my anger subsided.

After I had calmed my emotions, I put the gear in drive and pulled out of the parking lot. I drove to the nearest urgent treatment center and told them that I had fallen and hit my head. I decided that I would never tell anyone what had happened that night. It would be years later before I changed my mind.

Chapter 22: An Overdue Reunion

Raindrops fell heavily on my windshield as I drove. The rain-slicked streets were dark and bare. Only the occasional set of headlights passed by as I wound through the quiet suburban neighborhoods. I listened to the windshield wipers steady rhythm, a whisper of pssh... bmmp, pssh... bmmp, and over the stereo, a Dido song was playing through the speakers. It was a sad, melodic song with emotionally driven lyrics.

And I...

Just want to thank you...

For givin' me the best day...

Of, my life...

It was a song that I would listen to when I was feeling sorry for myself, and through the dark and dreary night, I felt like I was hanging on to the end of a very short rope. The summer season had turned into a cold, dreary fall. The passage of time and the change of season didn't offer any new solutions to the question of how I would pay my debt. If I paid Bullfrog what I owed him with what money I had, I would be left with nothing and still be in his debt. I needed the money that I had, or at least I believed I did, to sustain myself and be there as a safety net if my family fell on further hard times.

It had been several months since I had last seen Bullfrog. I hadn't seen him since the night when he had cornered me in the casino. I knew that I should have checked in with him weeks ago, but I didn't want to go back empty handed, and I didn't want to give him money from my own pocket. It may have been greedy, or it may have been out of self-preservation, but I wanted to have my money and spend it too. What I needed was a way to come up with a large amount of money, fast. As each week passed, and no new solutions became available, I grew desperate. I knew that if I didn't get the money soon, Bullfrog would send someone to find me, and I knew that I didn't want to be found. So after months of gnashing my teeth at the thought, I decided that I would have to resort to the only reasonable option I had left.

I slowed my Jeep and turned onto one of the many side-streets that connected to Nicholasville Road. On either side of the street, I passed by old

British-colonial style homes of brick and stone masonry. Tall, ancient trees with faded leaves of gold and brown hung above the homes like umbrellas, sheltering them from the rain. No streetlights illuminated the neighborhood. The only lights that could be seen were the headlights from my Jeep and the warm yellow lights glowing from within each home. I found the house that I was looking for, pulled into the driveway, and parked.

I gathered my courage and stepped out of my Jeep and into the rain. I trudged through the long, overgrown grass of the front lawn that was matted down from the steady fall of rain. I climbed several steps and stood on a porch landing of rough cement. I huddled under a slight overhang in the doorway to avoid the rain as I knocked on the front door of a quiet red brick house. From within the house, I heard a dog scrabble across the hardwood floor and crash into the door. I instinctively took a step back, then the door opened. Standing in the doorway, holding an overexcited black Labrador by the collar, I saw my dad.

My dad stood several inches taller than me and I noticed that his black hair had a touch of grey at the temples, which had never shown before. With his free hand, he welcomed me with a handshake.

"Hello, Charlie. It's been a long time." He said.

I returned his handshake. "Yeah. Mind if I come in?"

"Sure. As long as your mother didn't send you over here."

My expression turned sour. "No, Dad, I'm not here to argue tonight. I was just hoping we could talk."

"Well, come on in then."

I walked through the doorway and was nearly trounced by his dog as he released her collar. Her name was Britney. My sister had named her when she was a puppy. I could remember the days when I had worked at my dad's office with her at my feet, and judging by her excitement, it seemed as though she still remembered me too. Since I had seen her last, she had grown short and squat, resembling a black pig more than a Labrador Retriever, but she was cute in an ugly-duckling sort of way.

"Whoa! Easy, girl." I insisted mildly.

She bubbled like a ball of energy, hopping up and down in front of me. I petted her head and scratched her back to soothe her.

"She'll calm down in a minute, just let her wear herself out." My dad said, then looked through the open doorway and out into the rain. He shook his head grievously at the sight of his lawn and closed the door. "Did you happen to notice my grass when you came in?"

"Yeah. It's getting pretty long."

"I'd say it's about knee-high to a tall Indian, wouldn't you?"

I shrugged. He was suggesting that I should have my lawn-care company mow it for him, but his lawn was last on my priority list. He was living in one of the rental properties that we owned together. It was the first house that we had ever bought together. My lawn-care company had maintained the property from the time when we had purchased the house, but as our relationship grew further apart, his lawn grew further unkempt.

"It would be good if you could cut it one last time before the winter."

"Yeah. I'll see what I can do." I said, knowing that I had no intention of having his lawn mowed.

The living room where we stood was furnished with a leather couch and two leather chairs, a big-screen TV fit within a wooden entertainment center, and a wooden and glass coffee table that was littered with newspapers. A small, but warm fire crackled within the fireplace along the outside wall. My dad walked over to the cream-colored sofa and took a seat. I followed suit and sat in one of two green recliners. Britney anxiously continued to jostle for attention by my legs, so I continued to pet her as a long period of silence settled within the room.

"So, what is it that you want to talk about?" My dad finally asked.

I took a deep breath and sat forward in my seat. I knew what I needed to say, but I didn't know how to say it. "Well, Dad." I started, then paused.

"That's a deep subject." He prodded.

I smiled weakly. "Dad, I hate that things have turned out the way they have between you and me. I came here tonight to offer a truce. I don't want to fight anymore that's why—"

"It was never your fight to begin with." He interrupted smugly.

My temper flared and I no longer cared about the civility of what I said or how I said it. "Not my fight!?" I shouted, my voice rising with each repressed word that reached the surface. "You don't have a clue, do you!? No, of course you don't! You never have to see it, so how could you!? You don't know what it's like having to watch Mom cry because she can't even afford to buy groceries! You don't know what it's like, knowing that Blake and Sydney won't have anything for Christmas, because you're too cheap to do anything for anyone but yourself! You want to know when it became my fight!? *Do you!?* It became my fight when you stopped caring about your family and only started caring about your goddamn money!"

He stood from the couch in indignant anger.

"If this is why you came over here tonight, then you can get the fuck out of my house!"

I scoffed. "*Your house!? This is our house!* And *that* is exactly why I came here tonight! I want out! I want my half of the equity from all of our properties and I want out! I think it would be best for both of us if we dissolved our partnership, took our profits, and moved on!"

He sat down again and chuckled wryly to himself. "Well, good luck."

"*Good luck?* What the hell's that supposed to mean — *Good luck?*"

"It means good luck trying to pull any of the money out of the company. I refinanced all of the properties months ago. All of the equity is gone."

"It can't be *gone*! You can't do that without my signature!"

"I don't need *your* signature to do *anything*. I'm the managing partner and I can move money around, whenever and however I want to, and I *definitely* don't need your permission to do it!"

"What did you do with the money, Dad!?"

"It's none of your damn business what I did with the money!"

"It is my business, because my fucking name is on half of it! So, where's my half!?"

He leaned back against the back rest of the couch and softened his tone. "You never had a half."

"What?" My heart felt like it was trying to crawl up my throat. I didn't want to hear his next words but I forced myself to listen.

"You never had a half. Sure, it looks like you do on paper, but it was always mine. I'm in the middle of a divorce." He shrugged as if the word divorce should be enough to explain his actions. "A few years ago, when things between your mother and I started going south, I needed a way to protect my assets. That was when you came to me with your idea about buying properties together. I knew that if I involved you in my business transactions, your mother would never try to come after them."

"You used me..." I never could have imagined that my dad, the man who had raised me, could have done such a thing. It was beyond my comprehension. In that moment, I understood what the cartoon character, Elmer Fudd was intended to feel when he ignorantly stepped on a big red X and Bugs Bunny pulled the lever. The ground gave out beneath the unsuspecting dope, and somehow, I was the dope. "...How could you do that?"

"I'm just doing what I have to do to keep my head above water. I knew your mother would try to take me for everything I've got, but I'll be damned if I let her take me down with her."

"But, we agreed that you would sign over your half of the company when I graduated from college. This was the money that I was supposed to build a future with. All this time...it...it was a lie."

"No. I did really want to be in a position to do that for you when the time came, but your mother keeps dragging this divorce out. Don't worry about it though, you're young. You have plenty of time to build a future.

There's always more money to be made out there."

"Dad, you don't understand, I *need* that money."

"Just forget about the damn money!"

"You don't understand though--"

"I said forget about it! I refinanced the houses months ago and the equity's gone!"

"But, where'd it go? All that money can't just disappear."

He stood from the couch in a threatening stance above me. "I'm not going to say it again! It's none of your damn business what I do with my money!"

I stood from the recliner and stared into his cold, uncaring eyes. It was like looking into a mirror, but I was looking at a reflection that I never wanted to become.

"Then fuck you and your money!" I shouted.

I turned my back on him and stormed out of the house, slamming the door behind me. I stepped out into the rain and I didn't care that I was getting wet. I didn't care about anything. I walked to my Jeep, opened the door, and climbed inside. I backed out of the driveway and drove in no particular direction. I just drove and I didn't care where I went. Nothing seemed to matter anymore.

As my tires pounded mile after mile of pavement, I remembered how proud I had been, at the age of sixteen, when my dad and I closed the deal on our first rental property. I felt like I was on top of the world when I signed those papers, because I was well on my way to becoming a business man, just like my dad. But it was a lie. It was always a lie. And sometimes a lie can be so powerful that it can make you question everything that you have ever known, everything that you are and have always been, and everything that you ever hoped to be. And that night, the part of me that believed in hope died. It was like a tiny light within me had been snuffed out, and I was left in the dark. I knew that if I was ever going to find my way out of the dark, then there was only one option left for me to choose.

Chapter 23: Blue Skies

I walked down the staircase that led to the basement. Each step seemed to shift and sway like bodies under my feet as I walked. I pulled a hanging bed sheet aside and stepped into Devon's room. Devon, Luke, and Ethan were seated around the coffee table, laughing, joking, and as Devon would say, smoking copious amounts of marijuana. I stepped forward slightly and waited for their laughter to subside. They each slowly noticed my presence and turned their attention toward me. When I spoke, I spoke as a man defeated.

"Fuck it... I'm in." I announced.

Immediately, they knew what I was referring to. They welcomed me and cheered at my decision. They cheered as if I had been elected for mayor. I high-fived and shook hands with each of them, and Devon stood from his chair to give me a hug.

"I told you! I knew you would change your mind!"

He was right. Somehow, he had known all along. For some reason, he had continued to include me in his plans, despite my reluctance, yet more than a year after he had mentioned the idea, I decided to join. I had to admit, his persistence was admirable.

"But." I said, holding one finger in the air. "If we are going to do this, we are going to do it right."

"Of course we are." Luke answered. "We all know what's at stake here. If we screw this up, we could go to prison."

Devon laughed. "I don't know. They don't call it Federal pound-me-in-the-ass Prison for nothing. You might like it in there!"

"Fuck you, Devon! If anyone would like it in there, it would be you!"

Devon laughed wildly at the heated banter.

I attempted to steer the conversation back to my previous point. "Seriously, guys, we need to cover every angle of this thing if we are going to do it. This has to work. We have to make sure that everything goes smoothly and that we actually get away with it."

I still doubted myself, after what had happened at Bullfrog's casino. I had thought that I had every angle of my plan covered, but somehow, I still got caught. There had to be a mistake that I made somewhere along the way and didn't notice. Maybe the power to the apartment never went out. Maybe someone was watching us the entire time. Maybe someone saw us leaving and wrote down the license plate number of Luke's car. It had only been a temporary-tag, but still, it may have been traceable back to Luke and that may have been how Bullfrog knew his name. But however it happened, the fact that I had been caught was undeniable. I was deeply indebted to a dangerous man, and I no longer had any way to come up with the money. I once believed that I did, but the equity from the rental properties was gone, and it had never been mine to begin with. Sometimes, when you find yourself in a hole so deep, it seems like the only way out is to keep digging. So, I kept digging, but I was going to try to be more careful this time. This time, I wasn't going to be caught.

"It's not like this is our first time, Chas." Luke answered and looked at me with a conspiratorial glance. I turned away and avoided his eyes. "All four of us have done things like this before and we've never been caught. This plan is bigger than anything else that we've ever done, but we can get away with this too."

I didn't have the heart to tell Luke how wrong he was. Some things are best left unsaid, and I didn't see any reason to make Luke worry about what lurked in our past. The debt had fallen on my head and I held myself solely responsible to repay it.

Devon leaned against the backrest of the raggedy, leather computer-chair in which he sat. "But that's exactly why it's going to work! None of us have a criminal record. The police don't even have our fingerprints! They won't have any idea that it was four college kids that robbed them blind! They won't have a clue! They won't know what hit them!"

Devon's excitement continued to rise as he leaned forward to the edge of his seat. "We will become aristocracy overnight! Think about it! We are going to make twelve million dollars for one day's work! That's all it's going to take, boys! One day's work to do something that will be talked about for generations! This is our chance to make our mark on history! These books are a part of American history! This is our chance to be a part of something great! When we do this, our story will live on even after we're gone, because it will be attached to American history, and nothing can change that! Nothing!"

I didn't agree with most of what Devon had said, but I agreed with some of it. "That reminds me of something I read the other day, let's see if I can remember it. I think the quote went like this, 'Every great fortune originates from a great crime'. Yeah that's how it went."

"Well, they say if you're going to do it, do it big." Luke agreed. "I mean, look at the Kennedy's. I hear they made all their money bootlegging whiskey during the prohibition."

Ethan leaned forward in his yellow chair. "What about the Bluegrass Conspiracy? Did you guys ever read that?"

"Yeah, I read it." I answered and Devon also acknowledged that he had as he nodded his head in agreement.

"It talks about where all the money in Lexington came from."

"Yeah." Devon interrupted. "Supposedly, Lexington was built on crime. They were trafficking cocaine through the police department and made a fortune! In our own way, that's what we are going to do! Just like Chas said, we are going to commit a great crime and make a fortune! We are going to be the *new* Bluegrass Conspiracy!"

Ethan didn't speak often, but when he did, his words typically held a gravity of their own. Ethan cleared his throat and spoke up. "The other day I was at this Chinese restaurant, and the weirdest thing happened. I got this fortune cookie, right. It was so weird, I thought somebody was playing a joke on me or something. I opened it up, and I was thinking about all of this stuff, and the fortune cookie said, 'society creates the crime, the criminal commits it.'"

"Damn, Ethan. That's some deep shit!" Luke said with a laugh.

"Out of thousands of cookies, *you* got that one. There has to be a reason for that. In this situation, we would obviously be the criminals." We each nodded our assent as Luke attempted to decipher the fortune. "The crime, would be us stealing the books. And the society that creates the crime, that would have to be Transy. Think about it. They are holding millions of dollars worth of rare artifacts and during the daytime, they hardly even have a security system. They don't even have video cameras. It's almost like they are just waiting for someone to come along and commit the crime. I guess that's what it means by society creates the crime, but I don't really know if that's a good sign or a bad sign."

Devon was quick to respond. "It's good. It's got to be a good sign. Why else would Ethan get the fortune?"

For me to be able to commit such a crime, I had to find a rational explanation to out-weigh my conscience and make myself believe that the only thing wrong with committing the crime, was what could go wrong. I attempted to explain my rationalization to my friends. "Transylvania is covered by huge insurance policies on all of their valuable items. All of their books and paintings and manuscripts are covered. When we steal them, insurance will pay them back, so really, there won't be any loss. These insurance companies are major corporations who steal a small amount from a lot of people by denying thousands of claims each year. So, I think they can afford this claim."

"So, it's a win-win situation." Luke said. "We make our money, Transy gets their money back, and we get to screw the insurance companies back for all of the people they've screwed over the years."

"We are not just going to make money." Devon insisted. "We are going to make millions. Millions, boys. Just think about that for a minute. Let the numbers sink in. Do you have any idea how much that really is? Three million dollars for each of us! Do you know how much you can buy with that kind of money? I already know what I'm going to get first!"

"A sex change operation?" Luke jeered.

Ethan and I laughed as Devon ignored the comment.

"I'm going to buy a gyro-copter!" Devon announced, excitedly.

"A gyro-what?"

"A gyro-copter. It's a mini helicopter that's only big enough for one person to fly. It's so small, it could fit in a parking space. If I wanted to go to the grocery, I could just hop in my gyro-copter and fly there!"

"That has got to be the stupidest thing I've ever heard!" I chided as I burst into a fit of uncontrollable laughter.

"Yeah, you can laugh now, but you won't be laughing when I'm flying my own gyro-copter and you're stuck on the ground."

"Oh, we'll still be laughing." Luke said. "It will be hilarious when we shoot you and your dumb-ass gyro-copter out of the sky with a potato launcher!"

I mimicked as if I was holding a potato launcher and Luke took the lighter from the coffee table and lit the imaginary fuse.

"Boom! Mayday! Mayday! Devon and his dumb-ass gyro-copter are going down! I hope he has a parachute!"

In Devon's mind, his idea was untouchable. He wouldn't allow anyone to ruin his vision. Rather than stopping, he laughed at our jokes and expanded on his dreams.

"I don't have all the details ironed out yet, but I've got big plans for the future. I never want to have to worry about anything, ever again. Someday, I want to wake up, butt-ass naked, lying in a ditch on the side of the road in some third-world country like Thailand, and have no idea how I got there."

"Wow, that sounds great, Devon." I said, sarcastically. "You're really setting the bar high on that one... What about you Luke? What would you do with the money."

He sat back in his chair and stretched his arms wide. "I don't know yet. I'd like to become an entrepreneur. Maybe own some kind of business. One thing is for sure though, I'm going to get out of this country! Europe sounds good. Maybe Milan, Italy, Greece-- who cares! We could go anywhere! We could be our own boss! We could do anything and no one could tell us different!"

"Okay. What about you, Ethan? What would you do?"

"I would open my own art gallery. Maybe in New York. I would have a huge art show to showcase and sell all of my work."

Whether Ethan's career was financed by crime, or whether he let his artwork speak for itself, I knew that he would be successful someday. He was the most talented artist that I had ever seen, and I wanted to see him reach his dreams.

"That's all you're going to do with *three million dollars*?" Devon scoffed.

Ethan seemed pensive, but persisted. "Yeah, that's what I want to do. I've always wanted to own my own gallery."

"You don't need three million dollars to do that! But, don't get me wrong. If you opened your own gallery, it would be the most popular gallery in New York. I can already see it now! They're going to love your artwork!"

"Thanks, man."

"So, Chas, what about you?" Devon asked. "What are you going to do with your three million dollars?" His voice emphasized each syllable of the value.

I knew exactly what I was going to do. I was going to pay my debt to Bullfrog. After I was positive that I would never have to so much as see him again. I would ensure that my family was well taken care of. Then, I would begin building my future, one investment at a time. It was the same plan for a future that I had proposed to my dad, several years before, and it was the same plan that my life had been on, until I discovered that my dad had lied about it for his own financial gain. Rather than build a new, extravagant life, I merely wanted to preserve the life that I already had. What I wanted more than anything, was a future that I could look forward to again.

But, at the time, I felt no need to share all of my motivations with anyone, even my friends.

"Honestly," I said. "I wouldn't do much different at all. I would keep living the life that I am now, and slowly, over years of time, I would filter the money into legitimate businesses. Then, from there, the sky's the limit."

"Hey." Devon chimed in. "I was meaning to ask you about that. After this is all over, do you think you could help me invest some of my money? I want to make this money last as long as possible."

"Yeah, sure man. I could help you out."

"Okay, good. But, I'm still going to buy my gyro-copter first."

"Alright, that's cool." I laughed. "There is something else that I had been thinking about doing if all of this goes through. It may take years. I'm talking maybe twenty years. But, I plan on investing and growing my money so much that eventually I will be able to go through the black market and track down the books that we stole, and buy them back."

"Why would you want to buy them back?" Luke seemed bemused. "Have you lost your damn mind? What would you do *that* for?"

"Because, I want to buy them, and years after we stole them, donate them back to Transy. I don't know. It's just something that I want to do. That way, it will be like we borrowed the books--from the library--then returned them. They'll be pretty late, but I guess better late than never, right?"

No one responded and quickly we all drifted into a comfortable silence, each of us were lost within the fantasy of our future world. It was a world in which money was of no concern and we were free to dream. A place where we were free to live a life of our own choosing. A place where nothing could hold us back, but our own ambition. In our imaginations, the American Dream was alive. It was a life where anything was possible. It was the beautiful life.

"We have work to do." Devon said suddenly. And his voice scattered the dream-clouds that had floated blissfully on the horizon.

Chapter 24: The Big Day

And work we did. As most college students prepared for their final exams, we prepared for a multi-million dollar heist. Our daily routines were blended with the routines of dedicated criminals. We became like the bad-guys in my favorite movies, only we weren't acting. What we were doing was real, and we were the bad-guys. Each one of us continued to take care of our regular obligations such as school, family, and social events, but we also spent portions of our days in secret at the Transylvania library. We studied the coming and going of students, teachers, and staff. We watched the patrols of the campus police and triggered alarms to ensure the response time. We devised escape routes, both by car and on foot, and practiced each route during different times of day.

While we prepared for the crime, the four of us became a team. We were striving together toward the same goal, but ultimately, we were a team of individuals who were striving toward our own goals. We held heated debates around the stolen coffee-table in Devon's room. It became the communal where all of our decisions were made and where our plans evolved. One of our final debates was a dispute over the concept of disguises. As always, Devon had argued in favor of extravagance and I argued for simplicity. While we argued, Ethan molded masks of facial-putty and bald-caps to custom-fit each of us. He intertwined grey artificial-hair with layer after layer of facial putty to create masks with well-groomed, artificial beards and hair. With a touch of stage makeup to enhance wrinkles and the lines of age that had yet to show on our young faces, the masks made each of us look like an aged and withered version of ourselves. To complete the disguise of old men, we purchased vintage suits and hats and shoes from Goodwill, Devon's favorite second-hand store. On the day before the deadline, Devon and I reached a compromise. We agreed to test the disguises during a trial-run of the crime. But as we wore our disguises and limped with practiced arthritic gaits through the library, we quickly learned that it would take much more than clothes and facial putty to mask the tell-tale signs of youth when standing eye-to-eye with a stranger. In the end, we agreed on a simple plan with simple disguises. Devon and Luke would go into the building, Ethan would be a lookout, and in a personal attempt to maintain a low degree of risk versus reward, I would be the getaway driver.

When the day to follow through with our plan finally arrived, we were ready, or almost ready. Devon and Luke were waiting at the house and making their final preparations in Devon's room. Ethan was waiting patiently in his dorm-room at Transy. But I was seated in a large, auditorium-style classroom where row after row of stadium seats faced a podium and a wall of dry-erase boards. Nearly every seat in the classroom was filled by a nervous student who was anxiously awaiting their final exam. I could tell that some of the students were attempting to cram fragments of last minute knowledge before the professor stepped into the classroom. But the last minute study session didn't continue for long.

A door opened at the front of the room and the professor walked purposefully to the podium as two assistants followed at his heels. The professor of biology was a man with a quirky personality, wild, roaming eyes, and an even wilder nest of hair atop his head.

The professor dropped a stack of papers onto the podium and spoke into the microphone. "Hello, class. It looks like everyone is excited to take my test! I have to admit, I am one of the greatest test writers in the history of this school. Or, any school for that matter!" He joked. Unfortunately, he was encouraged with a few laughs from the front row. "What's so funny!? That wasn't a joke. Anyone that laughed automatically gets an F!" His sarcasm garnered several more brown-nosed chuckles.

"So, who's ready to take my test!? His eyes searched throughout the rows of stadium seats and found an unsuspecting volunteer. "You there. Yes you. The one digging the pencil in your ear. You look ready. Are you ready to take my test?"

A boy who was seated in the middle of the classroom turned as red as correction ink and sheepishly nodded his head.

"By the way, class. This is another lesson—free of charge. If you dig in your ear you won't find anything, but if you dig in your nose you might find gold!" The room erupted with laughter and the boy slunk down in his chair. "On that note class, it's time to put away all of your materials. Notes, study guides, books, or sophisticated machinery to attempt to probe the answers from my brain. It's too late for that. You had your chance earlier this semester, but now I have a metal plate in my head. I had it installed today!" He rapped his fist against his skull. "See! And by the way, NO CHEATING! I have eyes like a hawk and if I catch you I'll peck your eyes out! Plus, you'll be expelled."

The thought of being expelled from school seemed minute when compared to the other consequences that I would face throughout the day. Within several hours, I was going to commit a robbery during broad day-light, and I knew that I could potentially be arrested, shot, or even killed. The worries of expulsion or a poor grade on the exam were infantile worries that every other student in the room seemed to share and I alone was excluded from. When I looked around the room, I envied them all. I wished that like them, my performance in school was the most important concern in my life. Years before, I had been like them, but something had changed. Maybe it was the result of circumstance, or maybe it was the result of my own choices, or both. However it may have happened, the course of my life had led me down the road less traveled, and I understood that I was different from every other student in the classroom.

The professor's assistants passed the exams to each student, row by row. As soon as I received my exam, I began answering the questions and penciling in the multiple-choice bubbles. I hurried through the exam and finished quickly. I glanced around the room and realized that no one else had finished, so I stayed seated. I never liked to be the first person to turn in a test. I took a few quiet minutes to relax and consider what awaited me as soon as I stepped out of the classroom.

Shortly I noticed a girl stand from her seat in the front row and approach the podium. She handed her test to the professor with a smile of accomplishment and he winked conspiratorially in acknowledgement. Several more students followed. They walked to the front of the room, finished with the test, the class, and the semester. So was I. I was ready.

I walked to the podium and handed my exam to the wily-eyed professor. He looked at me as if he hadn't seen me in class all semester. I laughed to myself at his confusion, because I knew how unfamiliar I must have seemed. I had never attended any of his lectures and only saw him to receive a syllabus and to take the exams.

I walked out of the classroom and through the bustling sidewalks of campus. I walked to the teacher's parking lot and waved casually to the parking attendant whose pockets were used to my donations. I found my Jeep and drove several blocks to the residential out-skirts of campus, then across town.

Chapter 25: Heist

It was 10:15 in the morning when I pulled my Jeep into the driveway of my mom's house. I walked around to the side entrance where I was greeted excitedly at the door by our two black Labradors. I unlocked the door and stepped into the house as they pleaded for my attention. The house was quiet as I walked into the kitchen. I opened a drawer and shuffled through the contents as I searched for an extra set of car keys.

My aunt, my mom's twin sister, had recently sold her minivan to someone from out of town. The new owner would be taking the van to the other side of the state by mid-afternoon, and the coincidence was too perfect to let pass. I didn't like the idea of borrowing my aunts van to commit a crime, but I was desperate.

"Charlie!?" A familiar southern drawl exclaimed. Startled by the sudden noise. I jumped, then realized that it was only my mom's voice.

"Whoa, hey, Mom. You scared me."

"Really? Why are you so jumpy?"

"Oh, I don't know. I guess I've just got a lot on my mind."

I finally found the key-ring that I was looking for. I twirled the ring on my finger and closed the drawer.

"Where are you going with those keys?" She asked curiously.

I stared blankly at the minivan keys and they suddenly felt warm within my hand.

"Oh, I need to borrow the van for a couple hours."

"What for? It's awfully early for you to be out and about isn't it?"

"Yeah, I've got to help Luke move a mattress." I lied. "I thought it would be better to use the van."

"Okay, that's fine, I guess."

"Alright." I walked by her and walked toward the door. "I'll see you in a little while."

I really hoped I would. If things were to go wrong, horribly wrong, I knew I might never see her again. As I reached the door, I turned back. "Hey, Mom."

"Yeah?"

"I love you."

A warm smile spread across her face. It was her sincere smile that gave me the courage to do what I was about to do. I opened the door and walked out before she could respond. I wished that Blake and Sydney were home so that I could have seen them one last time and let them know that all of our problems would be over soon. And I wished that I could let them know how much I loved them, just one more time.

I climbed into the driver's seat of the periwinkle blue minivan and drove away.

I punched Luke's cell phone number into my phone and waited for him to answer. I would have called Devon, but he didn't own a cell phone. Luke answered on the first ring.

"Hello?"

"I'm on my way."

I ended the call and after a short drive through town, I pulled the van into our driveway. Devon and Luke were standing in the backyard as I parked. I stepped out of the driver's seat and met them in the yard. I could see my breath in the cool winter air as I walked. I looked at each of my friends and appraised their outfits that resembled my own. They each wore a plain black baseball cap with heavy overcoats and leather gloves. Luke had recently had a mole removed from his face and he wore a band-aid on his left cheek to cover the scar. Devon had bleached his long black hair blonde and buzzed it short so that the dyed hair was only visible around his ears and below the back of the cap. Around Devon's neck, he wore his lucky red scarf. Over my eyes, I wore my favorite sunglasses with the golden-brown polarized tint.

"Devon, did you set the appointment?" I asked.

"Yeah, we're set for eleven."

"Did you make the call from a payphone?"

"Of course."

"At least a mile from here?"

"I went downtown."

"Luke, did you get a temporary tag?

"Yeah, I'll swap out the license plate before we leave."

"Good." I looked at my circle of friends. I knew that we should have been anxious, but we weren't. We each seemed calm in our own way. We were relaxed and we were ready to go.

"From here on out we don't use names—only code names. Mr. Pink, Mr. Black, Mr. Green, and Mr. Yellow. Keep your gloves on at all times. Keep your faces covered. Only get what we came for, and leave nothing behind. Nothing. Everybody got that?"

They both nodded in agreement.

"This is it, boys." Mr. Yellow said. "It has all come down to this. Everything in our lives has built up and led us to this moment. As soon as we step into the van, there is no turning back. One way or another, our lives as we know them will never be the same. We will have moved on to something bigger and better, something that most people can only dream of! We are among the elite of society! Ninety-nine percent of all the people out there don't have the balls to do what we are about to do! That's what makes us different! We were never meant for the regular nickel-and-dime lifestyle, the fucking rat-race that goes on out there! We're above that!"

Mr. Black and I allowed Mr. Yellow's words to resonate within us for a moment. I made eye contact with Mr. Black and he nodded his head, letting me know that he was ready. I nodded in response. Mr. Yellow broke the silence when he understood that the time for talk was done and the time for action had begun.

"Alright, boys, let's go make history." He said with a sly smile.

Mr. Yellow and I climbed into the van and Mr. Black swapped the license plate with a temporary tag. He climbed in and we drove away from the safety and comfort of home. As I wove through the streets of downtown Lexington, I knew there would be no opportunities to back out when we reached our destination, but I kept driving. My decision had already been made.

Fortuitously, I pulled into a parking space that was only twenty feet from the emergency exit door. The door's alarm system had already been cut the day before. I parked and turned to face both of them in the back seat.

"Good luck." I stated evenly.

"Yeah, this ought to help." Mr. Yellow pulled what looked like two black magic markers from his coat and handed one to Mr. Black. "It's a stun pen. It's the smallest kind there is. Here. You take one and I'll take one."

Mr. Black looked at it strangely. He flipped a switch and a tiny band of electricity sparked between two metal prongs no wider than a pinky.

"What do you expect me to do with this?" Mr. Black balked.

"Just carry it in case you need it."

"Where did you get these things? These things look like toys!"

"Don't worry about it. I got them this morning because we might need them."

"We!? I'm not going into the room until you have her tied up. I already told you that."

"Fine. Don't take it then. I'll call you when I'm ready for you to come up."

Mr. Yellow wrapped his red scarf around his neck and chin to conceal his face. He took a deep breath, slid the side door of the van open, and stepped out.

Mr. Black and I watched Mr. Yellow walk into the library. From across the field, we could see Mr. Green. He sat atop the stone steps of a staircase that led to a red brick building. He sat with an art pad strewn across his lap and his cell phone ready at his side to alert us quickly in the event of unseen danger.

"Well, here I go." Mr. Black said distantly.

"Let me see your hands."

He held two gloved hands in front of his face.

"They're still steady." I grabbed one of his hands to give him a one-shouldered hug. "Good luck, man."

"Yeah." He covered his face with a neck-warmer until I could only see his eyes. He slid the stun pen that Mr. Yellow had given him under the seat, and stepped out of the van.

When Mr. Black stepped toward the entrance, Mr. Yellow had already walked through the library. Most students had finished testing and had already gone home for winter break, leaving the library deserted like a ghost-town of the old west as outlaws rode through in search of plunder. Mr. Yellow easily found his way to the circular staircase and walked upward. The first to arrive, he apprehensively approached the glass door and was surprised to see that no one was on the other side of the glass. Cautiously, he knocked on the door. When Ms. Bonner appeared, Mr. Yellow's heart began to race. She looked at him warily, because he was bundled beneath such heavy clothing. She reluctantly entered the security code and opened the door. Mr. Yellow smiled beneath the cover of his red scarf.

"Hello, Ms. Bonner. I'm Walter Beckman." He casually extended a gloved hand to her. She returned his handshake and he stepped into the Special Collections Room. Mr. Yellow was asked to sign an appointment ledger, and in his worst chicken scratch ever recorded, he scribbled what was intended to be Walter Beckman.

Anita Bonner led the way as Mr. Yellow's bundled figure walked by her side. "Okay, and through these doors are where we keep our most prized possessions." She opened a pair of intricately carved and polished, wooden doors. Inside, there was a rectangular room lined with tall bookshelves that climbed toward a high, vaulted ceiling. Large windows allowed natural light to enter the room freely and glass display cases adorned the central space. But the most noticeable feature of the room was a huge, antique cabinet that was positioned against the left wall. The cabinet's finish was polished to a shine and several drawers were laid open, each drawer lined with a brass box and lock that protected the Audubon books, Birds of America.

Mr. Yellow knew that he should take the unsuspecting woman down – hard and fast – just as he had planned. But, when the moment to act came, he was hesitant. For what seemed like an eternity, he held Ms. Bonner in conversation with meaningless chatter. Finally, he changed the topic of conversation.

"Do you mind if an associate of mine joins us?" He asked.

"Well, no, I suppose not."

Mr. Yellow pulled a cell phone from his pocket, a phone that he had stolen only hours before so that he could make one very important phone call, because despite his claims, he had never intended to do the dirty work alone. He dialed a number and waited for Mr. Black to answer.

Mr. Black answered on the first ring. "Yeah?"

"Hey, come on up."

Mr. Black dropped the cell phone deep into his coat pocket, then zipped the pocket closed. He walked up the round staircase and found the glass door locked. He had expected the door to be open and Anita Bonner to already be tied up and out of the way. He saw Mr. Yellow walk nonchalantly toward the door with Anita Bonner at his side.

She entered the security code and opened the door. Ms. Bonner held her hand in introduction to the unsuspecting Mr. Black. "Hello, I'm the caretaker here. My name is Anita Bonner."

Mr. Black returned the handshake uneasily.

"Please sign your name in the log."

Mr. Black scribbled a barely legible attempt at the name John and followed Ms. Bonner into the Special Collections Room. While her back was turned, Mr. Black shot Mr. Yellow a scathing look of surprise. Mr. Yellow returned the glare with a blank expression, void of all emotion. He removed the stun pen from his coat pocket and he flipped the switch. Anita Bonner stopped walking when she heard the crackle of electricity behind her. Before she could turn around, Mr. Yellow jammed the stun device into her shoulder. But there was no effect. The bands of electricity couldn't breach the fabric of her wool dress jacket.

Upon the intrusion of her space, Anita Bonner's breath was trapped in her chest like a bird within a cage. She looked back in disbelief, but it was too late. Mr. Yellow's weight was already on her. He wrestled her to the ground and she began to scream, but no one outside of the room could hear her cries for help, because the Special Collections Room was soundproof.

Mr. Yellow pinned her shoulders to the floor as she tried to kick and scream and fight her attackers.

Mr. Black hurried to Mr. Yellow's side with the zip ties. He wrapped the plastic binding around her ankles and pulled the cord tight. He moved higher, to her hands. He grabbed one hand as Mr. Yellow grabbed the other and Anita Bonner desperately struggled to keep them from tying her hands behind her back. One of her hands broke free of Mr. Yellow's grasp.

"Damnit 'Boner', stop! Do you want to feel more pain? You're only making it hurt worse if you keep moving." Mr. Yellow insisted.

She was confused by the use of the derogatory nickname, but yelled with her face to the floor. "Let me go! Why are you doing this!?"

"Listen, 'Boner', we're only here for the books. We don't want to hurt you. Just stop moving and this will all be over soon."

She relaxed her hands somewhat and Mr. Black took the opportunity to coil the plastic around her wrists and zip them together. Mr. Black attempted to reassure her of her safety. "As soon as we're gone, we'll make a call to let somebody know you're up here."

Mr. Yellow pulled a toboggan from his pocket and slipped it over her head, pulling the wool over her eyes. He then wrapped the toboggan with duct tape.

"'Boner'." Mr. Yellow prompted. "Where is the elevator key?" She only responded with panicked breaths and soft sobs in hope of relief.

"Where is the elevator key, 'Boner'!?"

"What?" She whimpered.

"The elevator key. Where is it?"

She hesitated, but answered. "It's in my pocket."

Mr. Yellow rummaged through the pocket of her dress jacket and found a small ring with nearly a dozen keys. He left her lying on the floor and moved across the room. He exposed the contents of the antique drawers as Mr. Black pulled a white bed sheet from his coat and spread it on the floor. Together, they hefted one of the leather bound elephant folios that contained a volume of John James Audubon's collection of paintings entitled, Birds of America. They stacked two of the huge books on the bed sheet, then Mr. Yellow spread a pink bed sheet on the floor. The two of them loaded another folio onto the pink sheet.

Mr. Yellow removed the next drawer that contained the fourth and final volume of the Birds of America collection. But somehow, the brass box that concealed the final folio was locked. The fourth book was needed to complete the collection. Mr. Yellow exploded in a fit of rage.

"Damnit, 'Boner'! Where's the key to this drawer !?"

She didn't respond to his anger. She lay quietly on the floor and waited for her attackers to leave.

Mr. Yellow frantically tried several of the keys within his hands, but none seemed to fit. Frustrated, he punched the brass lock with his gloved fist.

"Forget it!" Mr. Black urged. "Let's just get what we can."

Mr. Yellow was infuriated by the setback, but he was pressed for time. "Fine. Let's load the packs."

They removed the collapsible bags from their pockets and stuffed them with the contents of the room's display cases. Now full, they slung the heavy packs over their shoulders and strapped the bags to their backs. Mr. Black grabbed one end of the white bed sheet and prepared himself to heft half of the load, two elephant folios, each book weighing well over a hundred pounds.

But Mr. Yellow wasn't finished. He opened two small drawers of the antique cabinet and found that they were unlocked. The drawers contained another Audubon collection entitled, Quadrupeds of America. The collection was less than half the size of the set within the elephant folios and not nearly as valuable.

Mr. Yellow loaded two volumes of the Quadrupeds of America on top of the two elephant folios. He attempted to lift his end of the bed sheet and together they strained under the weight of more than three hundred pounds, but somehow, they managed to lift the items from the floor. They staggered through the room, waddling in an awkward effort to carry the heavy load. In their wake, they left the pink bed sheet behind with one of the Birds of America volumes lying on top of it, another volume of the collection locked within the cabinet, and the librarian who struggled desperately to free herself.

They reached the elevator and Devon tried a key. The key worked on the first try and the elevator door opened. They hauled the burdened bed sheet inside and let their load rest on the floor, attempting to regain their breath from the physical exertion.

Mr. Yellow pressed a button and the elevator lowered one floor. As the door slid open, Mr. Yellow and Mr. Black each lifted the corners of the sheet and hefted their load in preparation to make for the emergency exit, just as they had planned. But like all plans, there is always something that you can't plan for. The doors opened, and by chance, someone unknowingly blocked their path. A large woman in her early thirties walked aimlessly toward the elevator. Her hair was cropped short. She wore a pair of jeans and a t-shirt that were both several sizes too small. She looked as though she had shop-lifted a butcher for a small mountain of Christmas Ham. She made eye contact with Mr. Yellow and Mr. Black and she stopped dead in her tracks. She immediately recognized the Audubon books and knew that only Anita Bonner should be riding down the elevator, not the heavily burdened and bundled men who she saw.

"Hey, what are you doing!?" She shouted.

Mr. Yellow panicked and mashed another button on the control panel as she ran toward the door. The door closed before she could reach them and the elevator descended one floor.

"Fuck! This is the basement!" Mr. Black complained as the door opened. "We can't get out from here! We have to go back up!"

Mr. Yellow pressed another button and the elevator rose. When the doors opened the woman was nowhere in sight. They lifted the corners of the bed sheets and shuffled step by step from the elevator and turned around the corner that led to the exit ramp. Painfully, their muscles burning with each desperate step, they started the steep decline toward the door. They were exhausted from their efforts, but adrenaline pushed them on and held the sagging bed sheet from the floor.

"Hey! Stop!" Someone screamed from behind them.

They moved as fast as their bodies and their heavy burden would allow and they waddled faster. They were almost halfway down the ramp. They were only a dozen paces from the emergency exit-door.

"Stop!" Someone screamed again.

Over Mr. Black's shoulder, Mr. Yellow could see the large women barreling toward them. His eyes grew large with panic and Mr. Black turned his head to look back at her. Mr. Black's hand slipped and he lost his grip. The books crashed to the floor and began sliding down the ramp like a runaway priceless-work-of-art bobsled. Mr. Yellow dropped his end of the bed sheet and hurdled over the runaway books as he ran toward the door.

Chapter 26: The Driver

Waiting within the van, I patiently watched the emergency-exit from the van's rearview mirror. I adjusted my sunglasses casually and lowered the brim of my black hat. For some reason, the moment didn't seem real. Everything seemed distant as if something thicker than air separated me from the world. It almost felt as though I was underwater. I knew that I should have been anxious, or nervous, or fidgety as I waited, but for some reason, I was calm.

In the reflection of the van's rearview mirror, I watched the emergency door fly open. Mr. Yellow burst through the doorway in a sprint. He ran toward the van as I stepped out to help him load his cargo, but I noticed that all he carried was a backpack slung over his shoulders. I tried to corral Mr. Yellow toward the van, but he unexpectedly turned toward the heart of campus.

"Where the hell is he going?" I wondered aloud to myself. But I didn't have time to think about Mr. Yellow. Mr. Black exploded through the emergency exit with a large woman barreling after him like a one-woman stampede. I slammed the rear hatch closed, opened the sliding side door, and jumped into the driver's seat. I threw the van in reverse and kicked down the pedal. Mr. Black was much faster than the woman, but what her massive frame lacked in speed, she overcompensated for with tenacity. She rushed after him with roaring fury like an immense tornado of flesh. Mr. Black dove in the open side door of the van, and speeding in reverse, I nearly crashed into his pursuer, who huffing and puffing, bobbed and weaved toward the open door. I jammed the gear in drive and floored the gas. She lunged for the van, but her reach was too slow. As I pulled away, she attempted to memorize the fake license plate number.

"Good luck calling that one in." I mused.

The van caught up to Mr. Yellow as he frantically sprinted through the parking lot. I pulled alongside him and Mr. Black yelled to get his attention.

"Hey, dumb-ass! Get in the van!"

I hit the brakes and the tires screeched as the van skidded to a stop. Mr. Yellow turned and jumped into the van. Mr. Black slid the door closed behind him and I stomped the pedal to the floor. I drove thirty, forty, fifty miles per hour around the horse shoe parking lot. I came to the end of the lot and took a hard right onto the street. I broke into oncoming traffic like the van had been shot from a cannon. Cars swerved and honked their horns in frustration. I only drove faster. I wove through the slow procession of traffic with reckless abandon.

I took my eyes away from the road briefly to glance into the backseat. Mr. Black was on the edge of the bench, straining to watch the oncoming cars through the windshield. Mr. Yellow was gripping the side of the van with his head hanging out from the window. I wondered what he was doing, but then I understood. He spewed yellow chunks of vomit into the wind and the mess splashed onto the side of the van.

"What the fuck, man!?" I yelled, then spun my head back to the road. The car in front of me hit the brakes. I veered into the other lane, cutting off another car, nearly colliding with them both. I glanced back and saw Mr. Yellow wiping his face with the back of his hand. He pressed the button to roll up the window and the glass smeared with long streaks of yellow.

I spun the wheel and took a hard right. The tires squealed, searching for traction. The van skidded onto a one lane road. The traffic was sparse on each side. A silver minivan slowly putted along in front of our van, hogging the whole lane, blocking our getaway, so I took a risk. I pulled into the opposite lane of oncoming traffic in a desperate attempt to pass the minivan. The pedal was jammed to the floor, but we weren't going fast enough. I banged my hand against the steering wheel, and begged my ride to go faster.

"Come on! Come on!" I furiously prompted.

I turned my glance away from the oncoming line of cars and checked the silver minivan that I was trying to pass. A middle-aged black woman stared at me and I could only see the round, golf ball sized whites of her eyes. She turned her eyes from me to the car that was heading straight for me. She honked her horn and the approaching line of cars honked. The pedal and the steering wheel felt like an extension of my body. I could feel what the van was capable of. Horns blared and a blue sedan grew larger in my vision like the swell of an oncoming wave. At the moment of impact, I swerved back into the other lane, barely dodging both cars. Air buffeted the side of the van as the blue sedan rushed by. I looked ahead and noticed a fast approaching four-way stop. I pushed the van to the limit and blew through the intersection. I sped down a long stretch of road until the street narrowed and the traffic became non-existent. The road hooked around a rundown building within the housing projects and I slowed the van to a stop.

"Get out." I said flatly.

"What?" Mr. Black asked, unbelieving.

"Get out of the van! Hurry up!"

"What!? Why!? Where are we supposed to go?"

"Just get out! I'll explain later. Find somewhere to hide and I'll be back in a different car."

I knew the police would be on the lookout for a blue minivan. Especially, a blue minivan with three guys and a load of recently stolen items. I took a chance that the police wouldn't be on the lookout for two college kids on foot, walking through the projects. If I was pulled over while driving the van, the police would have nothing. But if I could drop the van off and come back in my Jeep, we would have an easy ride home.

Mr. Black and Mr. Yellow jumped out of the van and I watched as they ran across the street and disappeared behind a cluster of apartment buildings. I drove away and didn't look back.

As I drove, I felt as if every car I passed could potentially have a cop or an informant inside, calling in my exact location. I bit my lip and kept my eyes on the road. I pleaded with the van to carry me home. Instinctively, I clutched the Saint Christopher medallion that hung from my neck. I took every back road that I knew and I obeyed all of the traffic laws. I drove the speed limit and tried to appear calm as I drove through the upper middle-class neighborhoods.

When I pulled into the driveway of my mom's house, a feeling of relief washed over me. I parked and stepped out of the van. I popped the rear hatch and found the van's original license plate and a screwdriver. I removed the fake plate and replaced the original. With a garbage bag, I collected anything that was left inside the van. Two stun pens, a roll of duct tape, a few zip ties, and Mr. Yellow's lucky red scarf. I slid the door closed and looked at the yellow streaks of vomit on the van's exterior. I huffed, exasperated by the unsightly blemish. I couldn't let the new owner pick up the van with chunks of vomit clinging to the periwinkle blue paint job, so I ran to the side of the garage and turned on the hose. I sprayed the streaks of vomit and they ran down the side of the van and onto the driveway.

Clean, inside and out, I tossed the hose aside, stashed the van's keys in the driver's seat and jumped into my Jeep, bringing the trash bag with me. I backed out of the driveway and I called Mr. Black's phone as I approached the projects. The phone rang and rang, then clicked over to record a voicemail.

"Shit! Pick up your goddamn phone!" I yelled.

I tried his number again, but didn't get an answer. I turned my Jeep around a corner and stopped beside the rundown building where I had dropped off Mr. Black and Mr. Yellow. I looked around, but they were gone.

"Damnit, guys! Where the hell are you!?"

I drove down a road that led deeper into the complex. My eyes scanned every building, every corner, and every parking lot. I couldn't find them anywhere. I tried Mr. Black's phone, and again there was no answer. I pulled into an empty parking lot to turn around. I looked into my rearview mirror and I saw them. They were running through the parking lot yelling and waving their arms like two survivors stranded on a deserted island, trying desperately to flag me down. I threw the gear in reverse and sped across the lot. I reached into the backseat and popped open one of the doors. They dove through the open doorway as if they would land on the only remaining life-raft of a crash.

"Go! Go! Go!" They both yelled.

I slammed the gear into drive and the tires peeled against the pavement as I pressed down on the pedal. We drove out of the projects and back into downtown. When we reentered the flow of traffic, the flow of time and our racing hearts slowed to match the pace of our ordinary lives. As we hid behind my Jeep's tinted windows, we tried to relax and catch our breath and make sense of what we had done.

I pulled into our driveway and we hurried down to the basement. Mr. Yellow and Mr. Black each unloaded the contents of their backpacks onto the coffee table. The coffee table quickly became cluttered with books. We each shuffled through the small pile. There were six books in all. There was a pair of medical dictionaries with cream colored binding that had once belonged to Thomas Jefferson, titled "Hortus Sanitatis", dated circa 1500. There was a bound collection of pencil drawings by John James Audubon that were commissioned for "The Birds of America" books, the books that had been dropped, and also a text that he had written, titled, "A Synopsis of the Birds of North America", and both were dated prior to 1850. There was a small book with a light blue binding. A first edition of, "On the Origin of Species", by Sir Charles Darwin, which brought the theory of evolution to the world.

I lifted the final book from the table. It was a large, magnificently bound book of many colors, which was untitled, but labeled as an illuminated manuscript, dated circa 1425. I turned the pages reverently and watched the lights dance against the raised ink of gold and silver, red and green, blue and purple. The illuminated manuscript had once been in the possession of a king, and hundreds of years later, it was in my hands. Holding such a book, a book that had been passed down through time, for nearly six hundred years, generation after generation, through the rise and fall of kings and kingdoms, was an incredible feeling. Holding the illuminated manuscript in my hands felt like standing among kings. It didn't matter that the book was stolen. The book was in my possession as the book had been in the possession of other great men throughout history.

"What happened in there?" I finally asked.

"It's a long story." Mr. Black answered.

"Alright. We'll talk when I get back. I'm going to go get rid of all this stuff."

I carefully stacked the illuminated manuscript among the other books.

I stuffed several trash bags with the old men costumes – jackets, slacks, shoes, socks, bald caps, hats, and masks – the tazers and the temporary license plate, excess duct tape and zip-ties, the written plans and blueprints and sketches, and I took the gloves from their hands and the shoes from their feet. They emptied their pockets and we did one last search of the room for anything unwanted. The empty backpacks were added to the trash, then I walked out.

I drove each bag to a separate dumpster. I burned the documents and spread the ashes sporadically. When I was finally finished disposing of the evidence, I breathed easier and my steps became uncalculated, aimless, and relaxed.

I could have gone back to my house to celebrate with the other guys, but I didn't. I went home to spend the afternoon with my mom, because I was thankful that I could see her again. I waited for Blake and Sydney to come home from school. Seeing them again, watching them go about their day as if nothing had changed, warmed my heart. I knew that the crime I had committed was wrong, but if the proceeds could help them in any way, to at least live a childhood that they could enjoy and be proud of, then it didn't feel so wrong anymore. I may have done some wrongs in my life, but somewhere near the root of the wrongs, there was always a reason that I believed was right. Sometimes though, reasons and intentions aren't enough.

I left home and drove back to my house. When I walked through the front door, I could smell the scent of weed drifting through the air. The pungent aroma hit me like a wall as I threw aside one of Devon's hanging bed sheets and stepped into his room.

It was like the crime had never happened. Mr. Yellow, Mr. Black, and Mr. Green were once again, Devon, Luke, and Ethan. The three of them were gathered around the coffee table taking hits from a glass bong with psychedelic swirls of red and gold, or as Devon said, The Red Dragon.

"Here." Devon offered with a smile. "Have some of this Kentucky Bluegrass."

I sat down in one of the tangerine chairs and handed Devon his lucky scarf.

He looked at me for a moment in amazement. "Where did you get this!? I thought I lost it?"

"I don't know. I guess it was just magic." I answered sarcastically.

He stared at me with wide eyes and wrapped the scarf loosely around his neck. I shrugged and thought, why fight it? I pulled the bong toward me and lit the bowl.

"What took you so long?" Luke asked.

"I had to take care of a few things."

"Did you know we already made the news?" Devon asked.

"Oh yeah, really?"

"They haven't said how much the books are worth yet, but they said it might be the biggest heist in the history of Kentucky! Can you believe it!? We did it, boys!"

Luke reclined casually in his chair. "Some woman tried to call in the license plate number. She was way off though."

"That's good."

"They said the top spot is either between us or some jewel thieves back in the nineties." Devon exclaimed with pride.

I didn't care. I felt that we did what we had to do, and now, what was done, was done. I passed the bong to Luke and turned my attention to Ethan who was quietly enjoying his own thoughts. As always, he was watching, thinking, and observing each of us as the images of our lives unfolded. I wondered what he saw, as only an artist sees. I wondered if through his eyes he saw something different than what I could see. When I looked around the make-shift, basement room, I could only see four nineteen and twenty year old boys who had sealed their fate with destiny. We were either destined for greatness or destined for a great fall.

"Hey! Shhh! Look!" Devon pointed to the TV. "Listen, they're talking about us again!"

The camera focused on an anchorwoman as she read the breaking news. "A robbery took place on the campus of Transylvania University today. Police say that two men between the ages of twenty and twenty five entered the Special Collections Library around eleven o'clock this morning. The men bound a Transylvania employee, and stole a collection of rare books before escaping from the scene of the crime in a blue minivan. Police are on the lookout for the van, the license plate number is believed to be MT2333, if you have any information regarding the crime, please call this number." A telephone number appeared on the screen. "Officials at Transylvania believe the rare books which the thieves escaped with are worth more than one million dollars."

"We did it! One million, boys! That's huge!" Devon exclaimed.

"How much do you think the buyer will pay though?" I asked.

Devon calmed his excitement and puzzled over the question. "I don't know. I guess we will find out when I talk to him tomorrow."

As the day wound to an end, tomorrow couldn't arrive soon enough.

Chapter 27: Trouble in Paradise

"Well, boys, I've got some good news and some bad news." Devon said as he walked down the stairs with Ethan two steps behind him.

Luke and I had been sitting in Devon's room waiting for them to contact the buyer in Amsterdam. They had gone to the public library to send and receive emails.

"What do you mean *bad news*?" I asked, offensively.

The sale of the stolen books to a prearranged black market buyer was the most crucial part of the plan. The day after the crime was not a good time for bad news.

"Do you want the good news or the bad news first?"

"Stop playing around, man! What happened?" I demanded. "Just hurry up and tell me the bad news!"

Devon gritted his teeth and bit the bullet. "The buyer backed out. We told him what we have, but he said he wasn't interested. All he wanted was the Birds of America collection."

"What!?" I yelled, jumping to my feet.

"But!" Devon spoke hurriedly, "I have another buyer! A better buyer!"

The possibility relaxed me somewhat. He knew that he had both mine and Luke's attention.

"In New York we can sell the books through Christie's!"

"The auction house?" Luke asked.

"Yeah, I've done some research and they have a whole sector for private sales. Everything is kept quiet and done with nondisclosure agreements. If we go in the next few days then we could get this over with before the books get red flagged by the police."

"But what if the books are already red flagged?"

"They won't be. Not if we leave tomorrow."

I bit my lip, infuriated by the foolishness of what Devon had proposed and by how quickly the other two seemed to consider his idea as a feasible option.

"I set us up a meeting at Christie's in two days." Devon continued. "First they have to appraise the books, then they will find a private buyer—"

"Are you *that* fucking stupid!" I shouted, interrupting his speech that I could no longer tolerate.

The three of them looked at me slightly offended, but mostly shocked by my sudden outburst. I continued, uncaring of their response.

"We can't just walk into one of the biggest auction houses in the world and expect them to sell stolen books! That's just stupid! As soon as they look into the history of these books they are going to call the cops. That's how appraisals work! Personal property, real estate, rare books — whatever ! They're going to look them up to see where they came from and when they were last sold! They're going to see these books belong to Transy, then they're going to call the cops. Trust me. I know what I'm talking about! I do appraisals and I've worked in my dad's auction house for years. We need the buyer back that you lost! This idea with Christie's won't work!" I fumed.

Devon plowed forward like an unstoppable force. "This is different though." He said. Time is on our side. It won't be put in the stolen art database for at least another week. These books probably aren't even in the *Lexington* database yet. When we meet with Christie's it won't matter where they came from. Not yet. Not until it is put into the international database. We can get this done before then."

Like an immovable object, I felt I was right and I was not going to give him any ground by letting my point go unheard.

"If we go to Christie's, it won't work." I insisted. "What don't you understand about that!? If you're too fucking stupid to realize it, then I don't even know why I'm still here!"

The truth was, I was there because the money was there. We had the books, but now, we had to turn them into cash – without our original buyer.

"Just chill out, Chas." Luke said as he stood from his chair to stand beside me.

"We have one chance to do this, and we leave tomorrow." Devon said, already pushing for the majority of opinions.

"What's the rush?" I asked. "Think about it guys. The police have nothing on us. No leads, no prints, no pictures – nothing. We need to just take our time and finish this right. We need to just hang on to the books until we find another buyer." I turned to Luke and nudged his arm. "We could go over to Amsterdam, or Europe, and track down another buyer. This isn't something that we can just do a half-assed job with."

"How long would that take? Years!?" Devon scoffed.

"I don't know. Maybe. Maybe not."

"I don't have years! I'm tired of living like this! This *fucking existence*! Look at this!" He said, referring to his room with bed sheets for walls. "I can't take this shit anymore! You might be able to wait years, but I can't! We're sitting on a million dollars worth of books and I'm ready to start living like it! This is our chance, boys! If we go to New York we can make this happen! And in a week from now, we will have a million dollars! Who wouldn't be ready for that?"

"Okay, how about this?" I proposed. "How about we let each of us decide what we should do? Let's take a vote. Guys, who thinks we should wait until we can find another buyer overseas?"

I raised my hand, and my hand was the only hand in the air.

"What!?" I couldn't believe they didn't see the reason in my argument, especially Luke.

Devon took the opportunity and pounced.

"Alright," he said with an air of victory. "Who thinks we should go to New York?"

All three hands were raised. All hands but mine. Mr. Yellow. Mr. Black. Mr. Green. All but Mr. Pink.

I knew then that Devon's arrogance and his ignorance would be our downfall. We had walked together until then, but now he was taking a path that I didn't want to follow.

"You're an idiot." I said coldly as I looked at the smug expression on Devon's face. "You know that? All of you are!" I walked past them toward the stairs. "I don't give a shit what you all do from now on! From this point on, you all are on your own. If you all want to follow this fool," I pointed to Devon, "then that's your own fault. I hope everything works out for you guys in New York. If it does, that's great — but I'm out."

I walked up the staircase as they watched me in silence. I needed the money, but if I had to, I would wait or I would find another way to get it. I knew that the three of them were headed for disaster, and I wanted no part of their downfall. I walked to my room and shut the door behind me. I walked across my bedroom and sat heavily at my computer desk. I clicked a few buttons on the computer. The sounds of Ali Farka Toure, an African musician with laid back foreign lyrics and smooth guitar rhythms and drum lines flowed through the Bose speakers like a live concert. I propped my feet on the glass-top desk and let the music calm my thoughts.

Interrupting the slight semblance of peace I had acquired, there was a knock on the door. I ignored the knock, but the knock persisted. Then, without admittance, the door opened and someone ran up the stairs and into my room. I acknowledged Luke with a nod of my head, then turned back to the computer screen. From the corner of my eye, I watched him drag a chair across the room, place it beside me, and sit down.

"Hey, man, don't do this." He pleaded.

"Do what?" I asked, acting as if I didn't know or care what he was talking about.

"You can't back out now, the hard parts over. All we have to do now is sell 'em. You should really just come to New York with us."

"Why, Luke? Nothing good is going to happen there."

"We're going to find a buyer."

"Not in New York."

Luke exhaled, frustrated. He paused as he looked at me like an abandoned dog on the side of the road.

"Why are you doing this?" He asked.

"Doing what, Luke!?" I jabbed back.

"Why are you acting like this, man? Why are you being so difficult?"

"I'm not being difficult, Luke. I don't know about you, but I'm not trying to get caught. I've got too much to lose. There is too much riding on my shoulders right now. I'm not going to let Devon and his dumbass ideas take me down."

"At least he's trying."

"Trying what!? To get us caught!?"

"No, I mean he's trying to find another buyer."

"He shouldn't have lost the first one!"

"That wasn't his fault."

"Well, then who's was it?"

"We knew that could happen if we didn't get the whole Audubon collection. We all hoped the buyer would want whatever we got, but he didn't. There was nothing Devon could do. They just backed out."

"Here's a question for you, Luke. How can you really even trust anything Devon says? You know he's a liar. How do you even know he had a buyer in the first place?"

"I've seen the emails." He spoke confidently.

"Yeah, me too. But anyone could fake those. I could set up dual email accounts right now. One from me, and one from a buyer. I could sit right here, write two emails, print them out, then feed you some bullshit – just like Devon is."

Luke looked at me in perplexed silence as he contemplated the idea.

"Think about it, Luke. The one thing that Devon ever had to offer was a buyer, and now the buyer is gone – if he ever even existed in the first place. You have to look beyond Devon and his conniving angles. It doesn't matter what happened to get us to this point. We have a million dollars worth of books. The police have nothing. We need to get rid of these books the right way – with, or without Devon."

Luke's face was stern. He seemed at thought, teetering back and forth between the two sides like two fat kids on a seesaw, until one fat kid outweighed the other.

"I know what you're saying, man." Luke consented. "But I agree with Devon. I don't want to wait years to sell these things. I want to sell them now—"

"Why?" I interrupted. "You have enough money to wait."

"I'm tired of this lifestyle, man. I'm tired of going to school, hanging out with the same people, and going to the same parties and bars. I'm ready for something different, something better."

I had no counter argument for his statement. In a lot of ways, I was tired too. I felt like I was just going through the motions each day, I was ready to break free from my financial burdens, but to sell the books through Christie's, or any other auction house, was not the way. New York was not the way.

My desire for something better in life was outweighed by my desire to not get caught.

"I know, Luke." I said. "Trust me, I know where you're coming from, but we should just be patient. It will happen if we just wait."

"I'm not waiting. Neither are Devon and Ethan. I know I can't convince you to be a part of the deal at Christie's, but you should really just come to New York. It'll be an excuse to go party up there. Have you ever even been to New York?"

"No, have you?"

"Yeah, it's been years, but I've got some family near there. You should really come check it out."

"No, I'm good, man."

"What are you going to do if you stay here? Hang out with Claire?"

"Maybe."

"Come on, man. You should get out of town for a few days, at least until this thing cools down. It's going to be all over the news and you don't want to be stuck here with all that going on. You should come with us and take your mind off of Lexington for a while."

He had a good point. I could use a break from Lexington. If they wanted to put themselves at risk by going to Christie's, then that was their problem. But if somehow they succeeded, which I highly doubted, then I would be there to take my portion of the proceeds. If they failed, I would follow through with my own plan. Either way, I wanted to keep an eye on the books at all times.

"Alright, man. I'll go."

Chapter 28: We have arrived

We made reservations, packed our bags, established alibis, then hit the road. As far as anyone else knew, we were on a ski trip for the next few days. We would be home in time for Christmas. The four of us were loaded inside of Luke's Explorer for the twelve hour drive. The books were carefully stowed in the back with the luggage. Luke drove the speed limit with the speedometer set on cruise control as we made our way up the interstate. I rode shotgun, and controlled the music and the navigation. Devon and Ethan were in the backseat and were responsible for the consumption of marijuana.

Before we had driven twenty minutes outside of Lexington's borders, Devon packed a bowl. He flicked a lighter and took a long, slow hit, holding the smoke deep within his lungs.

"Smokey, smokey. Who wants a tokey?" Devon asked, then laughed as smoke billowed from his mouth.

A small, handheld pipe of blue glass went around and around and our mood grew light and carefree. It felt good to be on the open road. It felt good to be rolling toward something new.

The miles rolled by, but the bowl never seemed to end. When the top of the weed was burned, it would turn to ash, but the bottom would still be fresh. Most people would tap the bowl with a lighter to flip the cherry and expose the fresh underside, but Devon wasn't most people. A master of deception like the Devil himself, he had a quick-handed sleight that he thought no one ever noticed. When he assumed that no one was looking, he would palm another pinch of weed from the bag and nonchalantly tap the bowl with the lighter to flip the cherry, but in actuality would refill the bowl. Many miles and many cherry-flips later, Devon had his fill and the ashy bowl was emptied and laid to rest.

I flipped through a playlist on my mp3 player that was connected to Luke's car stereo. I smiled as I found the song that I was looking for. "Alright, here we go. I'd like to dedicate this song to the only bohemian I know – Devon Koli, this song's for you. So here it goes. Bohemian Rhapsody!"

I turned the volume up as loud as the speakers would allow. A guitar intro began and slow lyrics were sung in electronic harmony.

Is this the real life?..

Is this just fantasy?..

Caught in a landslide,

No escape from reality...

Open your eyes,

Look up to the skies,

And see...

Devon took over the lyrics; his voice rose above the stereo.

I'm just a poor boy,..

I need no sympathy,..

Because I'm easy come, easy go,

Little high, little low.

Any way the wind blows...

Doesn't really matter to me...

To me...

The interlude came on, and Luke and I picked up the chorus as Ethan followed. The three of us sang while we rolled along the interstate.

I see a little silhouette of a man,

Scaramouch,

Scaramouch,

Will you do the Fandango?!

Thunderbolt and lightening,

Very, very frightening me!..

Galileo, Galileo, Galileo, Galileo, Galileo,

Figaro, Magnifico!-o-o-o-o...

239

Devon: I'm just a poor boy and nobody loves me...

All: He's just a poor boy from a poor family!

Spare him his life from this monstrosity...

Devon: Easy come, easy go,

Will you let me go?

All: Bismilah!

No! We will not let you go!

Devon: let me go...

Oh, mamamia, mamamia, mamamia, mamamia,

Let me go...

Beelzebub has a devil put aside for me!..

For me!..

For me!..

An instrumental interlude continued and we danced along to the music. The instrumental faded, the music slowed, and the four of us sang the final lyrics in four-part harmony.

Nothing really matters...

Anyone can see...

Nothing really matters...

Nothing really matters to me...

Any way the wind blows...

The song slowly faded and as the miles rolled by, many more songs followed. We took turns driving. Every three hours a new driver took the wheel. When it was my turn to drive, we passed under the green highway signs of the New Jersey Turnpike. I looked through the passenger-side window as the landscape of Manhattan's skyscrapers stretched endlessly across the bay. The sight was awe inspiring. It was empowering to witness man's limitless capacity for progress. Each beam of the steel, high-rise horizon was a by-product of the universal human desire for more, the need to achieve, the need to improve the standard of living. My desires and needs were uniquely my own, but I too was human. I wanted what the majority of the world has always wanted. I wanted more.

We drove into the city of New York and checked into the Hilton of downtown Manhattan. The hotel was within walking distance of Christie's Auction House, which was located within Rockefeller Plaza. Throughout our first day and night in the city that never sleeps, we rented a limousine and toured the sights. The expansiveness of Central Park, the flash and flare of Times Square, the majesty of Lady Liberty, and the heart-heavy memorial of the World Trade Center appeared through the tinted windows of our limousine.

We explored Chinatown and gorged ourselves at an expensive restaurant while we downed shots of sake. After dinner, Luke and Ethan were ready to go back to the hotel, but Devon and I wanted to experience the New York night life. The driver stopped the limousine near the hotel entrance and Luke and Ethan stepped out. Ethan wanted a full night of rest before the meeting that was scheduled the following afternoon. Luke wanted to try his luck fishing for women at the bar in the hotel lobby.

The limousine pulled away from the hotel and Devon and I took in the city, one club, and several drinks, at a time. We drank as if we didn't want to live to see tomorrow. We shot Jaeger-bombs and downed Irish car bombs. We sloshed our way through Maker's Mark and Cokes, we sipped White Russians, and we savored Crown Royal and Sprites. And at some point, we stumbled into the China Club, a name we recognized from the Rick James episode of the Chappelle Show. Inside the club, there were platforms and stages where only girls were allowed to dance. Devon and I didn't care about rules. We climbed onto the stage and danced with the girls of our choice. We didn't care when the bouncers pulled us down from our elevated position. We climbed back up and danced until the bouncers carried us out of the club. As they escorted us out, I looked at them and laughed. "You can't kick me out! Don't you know who I am!? I'm Rick James, bitch!"

We walked to the limousine still laughing about our expulsion like rock-stars beyond reproach. I tipped the driver and dismissed him for the night.

Devon and I took to the streets on foot and the night became a drunken blur. We stopped at a hole-in-the-wall bodega where I haggled for Cuban cigars and Devon tried, unsuccessfully, to buy weed from an old middle-eastern man. Defeated, Devon returned to the hotel, but I ventured into the night on my own. I crashed through dive bars and after-hours restaurants. I found myself in the gift shop of a Planet Hollywood and I took a picture with an enormous, stuffed gorilla. I followed the lights, and through my aimless wandering, I stood in the center of Times Square. Lights flashed and flickered through my field of vision like beacons, ten stories tall. I scanned the streets, but there were no cars. I scanned the sidewalks, but there were no people. For a moment in time, I was the only soul at the center of the largest city in America, the most powerful nation in the world. The moment was mine, and mine alone. I felt as tall as the buildings that surrounded me. I felt like I was standing on top of the world. It was a feeling that I would never forget.

A taxi cab drove past and the moment was gone. I drug myself through the streets as the sky turned from black to the dull, ashen grey of a new day. I found the hotel room, which the four of us shared, crawled into my half of one of the room's two queen-size beds, and slept like the dead.

Chapter 29: The Meeting

When I woke, I woke to the sound of a ringing telephone. I lifted the phone from the receiver.

"Hello?" I asked, confused and groggy with sleep.

A computerized voice responded. "The time is twelve P.M.. This is a—"

I placed the phone back on the receiver. The room was dark. My head was cloudy with alcohol from the night before. I crawled out of bed wearing mesh shorts. I rubbed my eyes and stumbled toward the curtains where the noon sun shined around the edges of the thick, hanging fabric. I pulled the curtains aside and sunlight rushed into the room through the floor-to-ceiling windows.

"Aww... Bad form!" Devon complained as he shielded the light from his eyes with a hand.

"Personally, I don't care if you guys sleep all day. But if you plan on going to your meeting with Christie's, then you should get your asses out of bed."

Luke groaned. He swung his feet to the floor and sat on the edge of the bed that he and Devon had shared for the night. He walked to the window wearing a white t-shirt and soccer shorts. We both looked through the glass at the towering skyline of the city. From our elevation, the cars and the people down on the street seemed small and insignificant. I knew the hustle and bustle of the street was noisy, but within the comfort of our hotel room, there was only silence.

Devon disrupted the quiet as he yawned. I watched him from the reflection in the glass as he rolled out of bed and casually stretched his arms. I turned, unbelieving of what I saw. He was as naked as the day he was born.

"Damnit, Devon!" I yelled and turned back to the window.

Devon laughed. "What? Can't a guy have some naked time?"

"Not when you're in a room full of the other guys!"

"Did you sleep like that!?" Luke demanded.

Devon shrugged. "Yeah, so?"

"You slept a foot away from me, dickhead! That's disgusting!"

"There was plenty of room... It's a queen-size mattress."

"I don't care how big the bed is! I don't want your naked ass anywhere near me! You're sleeping on the floor tonight!"

"The floor's bad for my back..."

"I don't give a shit about your back! You're not sleeping next to me again!"

"Guys!" I interrupted. "We can figure this out later! Devon, for now, just shut up and go put some pants on!"

The conversation ended as Devon walked to the bathroom, sulking like a reprimanded child.

"Where's Ethan?" Luke asked.

"I don't know. I haven't seen him."

"Hey, Devon!" Luke shouted in the direction of the bathroom door. "Where's Ethan?"

"How should I know?" Devon replied over the sound of running water from the shower.

I reclined against the headboard of one of the empty beds. I found the remote control and flipped idly through the television channels. Nothing seemed to grab my interest.

"Here. See if you can find something to watch." I said as I tossed the remote across the room to Luke.

Luke sat at the end of the other bed and began searching through the channels. Program after program flickered to life then died with the press of a button. Finally, Luke grew frustrated and pressed the power button. The colors on the television screen faded to black as he tossed the remote into a corner of the room. "There's nothing but garbage on TV anymore."

"Yeah, I know what you mean. I think it all started when MTV stopped playing music. All they ever show now are these damn reality shows."

"But it's not just MTV!" Luke protested. "These stupid reality shows are on every channel! And what's worse, people actually watch that shit! I don't know how they do it!"

I shrugged. "I think some people just watch it, because it's on."

"I'm telling you, man, it really pisses me off. If I could shoot one person in the face and get away with it, I'd shoot whoever started these damn reality shows."

I laughed. "I don't know if they deserve to die over it, but they should definitely get a swift kick to the nuts."

"No, a guy like Jerry Springer, now *he* should get kicked in the nuts. He puts garbage on TV, and he knows it. But that's only one show. Whoever started these reality shows, single-handedly killed TV! If that guy got shot in the face, it would be like an eye for an eye kind of thing. You know?"

The bathroom door opened and clouds of steam rolled through the doorway. Devon stepped into the room wearing a towel around his waist. "I know who killed TV." He claimed.

"Oh yeah? Who was it then?"

"It was O.J. Simpson."

Luke and I both laughed. "And next you're going to tell me that Ted Bundy is responsible for every shitty movie that comes out." I joked.

"No, really! When O.J. was on trial for murder, it was a fucking media circus! It had the highest ratings on TV! When that crazy fucker held a gun to his head and took off down the highway in that white Bronco, the world was hooked! *That* was the day when reality TV was born!"

Luke turned and looked at me. "I think the druggie's got a point. You know what that means, don't you?"

I shook my head. "I don't know. What?"

"It means I gotta shoot O.J. Simpson in the face!"

We all laughed as Luke aimed a pointed finger and pretended to shoot the blank television screen. An electronic lock clicked and we each turned our attention toward the hallway door. The door opened and Ethan casually stepped into the room. I noticed that he was already dressed for the day. His face was shaved and his hair was coiffed and feathered like Patrick Swayze in the 80's. He wore a yellow suit with a matching yellow tie. The suit hung loosely on his small frame like a poncho on a scarecrow. Foam shoulder pads widened his shoulders to cartoonish proportions. The jacket collar flared out like a costume leftover from the disco era. The pants bunched in piles around his ankles and nearly overwhelmed his clean white sneakers.

I couldn't help but laugh at his outlandish appearance.

"What's so funny?" Ethan asked in a monotone voice, dryer than burnt toast.

"Your clothes, man! Where the hell did you get that thing, Halloween Express!?"

Ethan's face flushed red as he looked down at his suit. "No, it was my grandfather's."

"Who was your grandfather, Dick Tracey!?" Devon and Luke laughed along with me as Ethan grew more embarrassed. "Ethan, please tell me you don't plan on wearing that to the meeting."

"I do, why?"

"No one in their right mind could take you serious in that thing! When the people at Christie's see you in that yellow, Dick Tracey-looking get up, they're only going to have one question for you. They're going to want to know if you have any new leads on Flattop and the gang!"

Luke nearly doubled over with laughter as he walked to the bathroom. He gave Ethan a sympathetic pat on his over-sized foam shoulder and stepped into the bathroom.

Ethan reached into his jacket and withdrew what looked like a ball wrapped within white napkins. He unraveled the paper to reveal a blueberry muffin. He placed the muffin on a nearby dresser and produced two more muffins from the depths of his yellow suit pockets.

"The free breakfast downstairs closed a while ago, but I snuck some muffins out for you guys."

"Thanks, man." I said appreciatively, the kind gesture having caught me off guard.

With hungry eyes, I chose the largest of the three muffins from the dresser. I patted Ethan on the shoulder pad and resumed my reclined position against the headboard. I began eating the delicious ball of blueberry flavored bread as I turned my attention toward Devon. He had ignored the offering of muffins for the moment, because he was busy dressing himself. He wore black slacks, black wing-tips, and a white button-down shirt. His collar was popped and he was intensely focused on the process of tying a solid colored maroon tie. I watched in amusement as he struggled to make the proper combination of twists, loops, and pulls.

"Need some help?" I offered.

"Yeah. This tie won't cooperate."

I looked at him skeptically. "Are you sure it's the tie's fault?"

He didn't answer my rhetorical question. I stuffed the final bite of muffin into my mouth and wiped my hands on the floral-patterned bed comforter. He handed the tie to me with wary apprehension as if he sensed a trap.

I draped the tie around my neck. "What do you want? A half Windsor? A full Windsor?"

"I don't know. I want the knot that looks more like a rectangle than a triangle."

"Half Windsor it is then."

I proceeded to make the necessary twists while Devon watched each movement carefully. I looked up at him and stopped. I unraveled the twists.

"You don't know how to tie a tie, do you?"

Devon scoffed. "Of course I do."

"Here. Tie it then." I took the tie from my neck and held it in front of him. He looked at the tie then looked back at me without words. "That's what I thought." I placed the tie around my neck again. "Watch. I'm going to do this slowly, so pay attention."

I guided him through the process, step by step, and repeated the lesson until he could tie a passable knot on his own. As each minute passed, I had a terrible feeling about the meeting that they had scheduled with Christie's. Devon and Ethan were the two who would conduct the meeting. Devon's talkative and charismatic nature was intended to carry the conversation and Ethan's specialized knowledge of art was meant to answer questions regarding the books. But as I looked at the two of them, Ethan in his laughably large lampoon-suit, and Devon unable to tie his own necktie, their youth and inexperience was painfully obvious.

"Devon, it's not too late to cancel the meeting." I said, unable to hide my sense of impending doom.

"What are you talking about!? Of course it is! The meeting is in less than two hours!"

"I'm just saying, man, you can't even tie your own tie! If you can't even do that, how the hell are you going to negotiate a deal for a million dollars worth of stolen books!?"

"If you think you can do better, then why don't you come to the meeting?"

"Because the meeting's a terrible idea!"

"It's going to work, Chas!"

"If it does, that's great! But it's not looking good with your man over there wearing a goddamn clown suit!"

"He looks fine! He's wearing a suit and tie and that's all that matters!"

"Devon, you're not getting the point here! If this meeting goes bad, they're going to call the cops!"

"No they won't. Besides, we've got fake names and I.D.'s and everything!" Devon handed me a Massachusetts driver's license. Below Devon's picture was the name Jonathan Williams. "I'm Mr. Williams and he's Mr. Stephens! We're from Boston and we were sent here to sell the books for our employer!"

"And you think they're going to believe that!"

"Yeah. I do. And they're going to find us another buyer!"

"The bathroom door opened and Luke stepped into the room. Luke walked by, uncaring of our argument, wearing a towel around his waist.

"Whatever, man. Just do what you want." I relented. "I'm tired of all this, and honestly, I don't care anymore…"

I turned and walked into the bathroom. I shut the door as he began to respond, but I didn't listen to what he was saying. I stepped carefully on the floor tiles that were slick with moisture. I wiped the condensation from the mirror and looked at my reflection. I shook my head distastefully at what I saw. I realized that I had spoken the truth. I didn't care anymore. I didn't care if we got caught, and I didn't care if we got the money. Nothing seemed to matter anymore, because as I looked at myself in the mirror, I didn't like what I had become. But somewhere within me there was still an instinct to survive and enough willpower to carry me through the day.

I removed my shorts and boxers and stepped into a glass shower stall. I turned the water on and stood under the spray. I let the heat roll over me, the water steadily soaking into my skin. I tried to wash away everything – thoughts of the past, the future, and the moment that I was in – but no matter how hard I tried, nothing changed.

I stepped out of the shower, dried myself, and wrapped a towel around my waist. I brushed my teeth, rinsed, and spit, then opened the bathroom door. As I walked into the room, Devon was admiring his appearance in the mirror, Ethan was lounging in an armchair, and Luke was making the final adjustments to his suit. He wore a blackish—bluish suit, black wing tips, and a white shirt with a green tie.

"Looks good, Luke." I commented.

"Thanks."

"Are you going into the meeting?"

"No, I'm just going up there to drop them off."

"Alright, give me a minute and I'll walk up with you guys."

As I dressed myself, the three of them examined the books one last time before the appraiser's inspection. They carefully peeled away several certificates that signified the charitable donations from a third-party to Transylvania University. After all of the books were cleared by each of them, the books were tucked within white linen sheets and gently packed into a red suitcase. To properly represent Mr. Pink, I tightened a pink, diagonally striped tie around the collar of a white shirt. I tucked my shirt into a pair of grey slacks and slipped into a grey sports-coat. I laced my black wing tips tight, fearing that the need to run may arise. I draped a charcoal-grey overcoat onto my shoulders, and when I was sure that no one was watching, I pulled a silver .38 special Smith & Wesson revolver from my luggage. I slid the gun into the breast pocket within the lining of my coat.

"Hey, guys, we should probably go now." Ethan said, checking his watch.

I looked at the digital clock on the nightstand. The meeting was in forty-five minutes.

Devon looked around the room with a wide, alligator grin. "I'd say today is a good day to become a millionaire. What do you say, boys? Are we ready?"

The enthusiasm in the room was meager, but together, the four of us filed out of the room. We stepped onto the sidewalk of downtown Manhattan, walking side by side. The red suitcase rolled purposefully behind us, pushing us forward. Luke held the extended handle as if his hand was cuffed to the grip. The streets were packed with endless lines of traffic as we walked. Steam rose from exhaust pipes in the cold air and the constant commotion of car-horns and brakes and people's voices surrounded us. The wind whipped between the buildings and the cold air cut through my clothes like a harvest-blade made from ice.

We passed Radio City Music Hall, turned a corner, and walked into Rockefeller Plaza. Four stories tall, the Christmas tree of New York towered above us, glimmering with ornaments. We sat at an empty bench that overlooked an ice rink. Hordes of tightly packed skaters glided in loops around the small ellipse. I didn't know why, but the rink had always seemed bigger on television.

A short distance from where we sat, stood the monstrosity of Christie's auction house. The building was shaped like a stout, immovable block. The building seemed like a fortress from where we sat. I looked at Devon and Ethan and I knew that if I didn't stop them from entering the building, I would allow them to bring all of us one step closer to the clutches of the law enforcement that was surely hunting us. Every fiber within my body told me to stop them. I reached into my breast pocket and fingered the revolver. The wood-grain handle felt warm in my hand. I looked at them again and at the red suitcase that stood between us.

Devon and Ethan stood from the bench. "We're going to go in and make sure everything's on the up and up." Devon said. "If everything looks good, Ethan will run out here to get the suitcase."

I stood and faced them. I withdrew my hand from within my coat pocket. Devon looked at me strangely as I extended my open, empty hand to him. We shook hands.

"Good luck." I offered genuinely.

Devon smiled warmly. "Thanks."

I shook Ethan's hand and resumed my seat next to Luke on the bench. Disappointed, I watched them walk away. They crossed a street and disappeared through the revolving entrance of Christie's. Several minutes later, Ethan emerged from the building in a hurry. He rushed across the street. As he approached, I was worried that something had gone wrong. I stood from the bench and prepared myself to run. Ethan paused within several feet from where I stood.

"They want to see the books." He announced.

"How's it going in there?" Luke asked as he reluctantly released his grip from the handle of the red suitcase.

"Good, so far." Ethan grabbed the handle and rolled the suitcase away. He again vanished through the door to Christie's.

I tried to remain focused and maintain awareness of my surroundings, on guard for any signs of trouble, but more than anything, I people-watched as I waited. I watched the skaters go around and around and I watched the people who walked through the plaza. An Asian family walked by. A mother, a father, and two teenaged kids, a boy and a girl. They all wore big, bulky cameras strapped around their necks. Every few seconds, they stopped to take a picture. And every time the camera flashed, they seemed profoundly happy. I was amazed that such a simple thing was able to bring them so much joy. A stone's throw from where I sat, the children posed beside a lamppost. The father's camera flashed and the entire family laughed with genuine, heart-warming happiness. I smiled to myself, because I was glad to know that such a life was possible.

Luke nudged me with his elbow. "Look, here they come."

Devon and Ethan walked casually across the street with the red suitcase rolling safely in tow. Luke and I walked to meet them halfway.

"How did it go?" I asked when they were within earshot.

"It went great!" Devon said as he beamed with pride. "You should have seen us in action! We were flawless!"

"They bought the back stories and everything." Ethan added.

I looked over their shoulders to ensure myself that they weren't being followed. "That's good, guys. Let's keep walking. We can go over the rest when we get back to the room."

We walked back to the hotel without words. Devon was brimming with excitement, and I knew he was anxious to share the details from the meeting. We walked through the entrance of the Hilton hotel and rode the express elevator to the floor where our room was located. I slid a plastic key-card into an electronic lock, a green light flashed, and I opened the door. The four of us stepped into the room and the door locked behind us.

"Let's hear it, Devon." Luke prompted. "What did they say?"

"First of all, they *loved* the books! They were really impressed! Of course, they wanted to know where they came from. I fed them a line about our employer inheriting them, so that squashed that!"

"It really couldn't have gone any better." Ethan claimed. "We laid the books out on a table, some woman examined them, asked us a few questions, then it was over."

"That's it?" Luke asked,

"We haven't told you the best part yet…" Devon paused, letting the tension build within the room. He walked to the window, casually glanced toward the horizon, then leaned against the glass. "They're going to find us a buyer!"

"What!? Oh my God, that's great!" Luke cheered. "How long did they say it will take!?"

"They've got people lined up right now! They already know some people who would be interested! They're going to check with them then give us a call in a few days!"

"Wait, what did you just say?" I asked, walking across the room toward Devon.

"They're going to find us a buyer!"

"Yeah, but you said they're going to call us…"

Devon looked at me with an odd expression. He seemed apprehensive to proceed, but also accusatory, because I was ruining his moment of triumph. "Yeah. That's what I said. They're going to call us when they have a buyer."

"Call us where, Devon!?" I shouted.

All previous contacts had been made through emails, accessed from random, unmonitored, public terminals. Every name spoken had been false. Every identification used had been fake. Every transaction in furtherance of the crime had been in cash. Every step of the way, down to even the most insignificant details, measures had been taken to remain anonymous.

Devon could see the anger building within me and didn't respond to my question.

"Damn it, Devon! Where are they supposed to call you!?"

"On Ethan's cell phone." He finally answered.

"*What!?* You're telling me that you gave them the number to the phone that's in Ethan's pocket!?"

"Yeah. So?"

My entire body shook with rage. I wanted to fling Devon from the window that he was leaned so casually against. I walked toward Devon and pulled my cell phone from my pocket. I dialed Ethan's number and let each ring be heard through my phone's loudspeaker, and from the phone in Ethan's pocket. The ringing stopped and Ethan's voicemail sounded through the speaker.

"This is Ethan. Leave it."

"Does that sound like Mr. Stephens, Devon!?"

"That's no big deal." Devon protested. "He can change the name or just take it off."

"Devon. His name is registered to the phone. If Christie's gives the number to the cops, that's it! We're done! They'll trace it back to him and then back to us!"

"But they won't go to the cops."

"*You don't know that!*" I shouted.

I reached into the breast pocket of my coat and grabbed the revolver.

I wrapped my finger around the trigger of the loaded gun and aimed it at Devon's face.

"Whoa!" All three of them simultaneously responded. They tried to inch away, but there was nowhere to go. They were trapped. We all were.

"Listen to me, Devon! I don't care how you do it, but you have to go back into Christie's and get that number! Wherever she wrote it down, you have to get it back!"

"But, how? I can't."

"Did you *fucking hear me*!? I said I don't care! If you have to take this gun and rob the whole place, then do it!"

"Chas, it's too late. The number's gone. Just put the gun down. What are you going to do, shoot me?" He half-heartedly joked.

I stared down the silver barrel of the revolver and looked at Devon's face. I held the gun level with Devon's head and I turned and looked at Ethan and I looked at Luke. I despised each one of them for insisting that the books be sold at Christie's. But more than anything, I despised myself for ever choosing them as friends.

I yelled in anger and lowered the gun. "What the *fuck* was I thinking!" I don't know why I ever got involved with you idiots! Look at yourselves! You're a bunch of *goddamn morons*!"

They each stared at me blankly as I paced the room with the gun in my hand.

"Devon, you're nothing but an incompetent burned-out pathetic pot-head! You had one thing to do! *One thing*! And you screwed it up! I told you guys that this could happen! But, no, you didn't want to listen!" I raised the gun, using it as a pointer, and aimed it at Ethan. "And you! You need to grow your own set of balls and stop doing everything Devon tells you to do!" I swung the gun toward Luke. "And, you! You're just as bad as *these* two! The one time I ever needed you, you let me down! You decided to follow *this* idiot and try to sell the books in a hurry! What the hell were you thinking!?"

I slid the revolver into the interior pocket of my coat. I shook my head in disgust, opened the door and walked out of the room. I couldn't stand to be around them any longer. I took a long walk through the city to calm myself and clear my head. As I walked, I thought of a lot of things from my past. I tried to understand how at only nineteen years old, weeks away from my twentieth birthday, my life had become so different from how I had imagined it would be.

Someone close to me once said, "Tell me who your friends are, and I'll tell you who you are." I never wanted to believe those words. I wanted to believe that I was different. Somehow better, somehow smarter than they were. But what I wanted to believe didn't matter. The truth was, the four of us were bound together by our mutual decisions. For better or worse, they were my friends.

Chapter 30: A New Year

It was New Year's Eve. Back in Lexington, my roommates and I were throwing a house party to bring in the New Year. I walked through the crowded living room and unlocked the basement door. I closed and relocked the door behind me. Down the steps and through a hanging pink bed sheet, I found Devon, Luke, and Ethan having their own private party. Devon stood behind the bar as Luke and Ethan stood across the glass-topped wooden divide. The bass from the music upstairs vibrated through the floor. The indistinct voices of the crowd talking, yelling and laughing were muffled, but could still be heard.

"Does anyone have a razor blade?" Devon asked.

"Yeah, I happen to carry an extra one in my pocket." Luke answered sarcastically.

"Seriously. Just help me look. I need it to chop this up."

"Here, chill out druggie. Don't start having withdraws yet." I lifted one of the glass tumblers where he had absent-mindedly hidden the razor.

Devon laughed as he eyed the blade and quickly reached for it. He pulled a small white rock from his pocket and laid it atop the bar. It was the color of chalk and the size of a marble. He crushed the rock into powder and hashed the pile into twelve lines, one for each million that, according to Devon's plan, we should have already had by now.

"For this round, we've got three lines apiece." Devon announced. "Who wants to do the honors?"

Luke and I had sponsored the night's festivities, so I thought that one of us should go first. I pulled a hundred dollar bill from my wallet, ensuring that I only used the rarest of bills for myself and rolled it into a straw.

"I'll go." I volunteered. "But, we need some theme music or something."

Devon pushed a few buttons on the CD player at the end of the bar. He chose the Beastie Boys. He cranked the volume up loud, so loud that we could no longer hear anything from above us.

I put the straw to the powder, closed one nostril and snorted with the other, inhaling the line in one pass. I could feel the numb, burning sensation as the powder passed through my nasal cavities. My eyes watered from the sinus pressure, but I could feel the oncoming rush. I dropped the straw, then stepped away from the bar. The intensity, the power, and the excitement pushed through my veins. The music was all that I could hear and the rush was all that I could feel. Everything else was quiet, numb, silent. I listened to the Beastie Boys lyrics as if they were speaking only to me. The song was called Rhymin' and Stealin'.

Ali Baba and the Forty Thieves!

Ali Baba and the Forty Thieves!

Ali Baba and the Forty Thieves!

When everyone finished their lines, Devon improvised his own lyrics to the song.

"Transylvania and the Four Thieves!" Devon cheered. He looked around to each of us, grinning from ear to ear. His enthusiasm and natural charisma was infectious. With his hands, he invited us to chant the new lyrics.

We each joined in the chorus, feeling the excitement, the rush.

Transylvania and the Four Thieves!

Transylvania and the Four Thieves!

Transylvania and the Four Thieves!

I felt something vibrate within my pocket and I realized that it was my cell phone. I checked the caller ID to see a phone number and a smiling picture of Claire.

"Hey!" I yelled over the music. "Turn it down for a second!"

Devon scrunched his face, accusing me of killing the fun.

"Turn it down!" I yelled again, pointing to the CD player.

The volume was lowered and I answered my phone. "Hello!?" I yelled, unaware of how loud my voice was.

"Where are you?"

"I'm downstairs! Why!? Where are you!?"

"Stop talking so loud, you're screaming in my ear."

"Oh, sorry."

"Why are you downstairs?"

"I just wanted to get away from the crowd for a little while. You can come down if you want."

"Come open the door. The door's locked."

"Alright, bye." I put the phone back in my pocket. I slid the razor blade under the tumbler and left Devon to clean up the white residue on the glass bar-top. He licked his finger and rubbed the remaining powder on his gums. I walked up the stairs, unlocked the deadbolt, and slightly opened the door.

"Why's the door locked?" Claire asked, and from the tone of her voice, I knew she was upset with me. "What are you guys doing down there?"

"We just didn't want everyone down here." I answered dismissively.

She didn't agree with my occasional drug use. It was something that I chose to do, but out of respect for her, I wouldn't do it in front of her. I opened the door wider so that she could come down. I noticed that Rachel trailed a few steps behind her. The two girls walked past me as I started to close the door, but a hand caught it. I let the door open again, slightly, to see who it was.

Squint-eyed drunk with a toothy grin, Brandon Small stood in the doorway as I blocked his entrance to the basement. He was a friend from high school. He was a soccer player, built stocky and hairy like a caveman and he was almost always drunk or high. My roommate, Jeff, stood behind him, with eyes just as slanted and also wanted to be allowed downstairs. I looked at them as if asking what it was they wanted from me.

"I've been looking all over for you, man." Brandon said quickly. "What's going on down there? Do you guys still have some of that stuff? Can we come down?"

"No. But sure, come on."

The two of them walked past me and I shut and locked the door behind them. As I walked down the stairs, I pulled out a few pieces of mint flavored gum to get rid of the cocaine taste in the back of my throat.

I sat down in one of the tangerine chairs. The music had returned at full volume. The Beastie Boys were rapping about a sabotage. I tried to coax Claire to come sit with me by tapping my knee as if it were an empty seat. She looked at me from across the room and rolled her eyes. She watched Devon toss a bottle of vodka in the air as he poured White Russians. She tried not to, but she glanced back at me as I watched her. Her dark hair was straightened to fall smoothly over her slim shoulders. Her skin was pale without the summer sun and dotted with the occasional freckle. When I caught a glimpse of her aquamarine eyes, I tilted my head down and jokingly pouted my lips as I looked at her with sad puppy dog eyes.

She tried, but she couldn't stay mad at me any longer. She smiled accidentally, then attempted to disguise the smile with a light-hearted scowl. Slowly, she glided toward me and sat in my lap. I hugged her and held her close. I breathed deep, taking in as much scent as my cocaine-lined airways would allow. Somehow, she still got through. She always could. And she did it effortlessly. For the moment, I was content. I wished that time would stop so that I could live the rest of my life eternally frozen within one perfect moment.

My thoughts were disrupted by the sound of someone fumbling through the hanging bed sheet walls. I realized that Brandon was the cause of the disruption. I shot a glance at him over my shoulder.

"B Smalls, what are you doing, man?" I asked with a razor's edge to my tone.

"I'm trying to figure out what's behind these bed sheets." He answered in a grunting, guttural voice.

"It's just more sheets, Smalls." Luke answered quickly. "Come back and sit down, man. You'll get lost back there in all of that shit."

"More sheets? How many more are there?"

Behind a few rows of hanging bed sheets there was much more than more sheets. There was a hidden room that we had built. On the other side of plywood walls, a pad-locked door, and row after row of black plastic, there were two phototrons growing several pounds of marijuana and a million dollars worth of stolen property. Local law enforcement was still searching for the books, and the media was advertising a five thousand dollar reward for the return of the books, or for any information that could lead to an arrest.

"He's just messing with you, Smalls." I tersely responded. "I've got a bunch of stuff in storage back there. I don't want your drunk ass going through all that right now."

"Oh, my bad." He apologized and walked back through the sheet. He stood with Devon behind the bar and the few who knew what was located behind the sheets breathed easier.

I turned toward Rachel, who looked at her watch, then she hurried toward the television to raise the volume. "Hey! It's almost midnight!" She announced.

On the screen, I saw Times Square. There were thousands of people gathered in the streets. I thought about how I had been the only soul there, only days before. But no one knew that I had even been to New York. Not Claire, not my family. Only Devon, Luke, and Ethan could relate to what I was thinking. I looked at each of them as the countdown began. I knew that they were each thinking their own version of my thoughts. They were thoughts we shared and experiences we had been through together. But it was all in the past.

"7! 6!"

It was about to be a new year.

"5! 4!"

Things were going to change.

3! 2!

They had to.

"1!"

"HAPPY NEW YEAR!"

As the ball dropped and time jumped into a fresh three hundred and sixty five days, I could hear the muffled yells and the shuffling feet from the party upstairs, and also the excitement from the private party in the basement. I felt as if I was trapped somewhere between the two.

I turned and looked at Claire and we kissed through the first few seconds of the year. It was believed that such a kiss could bring good luck in the coming year, but I felt that it would take more than luck for me to change my circumstances for the better.

The first few hours of the New Year ticked by, and slowly, the crowd that occupied the house dwindled down to only a small group of stragglers. We moved the private party from downstairs and relocated to the living room of the main floor. Ethan had gone back to his dorm room at Transy and Rachel had left, leaving Claire to stay with me.

I lounged on a long, cream-colored leather sofa with Claire curled alongside me as Devon and Luke each sat at the table. I could tell that Claire was tired, but she was trying her hardest to stay awake.

Claire leaned back and whispered in my ear. "Let's go upstairs."

"You tired?" I whispered back.

"Kind of."

"Well, if you're tired, you can go ahead and go to sleep."

"Okay." She answered softly. "Are you coming?"

"Yeah, I'll be up in a few minutes."

She rubbed her eyes as she stood from the couch. She opened the door to my room, and I knew that I hadn't given her the answer that she had wanted to hear.

"Where are you going, Claire?" Luke asked.

"I'm going to sleep. I'm tired. Goodnight guys."

"Goodnight."

"Aww look at the poor baby." Devon mocked. "She's too tired to stay up anymore."

"Shut up, Devon." She fired back, then turned and walked up the stairs.

Devon stood from his seat. "I think we have a few lines left. What do you say, boys?"

Together, the three of us walked through the beer-splattered, trash-filled kitchen and stepped into Luke's bedroom. Devon dumped the remaining powder from a plastic bag onto Luke's wooden computer-desk. He used a stray piece of paper to hash the pile into three lines. Devon put the rolled one hundred dollar bill that we had used throughout the night to his nose and pulled a line through the make-shift straw. Luke took his turn next.

I watched Devon open the side door to Luke's room that led to the driveway. He stepped out into the night as Luke handed the rolled bill to me so that I could take my turn. I snorted the last line. As I inhaled, there was no more pain, no more burning. All thoughts went away, briefly. Everything was numb. I could feel a slight tingling sensation and a small rush, but most of all, I was numb.

I blew on the desk-top where the powder had been and wiped the surface clean with my hand. I shook the rolled bill and rubbed it on my shirt to rid it of any remaining residue and flattened it back to its original shape. I began to slip the bill into my wallet, but I realized that it was missing a few zeros. The hundred dollar bill had magically become a one dollar bill.

My anger flared like the lighting of a gas-fueled fireplace. "What the hell is this, Devon!" I shouted.

"What?" He answered from outside of the house.

I stepped through the door. Devon and I stood on a small concrete landing that was six steps from the ground. Luke walked curiously through the door behind me.

"What happened to the hundred dollar bill, Devon!?"

"What are you talking about?"

"The hundred dollar bill that we used is gone! You switched it with a one!" I crumpled the bill and threw it in his face.

"You better check your wallet! It was a one the whole time!"

"Where'd you put it Devon!?" I frisked his pant-pockets like an overzealous cop. Luke stepped forward as if to help, but only watched.

"I don't have it!" He yelled as he tried to push my hands away.

"Of course you don't have it! Not on you anyways – I know you hid it somewhere you slimy piece of shit! You think you're so slick, but I'm on to all your bullshit! I can see it coming from a mile away!"

"You think so?" Devon asked, no longer taking the defensive.

"No, I know so! You conniving bastard!"

Devon laughed. It was a dark, cynical laugh.

"No. You don't know anything! You think you do, but you don't!"

"What the hell is that supposed to mean?"

"You always want to blame everybody else when things go wrong! Take a look at yourself sometime, Chas! You make mistakes too!"

"Yeah, I'm sure I do. But I'm not the one who gave away Ethan's cell phone number!"

"Maybe not. But you've made your fair share of mistakes."

I scoffed. "Like what?"

"Like when you robbed that casino."

I stared at him in disbelief. I had never spoken to Devon about the casino, but I vividly remembered the night when Luke's money was taken from my room. I remembered walking into the kitchen as Luke spoke privately to Devon. And I remembered the way Devon smirked as he listened to Luke's words.

"Oh, you think I forgot?" Devon laughed. "No. I couldn't forget something like that. And you didn't think I would forget who made me lose my scholarship and my spot on the soccer team, did you?"

"That was your own fault, Devon! I warned you not to steal from my roommates!"

He stared at me with the coldest, most smug smile I had ever seen. "And I warned you not to cross me!"

Vaguely, I could remember Devon warning me on the day when Luke and I had confronted him in an empty parking lot. After I had forced him to get out of the car, I thought I heard him say that I had made the biggest mistake of my life. I didn't understand his words then, and I was only beginning to understand them now.

"Yeah. I talked to the guy you robbed." Devon continued. "What was his name again? Was it Bullfrog?"

I realized that my fists had instinctively clenched at my sides. I looked at Luke and he seemed unable to believe what he was hearing.

"All he wanted was your names. And he said he would handle the rest. He said you're in deep, but he wouldn't tell me how far. Really, I'm surprised he hasn't fucked you up yet."

Instantly, everything became crystal clear. I had doubted myself for months. I had wracked my brain, trying to understand how Bullfrog had known so much about the robbery. The answer had been obvious. It had always been Devon. He had used his friend's trust to further his plans for revenge and to further his own plans for the future. He had always known that I would participate in the heist, because he had always known that I would need the money to pay Bullfrog what I owed him.

"Devon, how could you do that?" Luke asked. "I trusted you."

Devon laughed. "I know. How did that work out for you?"

Luke didn't hesitate. He balled his fist and punched Devon in the sternum, knocking the wind from Devon's body. As Devon gasped for air, he hunched over and continued to amuse himself with a wheezing, gasping laugh of victory. I no longer felt the need to talk to Devon. There were no words for the violence within me. I threw a right uppercut into Devon's stomach. He coughed and staggered down the top two steps. Luke shoved him down the remaining four steps. His body tumbled down and he landed roughly on the asphalt driveway.

Devon laughed as he lay curled like a shriveled snake on the ground. "Payback's a bitch. Isn't it?" He said with intended irony as he stared into my eyes.

I realized that my own words had echoed through time and were spoken from Devon's mouth. I looked down at him and I wondered why I had ever considered him a friend. I had wanted to trust him, but time and time again, he had taken advantage of anyone and everyone around him. I wondered how he, an assumed friend, could have willingly inflicted such damage within my life.

I looked at Devon as he lay on the asphalt, writhing with laughter. I wanted to jump on top of him and punch him until he could no longer smile, or breathe another condescending laugh from his lungs, but I didn't want to give him such satisfaction. I turned away from Devon and looked to Luke, who stood beside me. We each were at a loss for words.

"What are we going to do?" Luke finally asked.

"About what?"

"If Bullfrog knows what happened, what are we going to do?"

I almost told Luke the truth, almost. But, I didn't. It would be years before I would tell him about the confrontation that I had with Bullfrog and the debt that Bullfrog insisted to be paid. I didn't tell Luke that night, because sometimes the truth is better left unsaid. And sometimes, we would rather believe a lie than know the truth.

"Don't worry about it. Bullfrog's not going to do anything. I know he won't." I lied. I knew that Luke wasn't in danger, but I couldn't honestly say the same for myself.

"You don't know that! We've got to do something!"

"Luke, just trust me. Everything is going to be fine."

"Trust you!? How do you expect me to trust you after what Devon did!? I don't trust *anybody* right now!"

"I know, but I'm not Devon. Have I ever given you a reason not to trust me?"

Luke gritted his teeth and flexed his jaw as he contemplated my question and the possibilities of the future. "No. You haven't." He finally declared.

"So trust me now. You have nothing to worry about from Bullfrog."

Luke nodded. We both stepped through the doorway and into the house, leaving Devon to fend for himself. I told Luke that I would see him in the morning and walked through the kitchen, the hallway, and into the bathroom.

I quickly brushed my teeth and made my way to my room. I locked the door behind me and walked up the stairs. I could barely see my hands in front of me as I groped through the darkness.

"Claire?" I whispered.

There was no answer. I approached the bed and could see the outline of her figure bundled beneath the covers. I paused as my eyes adjusted to the room and I could see her face, angelic amidst the darkness. She breathed softly and evenly in the quiet of the night, and I realized that she had already fallen asleep.

I changed out of my clothes and into a pair of mesh basketball shorts. Quietly, I slid under the covers, trying not to wake her. Somehow, she stirred as if she could sense my presence. She stretched her slender body and rolled over to face me.

"Where have you been?" She asked in a sleepy whisper as she nestled closer to me.

I kissed her forehead and put my arms around her. "I don't know. I definitely wasn't where I wanted to be." I could feel her soft breath on my chest. "I think maybe I've been in the wrong place for a long time now. It just seems like every time I think things are going to get better, they only get worse. You know? Claire? Claire?"

She was already asleep.

I laid awake for hours, unable to sleep. My mind and body raced at a frenetic pace, but I was tired. I was tired of nearly everything within my life, everything except for her, and my family. Everything else would have to change. It had to. It was a New Year.

Chapter 31: Someone's watching

The February weather was harsh, bitter, and cold. Within the house the temperature was warm, but far from comfortable. Devon, Luke, Ethan, and I were seated at the round table in the living room. The four of us had attempted to seclude ourselves from one another in recent weeks, sometimes unsuccessfully, but we set our differences aside and called a meeting to discuss our options for the future. I had decided to travel through Canada to find another buyer, and Luke had decided to go with me. The four of us were going to split the books two ways. One half for Luke and I, the other half for Devon and Ethan. All that remained undecided was the question of who would get which books.

"I don't know if it's just me." Luke said. "But have you guys noticed anyone following you lately?"

"No. Why? What makes you think that?" Devon asked.

"I don't know if I'm just being paranoid, or what, but I swear those were cops in the back of that theatre last night."

We had reluctantly gone as a group to see Ocean's 12. As the scenes unfolded, we felt we could relate to the movie. The places, the schemes, the art, and the heists reminded us of similar obstacles and successes that we had experienced in our own endeavors. The movie had recently hit the big screen, and was hugely popular, but there were only six people in the theatre as we watched from the front row-- the four of us and two men who sat together in the back row.

"Did you see them when the movie was over?" I asked. "When we were walking out they were staring right at us."

"Who cares?" Devon answered dismissively. "Maybe they were just gay. Think about it. Two grown men *alone*, in the back row of the theatre. They were probably just waiting for us to leave so they could get it on."

"Awww, come on man! That's just gross!"

"What!? I'm serious! Think about it."

"I think they were cops." Luke persisted.

"No, you're just being paranoid. You're starting to get like me. I think you smoked some bad weed or something."

"But what about the guy at the gas station the other night?" I asked. "Remember Luke? That guy that pulled up behind us in the unmarked car. That was a cop."

"Yeah, he was definitely a cop, but I'm not sure if he was following us. I was watching my rearview mirror the whole time. He wasn't behind us when we left the bar, so I don't know, it might have just been a coincidence."

"I don't think so, man."

I turned to Ethan whose eyes were squinted as if trying to see something far off in the distance. He was staring intensely toward the front windows of the house that looked out on to our porch, the front lawn, a few parked cars on the street, and a neighbor's house.

"Ethan, what are you looking at, man?"

His eyes snapped back into focus as if he had been lost in a trance. "What?"

"What was that all about? What were you doing?"

"Oh, I was just, I was just looking at this beam of light coming through the window."

I stared at him as if expecting a better explanation and he took the cue to continue talking.

"I was just trying to refract the light with my eyes in a way that makes it look like the beam of light is actually bending."

"Well, I'm sorry to interrupt and everything, but we're trying to figure out if the cops are on to us yet. Do you mind helping us out for a minute? Do you think you can handle that?"

He shook his head and seemed to refocus his attention on the conversation at hand. I nodded and continued.

"Have you seen anything going on at Transy? Has anyone been acting weird around you, or following you, or anything like that?"

"No. Not really."

"Nothing?"

"No. Not really. Well, there *has* been this girl coming up to me a lot lately though."

"Uh-oh, sounds like Ethan might have a girlfriend!" Luke taunted.

Ethan didn't rise to the bait, but seemed slightly embarrassed.

"What's she doing? Is she asking questions, or what?"

"I don't know. She just keeps trying to talk to me."

"Who is she? What's she look like?"

"It's some blonde girl that I've never seen before. She said she just transferred into the art program."

"Is she hot?" Luke chided. "Did you fuck her yet?"

Ethan didn't respond to Luke's derision.

"What do you think, Ethan? Do you think she could be some kind of undercover cop or something?"

"I don't know. She is kind of hot to be a cop."

"Hook up with her then, Ethan." Devon encouraged. "Cop or not, just fuck her. Then you could be like a rapper, because you 'fucked tha po-lice'."

Ethan laughed a quiet, almost internal laugh.

"Look, Ethan," I said, redirecting his attention. "I don't care what you do with this chick, just make sure you don't tell her anything. If she starts asking too many questions, that's when you know to back off."

"Yeah, I know."

"Guys, all of this isn't looking good. I don't know how much more time we have, but I don't think we have much. Luke and I are leaving in a week, so we need to go ahead and figure out who is taking what."

The three of them nodded their agreement and we each readjusted within our seats to lean closer to the center of the table.

"Alright. Here is what I'm thinking. We can do this like a draft. Luke and I'll pick a book, then you guys pick a book. How's that sound? We'll just go back and forth."

"Why do you get to go first?" Devon argued.

"Because we're selling the books and you two are staying here. Plus, you owe us because you're an asshole."

"Fine. Just take your pick."

"We'll take the Illuminated Manuscript."

"Damn. We'll take the Darwin then."

"Okay, you got us on that one." I pretended to concede so that I could position myself for my second and final selection. "We want the medical dictionaries."

"What!? No. That's two books! That's not fair!"

"Here. I'll tell you what I'll do, just to be fair. You two can have both of the other two picks. You can have the book of Audubon sketches and the book he wrote, the one that has his autograph. Those two books go together and our two dictionaries go together. That's fair. We can't split those things up."

I knew that I was getting the better end of the deal. After working for an auction house I had learned, among many other lessons, the most basic principle of antiques – age plays a large role in an items value. In our situation, the date on the Illuminated Manuscript was in the 1400's. The dates on the Medical Dictionaries were in the early 1500's. The dates on all of Devon's selections were post 1800. The items I had selected had been in existence 300 years prior to Devon's selection, which made them much older, and most likely, more rare and more valuable.

"Yeah, I guess that's fine." Devon conceded. "That sounds fair."

"Alright, cool. Luke, you cool with that?"

"Yep."

"What about you, Ethan?"

He was staring out the front window again.

"Hey, Ethan."

He stood from his seat—still staring—and pointed out the window. "There's a guy wearing a mask across the street. He's looking right at us."

I glanced out the window and saw a hooded figure in a white mask, crouched behind a parked car, watching us. I didn't flinch. Immediately, I bolted toward the door. I flung the door open to see the man turn and run.

Barefoot, at full speed, I jumped down the four steps of the porch and sprinted through the yard, through the street, rushing toward the man in the mask like a man on fire. His back was turned as he ran. He wore blue jeans, white sneakers, and a black, hooded sweatshirt that concealed the back of his head.

I gained on him with each purposeful stride. I crossed the street and chased him down the sidewalk at a furious pace.

He turned a corner and veered left onto a connecting street as I pounded the pavement in pursuit.

I turned the corner only seconds after he had, and somehow, he was gone.

It was as if he had vanished like the stage magicians of old. I knew he couldn't have gone far, he had to be close by, hiding somewhere. Luke, then Devon, then Ethan turned the corner, panting for air. They helped in the search as we frantically looked under parked cars, in the bushes, and behind nearby trees. But, it was no use. The man in the mask was gone.

"Where the hell did he go!?" Luke asked, standing by my side.

"I don't know. But if he comes back, we'll be ready!" I yelled, hoping that anyone in the nearby proximity could clearly understand my meaning.

We concluded our search and walked back to the house, glancing over our shoulders every step of the way. Each of us took a seat on the porch. I sat on the wooden porch-swing, Devon and Luke sat in wicker chairs, and Ethan sat along the brick and stone railing. We watched the cars drive by and the neighbors who walked along the sidewalk, hoping that we would catch a glimpse of the man in the mask.

"Who *was* that?" Devon asked.

"Who do you *think* it was!?" I snapped back in response. Devon turned away from my hateful glare and watched the road.

"I thought you said he wasn't going to do anything?" Luke asked.

"I know! I know, alright! I thought everything was under control, but I don't know anymore. Maybe if we're lucky, he'll think I live in the basement and I changed my name to Devon." I sardonically joked as I stared at Devon. "Do you see what you started? Sleep lightly, asshole. If you get beaten with a lead pipe in the middle of the night, just remember it was your own fault."

Devon didn't acknowledge my statement. He stared blankly toward the road. I stood from the porch-swing and walked into the house. Luke followed after me. He shut the front door behind him.

"We've got to go talk to Bullfrog." Luke insisted.

"And tell him what, Luke? That we're sorry? I think it's a bit late for that."

"Well, we can't just sit here and do nothing."

"Do you have an extra hundred grand lying around that I don't know about?"

"No."

"Exactly. So that's what we're going to do. We're going to sit here and wait until we get out of town. I know we were supposed to leave next week, but I think we should go tomorrow."

"That's fine with me, but I still have to take my furniture and clothes and all that stuff to my parent's house."

"We can do that tomorrow on our way out of town."

I walked to my room and locked the door behind me. I knew I would have to speak with Bullfrog before we went on the lam. I couldn't leave, knowing my family would still be there and be at the mercy of my mistakes. I would approach Bullfrog carefully the following day with a down payment toward my debt. It would be expensive to make such a payment before Luke and I found a new buyer and sold the books, but I couldn't put a price on my family's safety and my own peace of mind.

I spent the remainder of the afternoon alone. I listened to music and watched my favorite movies. I cleaned my revolver, loaded the six-bullet chamber with high impact hollow-point rounds, and stashed the gun in the closet nearest to my bed. When night fell, I grew hungry and ordered a pizza to be delivered. A handful of minutes later, there was a knock at the door to my room.

"Who is it!?" I yelled down the stairs toward the door.

"It's me." Claire responded.

I had forgotten that we had made plans to spend the night together. I hurried down the stairs and unlocked the door for her.

"Hey." She smiled as I opened the door.

For a brief moment, I forgot all of the worries that had been overwhelming my thoughts, and I only saw her. My heart raced as I returned my own smile in response. She stepped by me and walked up the stairs as I closed and locked the door behind her. She dropped her purse and car keys to the floor and hung her coat on the back of a chair.

"You hungry?" I asked.

She shrugged. "Not really."

"I just ordered a pizza a while ago, it should be here in a few minutes."

"Okay."

I stacked several pillows against the headboard and sat comfortably on the bed. I stacked several more pillows beside me in suggestion that she join me. She stepped out of her tennis shoes and crawled onto the bed wearing baby blue sweatpants and a matching North Carolina Tarheels t-shirt.

"Baby, we really need to do something about your clothes."

"Why? What's wrong with what I'm wearing?" She asked, defensively.

"It's the wrong blue. It's supposed to be U.K. blue, not U.N.C. blue!" I joked.

She laughed. "Those rules don't apply to me, because neither one of them is my *real* team. My *real* team is the Pittsburg Steelers!"

I acted as if I contemplated her answer. "Nope. That excuse won't work here in Lexington. It might work for you Yankees from up north, but not for me. But don't worry. I know how we can fix this problem. All you have to do is take your clothes off."

She feigned indignation at my suggestion. "I don't think so!"

I rolled over and playfully wrestled with her. We rolled across the bed, tussling from side to side. She pinned me down and raised her arms in victory. I took the opportunity to tickle her along the sides of her ribs. She flopped down to the bed laughing, trying to cover her ticklish sides. I rolled on top of her and continued my assault.

"That's not fair!" She giggled as she gasped for air. "You're cheating!"

"That's what you get for being a Tarheels fan!"

The front doorbell rang, but I continued to tickle her.

"Stop! Stop!" She pleaded through fits of laughter. "Someone's at the door!"

I sighed and rested my hands on her stomach. "Saved by the bell. You got lucky this time."

I rolled off the bed. I grabbed my wallet from the nightstand, tied a pair of tennis shoes on my feet, and stepped to the closet where I had hidden my gun. I felt ridiculous for even thinking such a thought, but I tucked the gun behind my back, under the waistband of my mesh shorts. I made sure that my t-shirt concealed the gun from Claire's view, then I stepped away from the closet. The doorbell rang again and again.

"What are you doing?" Claire asked. "Aren't you going to answer that?

"Yep. I'll be right back."

I hurried down the stairs, skipping steps along the way. When I stepped into the living room, I slowed my pace. The doorbell continued to ring as I warily approached the door like a reluctant victim within a horror movie. I braced myself for the possibility that the man in the mask could be waiting for me on the other side. I quickly glanced through a rectangular window near the top of the heavy, wooden door. A man wearing a pizza delivery uniform, holding a pizza box, stood impatiently on the porch.

In one fluid motion, I unlocked the dead bolt and swung the door open, keeping one hand gripped to the gun behind my back. The sudden movement startled the unsuspecting delivery guy. He bobbled the pizza box, but quickly regained his composure. He wore glasses beneath the bill of his uniform hat. He seemed to be slightly older than I was, possibly in his mid-twenties. Bushy, black sideburns nearly covered his ears. He wore a red uniform coat, blue jeans, and white sneakers. I knew better than to trust him.

He held the box toward me. "Your total is twelve sixty eight." He said suspiciously.

I eyed him with a steely gaze, attempting to see through any attempts at trickery. When satisfied with what I saw, I handed him a twenty-dollar bill with my free hand. He took the money with one hand and I took the box. He pulled a wad of one-dollar bills from his pocket to give me my change.

I shut the door in his face. "Just keep the money."

I locked the door and walked to my room, shaking my head in disbelief at how paranoid I had become. I laughed at myself for treating the pizza delivery guy as if he could have been a hired hit man. I felt absurdly foolish as I locked the door to my room and climbed the stairs. I removed the gun from the back of my waistband, careful to hide the weapon from Claire's view, stashed it in the closet again, then I repositioned myself on the bed.

"Pizza's here." I said, giving the box to Claire. "I just got pepperoni this time."

Claire opened the box and took the first slice. She took a bite, then covered her mouth with a hand as she spoke. "It's good. Hey, what are you watching?" She asked, referring to the frozen image on the television screen.

"Pulp Fiction. I'm in the middle of it, but I can start it over if you want to watch it."

"That's by that guy you like, isn't it?"

"Yeah, Quentin Tarantino."

"I don't care." She shrugged. "I guess you can start it over if you want. I don't think I've ever seen it all the way through."

I pressed a button on the remote and the movie began again from the opening scene. I dimmed the overhead lights until the room was dark. I took a slice of pizza from the box and ate while the movie played. After several slices and several scenes of the profane and violent movie, I looked away from the screen to see Claire engrossed in the dialogue. I smiled as I looked at her, looking at the screen. I knew there was something special about a girl who could watch a movie about the misdeeds of criminals and be undeterred. I leaned across the space that separated us and kissed her cheek. She nuzzled her head against my own, then turned to meet my lips with a kiss. I moved closer to her as her slender body slid down from the stack of pillows to lie flat against the bed. My lips moved with soft kisses across her face, her cheek, her ear, then brushed lightly down the sensitive skin of her neck, lower and lower. Her breath quickened and I touched her skin with my teeth as I smiled, then kissed her again.

At the base of the stairs to my room, there was a knock on the door. Annoyed by the interruption, I grumbled something indistinguishable under my breath and slumped my face into the bed. I turned and paused the movie as the knocking persisted.

"What!?" I exploded. "What is it!? What do you want!"

"Hey, Chas!" Luke yelled through the locked door, hoping his voice would carry up the stairs and into my room.

"Yeah! What!?"

"Devon got arrested! He's over at the county jail!"

"What for!? A grim scenario quickly flashed through my thoughts.

"He said he got caught shoplifting a TV dinner from the grocery store!"

"Are you serious!?"

"Yeah, I'm going to bail him out!"

"Why!?"

Luke didn't respond, so I answered my own question with a statement. "Fuck him! Just let him stay there! He deserves it!"

There was a long silence as Luke considered my words.

"No." He finally answered. "I'm going to get him."

I turned my attention back to Claire. "Now, where were we?"

"Did he say Devon got arrested for stealing a TV dinner?"

I laughed disparagingly at the thought of Devon. He had more than a million dollars worth of stolen property hidden within his basement hideout, but he still felt the need to stuff a box of frozen chicken parmesan under his shirt in a grocery aisle.

"Yeah, that's what he said." I regretfully admitted.

"What's wrong with your friends?"

In answer, I could only lift my arms in defeat, shrug, sigh, and shake my head, completely bewildered. There was a topic of conversation that I had been dreading to broach from the moment when Claire had stepped into my room, and I decided that it was time to tell her.

"Hey, remember how I told you that I was going out of town next week?"

"Yeah..."

"I'm going to leave tomorrow instead."

"*What? Why?*"

"It would just make things easier if I go ahead and go tomorrow."

Claire's eyebrows furrowed in frustration. "Why? I don't even understand why you're going. What are you going to do about your classes while you're gone?"

I wasn't proud of the truth, but I needed to tell her. "Claire, I didn't sign up for classes this semester. I'm taking the semester off. I'm not even *enrolled* right now."

"What!? What's *wrong* with you? Why are you taking the semester off?"

"Because I feel like my life is spinning out of control, Claire. I just need to take some time to put everything back together."

"And how is dropping out of school and going to Charleston, South Carolina going to help you do that?"

Charleston was where Luke and I had decided to rent an apartment so that we would have a place to stay between intermittent trips to Canada and Europe. We weren't sure how many trips, or how long it would take to locate a buyer, but we couldn't afford the excessive expense of travel and living abroad for more than a few months. A buyer would have to be found quickly.

"It just is, okay." I answered. "I need you to trust me."

"How am I supposed to trust you when I don't even understand what you're doing? I don't even know who you are anymore."

I sighed, unable to answer her question. I wanted nothing more than to let her understand what it was that I was dealing with everyday, and understand why I was doing what I was doing. Every reason, every decision that I had made, everything that I hadn't shared with her was at the forefront of my thoughts. Halfway out of my mouth and beyond the tip of my tongue was everything that I wanted to tell her – the heist, the stolen books, the trip to New York, the police that I feared were following me, the false partnership with my dad, my family's finances, the theft of the underground casino, my debt to Bullfrog, Devon's deceit, the man in the mask – everything. But after everything that I had been through, something prevented me from trusting anyone other than myself.

It may have been selfish, but I decided to ask Claire to give something to me that I couldn't give to her. "I really, really need you to trust me right now. I'm doing the best I know how to make things right, but I just need you to trust me."

Claire looked at me evenly with her beautiful blue-green eyes and didn't respond.

"I don't know how long it's going to take to make things right. It may be two weeks, it may be two months, but as soon as I come home, everything is going to be okay. And while I'm gone I'll be missing you everyday that I'm away from you. And no matter how long it takes, and no matter what happens, I want you to know that I will always love you. Don't ever forget that, okay?"

"Chas, you're scaring me. Why won't you just tell me what's going on?"

"Because right now, all you need to know is that I love you, and that I need you to trust me."

Claire stubbornly shook her head and looked away. I gently nudged her chin with the tip of my thumb and forefinger until she faced me again, but she refused to meet my eyes with her own.

"You can't hide those beautiful eyes from me forever." I teased.

She smiled, and reluctantly, she raised her eyes. There was sorrow within the depths of blue and fear for the future within the fathoms of green. I wished that I could take away her pain and fill her eyes with happiness and love as I knew they should be.

"You know me better than anyone, Claire, the real me. Look at me, and tell me honestly. Do you trust me?"

As we looked into each others eyes, she searched my heart for the answer she most needed to know, and for the answer I most needed to hear. As she searched, I lowered every boundary and every wall that had blocked my heart and I tried to let her know that I was still the same person she had once fallen in love with. Circumstances and choices had pulled me away, but somewhere beneath it all, I was still there. At one point in time, I had intended to help my family through a difficult situation, but good intentions weren't enough to protect me from the consequences of my wrongful acts. I was in too deep to stop, so I felt that I had no choice but to keep going. But I was almost finished. The nightmare that had become my reality would soon be over and everything would be as it should. If only she could trust me, and wait.

"I do." She whispered sweetly. "I just don't understand why things can't be the way they used to be. Everything was so much easier when we first started dating."

"We were kids then, Claire. We were sophomores in high school."

"I know, but…"

"I'll tell you what. I'll make you a promise. When I get back, we'll start over. We'll start our relationship from scratch, all over again, and we'll start with the little things, like this."

I placed her hand in mine as I had done when we were fifteen years old and falling in love. We had grown older and more mature in the five years that we had been together, but the simple touch of her hand in mine still sent a warm, thawing sensation to the core of my heart. She smiled then, and it was my favorite of all her smiles. It was the smile that only said, I love you. And in such moments, I felt as though there was nothing else in the world that I needed, because her love was more than enough.

"You promise?" Claire asked.

I smiled as I noticed that the sorrow and the fear had disappeared from her eyes and I kissed her lips once, then pulled away.

"I promise."

She kissed me passionately, and together, we allowed our love to guide our actions. We were both ready to look beyond the troubles of the past and look forward to a brighter future. I no longer believed in hope, but I believed that I could make everything right with Claire, with my family, and with myself, as soon as I finished what I had wrongfully began.

It was well after midnight when the flames of our passion died down, but the embers of our love continued to smolder on into the night. The movie was paused on the screen as we lay together, whispering to one another in the dark.

Disrupting our quiet conversation, there was a knock on the door at the foot of my stairs. "Hey, Chas?" Luke's voice called through the darkness.

"Tell him I'm not here." I whispered to Claire. "Tell him to leave a message."

"He's not here, Luke." Claire said, trying to hold back her laughter.

"Where is he?"

"Tell him I moved without him." I whispered.

"He already left, Luke. He said he was going to Mexico."

Claire couldn't contain her laughter any longer. She held a pillow to her face so that Luke couldn't hear her through the door.

"Mexico?" Luke asked, perplexed by the possibility.

"Yeah! He's probably across the border by now!" Clair said through an uncontrollable fit of laughter that the pillow couldn't contain.

"Okay, that's real funny, Claire. Is he up there with you or not."

I waved my hands and shook my head to signal that I wasn't there.

"No. He's not here. Do you want to leave a message?"

I could hear Luke grumble to himself through the door. "Claire, if he's up there, tell him that I picked Devon up from the county jail and I didn't even have to bail him out. They just let him go."

"Okay, I'll tell him." She laughed, and I could hear Luke's footsteps walking away from the door.

Claire and I didn't acknowledge Devon's stroke of good luck. We repositioned ourselves closer within each others arms and resumed our quiet conversation until late into the night, when we finally fell asleep.

Chapter 32: Fear

The following morning came before dawn.

"Chas! Get up!" Someone screamed.

I could feel someone desperately shaking me. A voice, Claire's voice, rang through the fog of sleep like a siren through the sea. Her words seemed distorted and filled with fear. I opened my eyes to a blurred vision of darkness all around me.

"What... what?" I sputtered, trying to comprehend her fear.

"Chas! Oh my God, Chas! Someone's trying to break in the house!" She screamed, still desperately shaking my arm.

I paused and listened, and I understood why Claire was afraid. Crashes as loud as thunder rolled through the house and up to my room as forceful blows fell against the front door. One loud crack like the lash of a whip resounded as the heavy, wooden door broke loose from its frame. A percussion of scattered footsteps stormed through the entrance and I knew the man in the mask had returned and he was not alone.

As my eyes began to focus, I could barely see the outline of Claire's face as she sat upright in the bed. Of her face, I could only see the whites of her terror stricken eyes.

Disoriented, I threw the covers back and jumped out of bed. I fumbled through the dark until I turned the overhead lights on to a low, dim level. I could hear screams, blood curdling screams from girls on the first floor below who had stayed the night with my roommates. Angry shouts were exchanged and the meanings of the words were lost as the vibrations were muffled through the floor. I didn't need to understand what was said to know what the intruders wanted. It was me they were looking for, and they would want money, or worse.

I rushed around my bed to the nearest closet. I opened the door and fumbled through a pile of clothes. I wove my hand under several layers of soft fabric until I felt the cold steel barrel of my .38 revolver. I lifted the gun from beneath the pile of clothes, and instantly, I felt more secure with a gun in the grip of my hand. I opened the six-round chamber and felt the high impact hollow-point bullets that filled each chamber. With a flick of my wrist, I snapped the loaded chamber into position. I rushed to grab a box of ammo and dumped extra bullets into my palm, but in my hurry, several fell from my hand and bounced on the carpet. I stuffed a handful of ammunition into a pocket in my mesh shorts and turned toward the stairs.

Then I saw Claire. She looked as fragile as a porcelain doll amidst the shouts and the commotion and the chaos that had been unleashed within my house. She stood beside the bed wearing one of my blue t-shirts and her own pair of short, mesh shorts. Her hands were clenched together at her chest as she listened to the violent sounds that were bound to reach us.

"Claire!" I shouted.

Her eyes jumped toward me and she looked at the gun in my hand. "What are you going to do?" She asked.

"I don't know." I answered honestly. "Come here."

She shuffled toward my open left arm. I pulled her close to me, and as I held her within my arms, I knew that I would do anything to protect her. If I had to die, or kill to keep her safe, then I would die a thousand deaths and I would kill a thousand more, because I loved her.

Claire's head turned toward the stairs as someone began to beat against the door to my bedroom. "Chas, what's happening?"

"I don't know, Claire. Look at me." I waited for her eyes to meet mine. I held her as streaks of fear streamed down her face. "Look at me. Baby, I don't know what's going to happen. Just hide in here, and no matter what happens – don't come out."

"What? In the closet? Why?"

"Just do it, Claire. Get in the closet."

She hesitantly stepped into the small space, but refused to let go of my arm.

"No matter what happens – just stay in there, okay? Promise me. Promise me that no matter what you hear, you'll stay in there."

She nodded, but her eyes darted toward the stairs as the violent crashes continued to fall against the thin, wooden door.

"Don't worry, Baby." I tried to refocus her attention. "Everything is going to be alright. I promise."

I didn't know if I had spoken the truth, but I was willing to risk my life to keep my word. I kissed her one last time and I kissed her with lips that feared they may never meet her lips again. I pried myself away, closed the closet door, and left her hidden from danger. I could still feel her tears cold and drying on my cheeks as I walked away. I gripped the gun firmly and the extra bullets jingled in my pocket as I moved across the long, narrow room. I stopped and stood at the top of the stairs. Twelve steps separated me from the door, where the butt of a shotgun slammed against the wood, again and again. The door shook on its frame like a frightened child against the relentless onslaught.

I planted my feet in a wide, firm stance as I waited for the inevitable. I held the gun with both hands steady and thumbed back the hammer. I aimed down into the dark void at the bottom of the stairs, where the intruder would soon stand, turn to his left to find the stairs, me, my gun, and my bullet.

A loud crack split through the air like a bolt of lightning as the wood began to splinter. A small crack became a wide gap as each blow from the shotgun chopped at the door like an ax. Streams of light from the living room began to push through the hole. A gloved hand reached through the splintered door, searching for the knob to unfasten the lock. I took aim, but waited. The gloved hand twisted the knob and the door swung open. A man nearly as large as the doorway itself took two steps into the void where his massive frame was encased by a soft light.

The sight at the end of my gun was aimed at the center of the man's head. My finger was wrapped tensely around the trigger and within the time it took for a man's life to flash before his eyes, I observed the man who stood below me. He was dressed in black clothing, from head to toe. He wore a black hat and his chest bulged from the block pattern of a bullet-proof vest. He turned his head to see me, and the gun that was aimed at his face. Our eyes locked like the horns of two butting rams and I watched as fear overwhelmed his features. I could clearly see his face as he realized that he was about to die. He looked ageless within the depths of his soul and unprepared for death's final call. We stared at one another for an instant that seemed to last a lifetime as my focus blurred and I felt the trigger tightening beneath my finger. I glanced down the barrel, looking beyond the sight to the target of the man's head, then I noticed the white letters that were boldly printed across his hat – F.B.I.

I hesitated, because I couldn't believe my eyes. The man noticed my hesitation and swung his shotgun toward me. "Drop the gun!" He demanded.

I held the gun firm as I stared, awestruck by the bold white letters that were written across his bullet-proof vest – S.W.A.T.

People say that time slows down, or that everything happens in slow motion during extreme moments of our lives. As I realized that federal agents were raiding my house, time didn't slow down, time stood still. I lost all ability to think or react or move. And within an instant, the balance of power shifted. I was at the mercy of the man who stood at the base of the stairs. He had the power to end my life and the power to forever alter it. He spoke an inaudible demand, but somehow, I understood that he was asking me to choose one of the two options that were within his power. I unconsciously made my choice. I felt my arms drop heavily to my sides. My right hand remained glued to the grip of the gun. A long black line funneled up the stairs, rushing straight for me.

The gun was knocked from my grip and I was thrown to the floor. The man pounced on me and pinned my face to the floor as an accomplice crashed into the center of my back with an elbow.

It was the feeling of white hot pain that caused time to begin again. My arms were twisted behind my back to fit my wrists into handcuffs. The icy, metal grip clinched tight around my skin as my bedroom filled with more and more black suits. My face remained pinned to the carpet, and from the vantage point of a cockroach, I noticed a pair of black boots approach.

"Let him up." A man ordered.

The two overzealous men removed their combined weight from my back and I struggled to sit up with my hands cuffed behind me.

"Mr. Allen?"

"Yes."

"I'm Special Agent Markum. I am here on a federal warrant for the search of the premises and the arrest of Devon Koli."

He said Devon, only Devon, I thought optimistically. Maybe I was still in the clear.

"What is this all about? What's going on?" I asked acting as if I was appalled by the unexpected intrusion on the life of an upstanding citizen.

I took a good look at the agent. His eyes were his most prominent feature. They were beady and black like a serpent. His skin was pale and his red hair was cut short under the edges of a black hat.

"We would like you to come down to the station to answer some questions for us."

All I had to say was no. If they didn't have a warrant for my arrest, then no. But, I was confident that they didn't have any evidence against me.

I shrugged affably. "Can I at least put some clothes on?"

He looked at me, sizing me up, then agreed.

"Take the cuffs off." He ordered.

"Thanks." I removed my shorts, the pockets of which were filled with extra ammunition that jingled as I threw them into the laundry hamper. I dressed myself with the first warm clothes that I could find, a light blue and white pair of striped pajama pants and a grey cashmere sweater. I slipped a pair of tennis shoes over my bare feet.

"Okay, put the cuffs back on him."

My arms were twisted behind my back and I was hand cuffed again.

"Sir." A young-looking man said, addressing the special agent. "You should come take a look at this. We recovered the items and also found a few more interesting things. It looks like a grow operation."

"Okay, I'll be right there. Any word from Bravo Team?"

A woman with blonde hair tucked beneath her hat spoke. "Yes sir. Bravo Team apprehended the other suspect at Transylvania several minutes ago."

Special Agent Markum nodded.

I wasn't exactly sure what they were talking about, but I took their words to mean that they had arrested Ethan.

"Okay, take Mr. Allen to the car."

I was forcefully pushed, led toward the stairs. When I reached the first step, I looked across my bedroom and saw Claire. She was standing outside of the closet with her hands held to her chest as if she feared her heart would leap from its cage. She looked at me and she looked at the federal agents who had overwhelmed the room. And within an instant, everything that she had ever known about the boy who she had loved for more than five years became uncertain. I could almost feel her world being torn apart as she witnessed the truth that I had hidden from her, the truth that I was a criminal.

Our eyes met, and something shattered within me. A hollow, empty feeling consumed my chest and I could barely breathe. Claire stared at me and her blue-green, aquamarine eyes had never looked more vibrant than they did then. Her eyes were wet with tears as she hoped, begged, and pleaded that I would give her a smile, a nod, a wink – anything that would let her know that what she saw was a mistake. But my eyes only confessed my shame.

I tried to reach out to her, but my hands were locked behind my back and she was too far away. I was led down the stairs and taken away from Claire. But the image of her face, streaked with tears, would haunt me for years to come.

Chapter 33: Back to Present & County Jail

I was taken into federal custody for questioning. I was confident that there was no evidence against me when I stepped into a dark room with two F.B.I. agents. But evidence wasn't necessary when two of my friends had already attested to my guilt. After a short interrogation, I was arrested, and it was then that I had asked to speak to an attorney.

It was Harvey Bird who I eventually spoke to in a small, concrete room within the Fayette County Detention Center. During a series of attorney-client privileged conversations, I spoke through a perforated glass window and told him everything that had led to my arrest--things that I had never shared with another soul. When I finally finished speaking, I leaned back from the window and repositioned myself on the concrete square where I sat.

Harvey sat in the opposite room and gravely nodded. He leaned back in his chair, one leg folded across the other, and let out a sigh like a slow leak in a tire. He clasped his hands behind his head without disturbing his professional attire. He wore a grey suit, white shirt, and a red tie. As I had learned to expect, his blonde hair was neatly combed to one side.

"Is there anything else?" He asked, almost hesitant.

I considered the question for a moment, then shook my head. "No. I'd say we've covered just about all the bases."

He seemed relieved as he sat forward again, his elbows on a metal ledge attached to the window.

"Well, what do you think?" I asked.

"For starters, I think you should never repeat anything that you told me."

I laughed. "Yeah, I know that. I'm just saying, what are my chances. Is there any way that I can beat this."

"There is always a chance, and I can attempt to take it to trial if you want to go that route. But, I wouldn't advise it."

"Why not?"

"There are already two corroborating stories that put you at the crime, and also thereafter. Let's see." He quickly scanned through the pile of papers on the ledge. "There were statements made by Ethan Burnett and Devon Koli. Am I saying that right?"

I nodded with a heavy heart. The mention of Ethan's statement didn't bother me, but for some reason, Devon's did. For all that we had been through together, I had loved him like a brother, and for all the damage that he had caused in my life, I hated him like a bitter rival. It was a hard truth, but time and time again, he had proven himself a greater enemy than he had ever been a friend.

"The only feasible path that I see for you to take is to go ahead and plead guilty. That way, you will receive a three point reduction under the sentencing guidelines."

"What does that mean?"

"Basically, you would be having a trial by court. The judge would decide your sentence and the three point reduction could shave a few years off for your acceptance of responsibility."

"So, there would be no jury?"

"No, a jury would be necessary to decide guilt or innocence. And, I think it's safe to say there isn't much question in this case."

My eyebrows arched at his blunt remark, but I appreciated his honesty. "So, realistically, what are we talking here? What am I looking at?"

"Well, this is definitely a unique case, so it makes it hard to say. I'm sure you've seen yourself on the news lately, and if for some reason the public latches on to this case like I think they may, we could be in for an uphill battle. But as far as the sentence itself goes, it depends on a series of variables, one of which is the judge that we are assigned. More or less, that comes down to the luck of the draw. If we get lucky and draw a liberal judge, then we may be looking at a few years, possibly even a lengthy probation."

"Okay, okay." I said, trying to take it all in. My mind seemed to be operating on only adrenaline and fear. "So, how long until I get out of here?"

"It depends. I'm trying to get a bond hearing as soon as possible. Your likelihood of receiving a bond would be better if you were to plead guilty."

I couldn't seem to shake a depressing, sinking feeling in the pit of my stomach as I looked through the glass. I felt as if I had run out of options.

"Alright, alright. When do you need an answer by?"

"I'll be back in a few days. How about then?"

"Okay."

He gathered and stacked the pile of papers before him, then slid them into a black leather briefcase. He snapped the gold clasps closed and nodded his head. I nodded cordially in return and watched him exit the room. As with all attorneys, he was excellent at ending conversations. One second we had been talking, the next, he was gone. I leaned back and sat in quiet contemplation of the impending future as I waited for a guard to place me in handcuffs and escort me from the room.

An electronic lock clicked and a steel door swung into the room. A dumpy-looking correction officer with salt and pepper hair and a scruffy mustache stood in the doorway.

"You know the drill." He announced.

I stood and turned away from him, placing my hands behind my back. Steel cuffs locked into place around my wrists. The officer led me by the arm onto a second tier catwalk that overlooked a large, open room. There was a circular control station in the center of the room where two more officers sat and idly surfed the internet to pass the time. Occasionally, they would glance through the glass walls that enclosed the concrete-block cells that surrounded them. There was one man confined within each cell of Cell-Block D.

A green canvas jumpsuit hung loosely on my frame as I walked along the catwalk. My Saint Christopher medallion had been taken from me when I was admitted into the county jail. I had worn the necklace every day for several years, and without it, I felt naked. I was led to a stairway and my canvas slippers slapped against the corrugated steel steps. From my vantage point, I could see clearly into more than a dozen cells. Luke was leaning against the glass that confined him. We looked at one another, shook our heads heavily, and shrugged. We knew that we had reached the end of the road. We were beyond redemption and the lives that we had envisioned for the future seemed like long-forgotten dreams of the past. My heart felt for Luke as he stood there, caged like a punished animal, looking back at me with the distant expression of defeat. I looked into Ethan's cell, but he was in bed, bundled beneath a paper-thin blanket.

At the base of the stairs, I turned to the right and walked toward my cell. Devon's cell was next door to my own. He sat on the edge of his bed with his head in his hands. He heard the officer's keys jingle as we approached and he turned his head. He weakly offered a wave and an ashamed smile. I looked to my cell as if I didn't know him.

I paused in front of the door to my cell. An officer within the control station momentarily turned away from the computer screen and pressed a button to electronically open the door. The lock clicked and the thick, metal door slid within a wall of glass and steel. The officer at my arm unfastened the handcuffs and the door closed and locked behind me.

The cinderblock box where I was confined had only enough space for the essentials. There was a bed, a desk, a sink that had been combined with a toilet, and a mirror. Everything was metal, the color of cold, uncaring grey or painted with thick coats of deep, depressing blue.

I kicked my slippers off and lay down on the bed. I stared at the ceiling for what felt like an eternity. Hour after hour, I wasted away in my lonely cell, loathing myself for the choices I had made. The unbearable amount of stress that my thoughts created manifested itself as a physical pain. I had tried to force myself to eat, but it had been nearly a week since I had eaten a full meal. My heart was pumping what felt like cold battery acid through my veins. My heart felt as if it were two sizes too large and I couldn't breathe. Everything else within me seemed shrunken, hollow, and empty like the void within a vacuum.

Unwittingly, I had become the architect of my own demise. The way of life and the reputation of my family that I had fought to preserve, would be destroyed, shattered, and crushed. In my attempt to save them, I had become their downfall. I had promised Claire that I would fix everything, and I had thought that I could. I had thought that I could fix it all, for everyone. But, I failed. Each step of the way I had dug myself deeper into a hole, thinking that I was always only one step away from finding the solution. But all I had been doing was digging my own grave.

I stood and stepped to the metallic-sheet mirror that hung above the toilet-sink. I looked into the unsympathetic grey image and I no longer recognized myself. My eyes had sunken into dark circles within each socket. My cheekbones had protruded. My face looked like it was a meal away from being emaciated. Worry lines had creased deep into my brow. There was no color within my reflection, only a ghostly, pallid, pale grey. I despised the image of what I had become. The familiar image that I had once known was gone.

I lay down on the blue mat again and I felt lower than I had ever felt before. The mat felt as if it were the hard, rock bottom of a dark and deep well. The white ceiling seemed an impossible distance above me. Then I heard a voice from far away. It seemed to echo through my thoughts. I knew the voice to be Devon's. He sounded angry and overwhelmed with grief.

"Satan!" He shouted. "Can you hear me!? If you're real, I want you to hear me!"

I tried to turn away from his words, but his words were all around me.

"Satan! I will sell you my soul for the powers of Magneto! I'll blow this fucking door right off its frame and get out of this goddamn cell! Do you hear me!?"

To block the sound of Devon's words I had to drown them with words of my own. I focused on the white above me as if it were the light at the end of an infinite tunnel and prayed. I wasn't sure who it was that I prayed to, because it had been years since I believed in anything more than myself. But in my hour of need, I spoke from the depths of my heart and confessed the wrongs that had been weighing heavily on my conscience, and I prayed for forgiveness. The prayers spilled from my heart and overflowed from my soul. And as my words continued to roll, something unexpected happened. I felt a response to my prayers. I wasn't sure whether it was God, Allah, Buddha, Shiva, the collective unconscious, the Dali Llama, or Dolly Parton, but somehow, a gentle wave of calm washed away my worries, my fears, and my doubts. I felt lighter of spirit than I had ever felt before. I took a deep, refreshing breath that filled my lungs to capacity. The white ceiling looked like a clean state above me and everything around me seemed to burst with newfound light.

I stood from the bed and I felt as though I had dropped a thousand pound weight from my shoulders. I stepped to the mirror to look at my reflection and I was surprised by what I saw. I was smiling. It was a carefree smile of pure happiness and joy. Tears streaked in lines down my face as I looked into the image of my reflection, and I was happier than I could ever remember.

An empty space within my life had been filled. I felt no stress, no worries, and no fears. I knew that from that moment on, everything would always be okay, no matter what the future held, because I would face it with an open and honest heart and I would face the consequences of my actions with my head held high.

Sometime throughout the night, I decided to plead guilty to my crime and hope the court would have mercy on me. Whatever the punishment would be, I would accept my fate. But first, if I was given a bond and released from jail, I would have to face Bullfrog.

Chapter 34: A Burden Lifted

Devon, Ethan, Luke, and I entered a plea of guilty during an arraignment hearing and we were released from county jail on a bond while we awaited sentencing. We each moved home to live with our families. I moved into my mom's house, and each morning that I woke there, I awoke with an appreciation for life known only to those who are dying. Each additional day that I was able to spend with my family became a cherished gift.

It was more than a month after I was released when I went to speak with Bullfrog. I drove across town in my mom's X5 and parked in a vacant space outside of the apartment complex. I walked through the familiar maze of sidewalks on a damp morning of April wearing khaki pants, a blue polo shirt, and a brown leather jacket. The air was cool and the sun glistened from the dew covered grass as I walked along the footpath. I entered the building that housed Bullfrog's casino and walked up the stairs to the second floor. I ignored the cameras that watched my every move and I knocked on the door. There was no response. I pressed my ear to the door, but everything within the apartment was quiet. I knocked again to no response, then stepped away from the door. I walked down the stairs and sat comfortably at the foot of the staircase as I waited for Bullfrog to enter the building.

I was aware of the potential danger that I could soon face, trapped in a stairwell with a dangerous, and most likely, armed man who I was deeply indebted to. But I wasn't afraid or worried or nervous as I had been in the past. I was confident that I was doing the right thing, and nothing else seemed to matter.

It was almost noon when I heard footsteps approach the door. The door opened and light flooded the dark stairwell. I squinted to shield my eyes from the sun as Bullfrog's massive body slumped through the doorway. He paused when he noticed me. He seemed startled by my presence. He stared at me as if he were calculating my intentions. I remained seated to let him know that I meant him no harm and that there was no cause for him to harm me. Slowly, he closed the door behind him and the stairwell succumbed to darkness.

Bullfrog licked his lips and cleared his throat. "You're about the last person I expected to see, kid. I seen you all over the news. What the hell ya doin' around here?"

"Frog, I know it doesn't do much good now, but I came to apologize for what I did. I was in a bad place at the time and I thought money could fix all of my problems, but really, it just seemed to make things worse."

Bullfrog worked his teeth like a coffee grinder as he stared at me. "You're tellin' me ya waited inside my building and scared tha shit outta me, because ya wanted to apologize."

"Yeah. I'm really sorry for what I did and I wanted to tell you that in person."

"No. I'm not buyin' it. What are ya tryin' to do, set me up? Are the feds outside?"

He flung the door open and looked out into the sun-filled courtyard. When he was sufficiently satisfied that we were alone, he closed the door. I pulled an envelope from a pocket within the lining of my jacket. I stood and approached him calmly.

"This isn't what I owe you, but it's all I have." I offered.

He apprehensively accepted the envelope and scanned the contents. "How much is this?"

"It's twenty-five thousand."

"That's a start, but where's the rest?"

"It's gone, Frog. After that, I don't have any money left to my name. I sold everything I owned. I sold my car, cashed out of my stocks and mutual funds. I even cashed out savings bonds that I had since I was three years old."

"Why don't ya just get your parents to loan ya tha money like I told ya before?"

"I'm the one who messed up and it wouldn't be right for me to ask them to pay for my mistakes, even if they could afford it. If I had anything more to give you, I would, but I have nothing left. I took all the money I had, split it in half, and gave one half to an attorney, and the other half to you."

He drew a deep, labored breath as he rubbed his chin with a bloated hand that vaguely resembled a leather catcher's mitt. "So what are ya expecting me ta do about all this?"

"I expect you to do whatever you have to do. But I'm asking you to forgive me."

"This isn't that kinda business, kid."

"I know." I sighed.

He flipped through the money within the envelope, then returned his gaze to meet my own. "Go on. Get outta here." He gestured toward the door. "You're already in enough trouble as it is. I don't need to be givin' ya anymore."

I hesitantly smiled. "So, for now, does this mean we're even?"

He chuckled dryly. "Ya always have to push your luck, don't ya?"

"Yeah, I've always said I'd rather be lucky than good at anything."

He extended an open hand and smiled an ugly, but friendly smile. "Consider it your goin' away present."

I shook his hand, unsure whether his words were intended to be rude or heartfelt, but either way, I appreciated the generous offer.

"Thanks." I said. "But whenever I can get enough money, the honest way, I'm going to pay you back."

He looked at me as if appraising my words, then nodded in approval.

"Good luck, kid. I hope everything works out for you."

"Thanks, you too."

I stepped past him and opened the door. Sunlight blinded my eyes as I walked out of the building. The door closed behind me. After I had taken nearly a dozen steps, the door opened again. Bullfrog stood in the doorway, half of his massive body shown in the sunlight, while the other half remained hidden within the shadows.

"Hey, kid." He called to get my attention. "If ya needed the money that bad, ya never had to take it in the first place. All ya had to do was ask. Remember that next time, will ya?"

I nodded and smiled, abashed by his unexpected show of kindness. He smiled a wide, alligator smile that only a mother could adore, and stepped back within the stairwell. He closed the door and I walked away. I wove through the memorized maze of sidewalks toward the parking lot.

At one point in time, I had hated Bullfrog and perceived him as a monster, but he had only responded in kind to my own actions. I had been afraid to admit my faults and speak to him honestly, but when I did, he proved himself a more generous friend than he had ever been a ruthless enemy. I had expected to feel relieved if he accepted my partial payment, but as I walked away, I wished I could have paid him in full. I had given him my last dollar, but the offering of money was worthless when compared to the undeserved mercy and kindness he had given in return.

I climbed into my mom's X5 that I had borrowed for the day and drove away from the apartment complex. As I drove along the busy downtown streets of Lexington, I hoped the justice system could grant me even a fraction of the mercy that Bullfrog, a life-long criminal, had been willing to give.

Chapter 35: Court

Spring became summer, summer turned to autumn, and autumn became winter as the impending day of sentencing approached. Media coverage of the crime and rumors that stirred within Lexington exacerbated the difficulty of each day. There were many days when I felt lonely and ashamed as the dread of potential imprisonment hung over my thoughts like a persistent black cloud on the horizon. My reputation had become tainted and I no longer had, or wanted, money to burn. People who I had once believed to be friends shied away as if I were a leper when I reached out to them for company or moral support. And Claire, whose love I needed more than ever, turned her back on me. She claimed that the persistent negative publicity was too much to bear. I didn't blame her for leaving, but my heart mourned her loss.

There may have been an ever-present cloud on the horizon of my thoughts, but the remainder of the sky was a beautiful, clear blue. I cherished each and every moment that I shared with my family, I reestablished friendships that had been forgotten, but not lost, and I made new, amazing friendships along the way. I thrived on the love and support that I received from family and true friends, and when the day of sentencing arrived, I was filled with positivity and hope for the future.

My attorney and I were the first to enter the federal courtroom on a cold, bright morning of December. The room was an enormous chamber, the ceiling more than three stories above me. The wooden benches, podiums, paneling, and trim were a rich cherry. The carpet was a plush, deep blue. Paintings of judges past hung from the walls and they seemed to stare down at me with accusatory eyes.

My attorney, Harvey, directed me toward a row of leather-backed chairs behind a long table designated for the defendants. It was an uncomfortable place to be, but we each took a seat and saddled up to the table. An immense and ornate set of cherry double-doors opened as Luke and his attorney, followed by Ethan and a partnership of attorneys, entered the courtroom. The attorneys positioned themselves between each of the defendants and everyone sat among the row of chairs. The attorneys, including Harvey, proceeded to quietly coach their clients on the procedures of the day. It was several minutes later when Devon casually strolled into the courtroom with his shoulders thrown back and his head held high. A female, his court-appointed attorney, walked by his side. I smiled to myself when I noticed that Devon wore his lucky red scarf around his neck. Devon and his attorney sat at the far end of the table, opposite from my own seat. Down the row of attorneys, I looked at my friends who had become my co-defendants. They each wore a suit and tie and appeared professional in their attire. We hadn't been together as a group since the day when we were released from county jail, nearly a year ago. I held no grudges against any of them for the past and I wished the best for each of them in the future.

"Good luck today, guys." I said, looking at each of them along the table.

They wished me, and one another, luck as well, then we turned our attention toward the cherry double-doors as the prosecutor entered the room. He was a tall man with short wavy hair of dark grey. He walked with the confidence of a man able to achieve high conviction rates and higher sentences for anyone who had the misfortune to oppose him. Walking by his side was Special Agent Markum of the F.B.I. and the victimized librarian, Anita Bonner, and a spindly wisp of a man who trailed behind her. Ms. Bonner sat in a booth designated for witnesses. The prosecutor and Markum sat at the prosecution table, parallel to the defense. But the spindly man remained on his feet. He crossed the center of the courtroom and approached each of the defendants in turn. He approached me last. He cordially handed a small stack of legal documents to me.

"A parting gift from Ms. Bonner." He said with a spiteful smirk that curled his lips like bacon in hot grease.

I looked at the documents and realized that I had been given a lawsuit filed by Ms. Bonner. She was suing the four of us for a total of one hundred thousand dollars. I wondered if the scales against me would ever balance. I looked at Ms. Bonner across the courtroom as she looked in the opposite direction, pretending to be aloof of the situation, and I pitied her. I felt sorry for what she had been forced to endure, but more than anything, I felt sorry for her, because she sought money to console her for the past, and from my experience, I had never known money to be anything but a false friend. I wished there was some way that I could change the past and prevent her present pain, but I didn't know how. If she believed that money could console her, then I would eventually find a way to pay my portion of the amount she desired, but for her sake, I hoped money would treat her better than it had treated me.

Row after row of wooden benches within the gallery began to fill with people. Soon, every seat was taken and those who didn't have a seat stood in the aisles. The massive double-doors were propped open and people who couldn't fit in the courtroom stood in the adjoining hall. I looked across the bustling crowd of people and I realized that nearly everyone I saw was gathered there for my support. I had never witnessed an outpouring of love in such volume. My heart swelled with adoration as I saw so many supportive faces. My mom, Blake, Sydney, and my cousin, Lynsey, sat in the first row, directly behind me. Many of the people I saw were family members, family-friends, cousins, aunts, uncles, and grandparents. I saw old friends and new friends and I knew every one of them were true friends. There were teachers and coaches who had known me as a child, before I had gone astray. In the centre of the crowd, I saw Claire. She sat with her younger sister, and when our eyes met, she smiled. It was a hesitant and forced smile, but still, it was a smile I loved. I looked to the back of the crowd, and standing by the open doorway, I saw my dad. He nodded encouragingly and I nodded in response.

A door opened at the front of the room and a procession of court officials entered.

"All rise for the honorable Judge Milner." A bailiff announced.

Everyone within the room stood as Judge Milner took her seat behind the bench. She was and attractive woman who appeared younger than her stature as a federal judge implied. She wore her dark brown hair short and styled in curls. Her posture and her facial expression was stern but her eyes were not uncaring. They seemed to be the calm centre of a harsh and threatening hurricane as she looked down upon me from her high seat of honor.

"Thank you." She announced. "You may be seated."

Everyone resumed their seat if they had one, or remained standing if they had no seat to return to. The proceedings that I had waited nearly a year for, waiting in both dreadful and hopeful anticipation, finally began. Arguments were waged by the two opposing sides and the momentum swayed, rose, and fell as the hours passed, and all the while, my future hung in the balance. Morning had become night when the proceedings were near an end.

"Mr. Allen." Judge Milner said, addressing me directly. "At this time, I would like to give you the opportunity to exercise your right of elocution. If you have anything that you would like to say before I issue your sentence, please approach the podium."

I gave Harvey a quick nod of confidence and stood from my seat. I nodded to each of my co-defendants, then turned toward the crowd of supportive eyes that were upon me. I smiled to thank them all for being with me when I needed them most. It was their support and their show of love that gave me courage as I stepped to the podium. I adjusted the microphone to speak and cleared my throat.

"Thank you, Your Honor." I began mildly, surprised by my own voice as it boomed throughout the entire room. I felt small compared to the immensity and vastness of the federal courtroom. Everything within the room was an embodiment of the power which I had opposed. I had broken the law and as I stood there, I stood alone, Charles Allen II v. The United States of America. I eased back from the microphone, cleared my throat, and continued.

"Your Honor, I have nothing to say in defense of the crime that was committed. What I did was illegal. What I did was wrong. And I'm sorry, deeply sorry, on more levels than I even know how to relate, for my wrongful actions and for the pain I have caused my family, my friends, and the victims of this crime, Ms. Bonner and Transylvania University. From the depths of my heart, I'm sorry and I hope that some day each of them may be able to forgive me."

"I have made terrible mistakes in my life, but it is in our mistakes that we find opportunities to better ourselves. Through my struggles, I have become a better person, and finally, I have found peace in my life. Your honor, I have learned my lesson and never again will I knowingly break the law. As you impose your punishment, I ask only that you have mercy on me."

"Thank you, Your Honor."

"Thank you, Mr. Allen. You may be seated."

I stepped away from the podium and walked back toward my seat. I looked across the crowd and smiled warmly, thanking them again for their support and for their love.

"Now." Judge Milner said. "I would like all four of the defendants to please approach the bench."

Devon, Luke, Ethan, and I stepped forward and stood in the center of the courtroom. Our attorneys stood staggered between us. Tension within the room rose thick and heavy like murky water from the depths of a river. I fought the urge to hold my breath as I awaited the words that would determine my fate.

"Despite the nature of this sentence, I am going to pass judgment on each of you individually. I ask that you step forward when your name is called."

We nodded our assent.

"Mr. Allen."

I stepped forward, and in my thoughts I prayed for mercy.

"Charles Thomas Allen II."

"Yes, Your Honor."

"Mr. Allen, I hereby sentence you to incarceration for a term of eighty seven months."

Eighty seven months. The number sounded like a foreign language. Eighty seven months. Numbers began clipping through my thoughts as I did the math. Five years was sixty months. Six years was seventy two months. Seven years and the numbers kept climbing, but they were more than numbers, they were years of my life, and they were years that were taken from me in an instant. Seven years and three months of my life were no longer mine to live. The time belonged to the justice system. I realized that the sentence she imposed was more than a third of the entirety of my twenty year old life. All of the air vanished from within the room and I stood breathless and shocked as I looked into the pale face of the repercussions for my actions. Incarceration, years of incarceration. I could no longer hear the words that Judge Milner spoke. Harvey prompted me with a nudge and I took a step back. He pointed with a pen to the calculation he had done on his notebook paper. Seven years and three months.

I waved him and his numbers away. I wanted to walk out of the courtroom, but I wasn't sure whether my legs could carry me. I considered dropping to my knees, slumping and crumbling under the weight of the punishment I had been made to bear. I could feel the crushing downward pull of the years, months, weeks, days, and endless hours that I would be forced to live in prison. I wanted to give up and give in to the welcoming company of defeat, but I stopped wallowing in my own self-pity and thought of my family and how they must have felt. I thought of all the people who were there to support me and I realized that it was my turn to return the favor. I stood straight-backed, held my head high and decided that if I wouldn't be strong for myself, I would be strong for them.

Judge Milner proceeded to issue sentences down the row of defendants, issuing the same sentence for us all. Each of us were ordered to serve eighty seven months in federal prison. Between the four of us, our combined sentences were three hundred and forty eight months, a total of twenty nine years to be served between four twenty year old boys, four college kids, four friends.

Judge Milner announced that each of us had forty days until we were ordered to self-surrender to our designated prison facility. She dropped the gavel like an executioner's ax and her words became law.

I turned to face the disappointed crowd, and my eyes rested on the wounded souls of my family.

My mom sobbed uncontrollably into her hands. My brother pushed back tears of anger and frustration and yelled obscenities in his rage. My little sister looked up at me and our eyes met. She looked at me with pure, heart-wrenching sadness that only a child can muster. And once again my heart was broken.

I went to them and hugged them as if through our embrace I could take their pain away and make it my own. Together, we walked out of the courtroom. I shook hands and gave and received hugs of grief and anguish and support every step of the way.

I pushed through the glass doors of the courthouse to face the cold, outside world. It was a black, starless night, but the exit was bright with photography flashes and cameras and microphones and reporters. Like vultures, they had gathered to capitalize on our loss.

I looked straight ahead into the distance, into the night, and pushed through the barrage of nosey questions that were shouted from every direction. I pushed through, then I crossed a street. I was alone as I walked under streetlamps that glowed desperately against the dark of night. And somehow, I found my way home.

Chapter 36: Home

Like all things, good and bad, my final forty days of freedom came to an end.

Throughout my final night, friends and relatives came by my mom's house to wish me well. Luke, and then later Devon, each came to say goodbye and to wish me luck. We had been assigned to different prisons, so it could be more than seven years before I would see them again. I didn't hear anything from Ethan, but I hoped he was prepared for what awaited each of us the following day.

I turned and checked the neon blue glow of a microwave clock that glared within the nearby kitchen. The time was 11:30 A.M..

"My ride should be here any minute now." I announced sadly.

I was ordered to self-surrender to a federal prison on the outskirts of Lexington. The facility was only fifteen minutes away from home. It was both a blessing and a curse to be so close to home, yet so far away. But for the sake of my family and friends, I was glad that I would only be a fifteen minute drive away from them if they wanted to visit me within the prison.

I stood from the couch and walked to the entrance foyer. I opened a set of wooden double-doors and looked through doors of glass that overlooked the front lawn. Outside of the yellow and white warmth of my family's home, the world seemed grey and dreary. It was raining. It was a bitter and wet January morning where even the birch trees in the yard looked miserable. They had been stripped of their leaves, their color, and they seemed to be weighed down and waterlogged by the effects of the world.

I turned my attention back within the house and noticed that I wasn't alone. I looked around the foyer at my family and friends, and I smiled warmly. I had once believed that money was the key to happiness. But I had learned that true happiness was found in the relationships that we as people share and the bonds we grow. I was down to the last few minutes, even seconds, of the time that I had left with the people I loved, and in such moments I understood the value of the time that we were able to share together. It would be seven years before I would see them again, outside of prison walls. As I looked around the room of loving, sad, and crying faces, I was so filled with emotion that I tried to smile, but I laughed as tears came out instead.

I watched their eyes turn toward the street behind me and I knew my ride had arrived. I turned and noticed that my dad had pulled along the curb in his black H2 Hummer. He didn't honk. He simply parked and let the rain fall against his windshield.

"Well, I guess this is it." I stated simply.

Stanley came toward me with arms open wide and I hugged him goodbye. He had been the first friend to stand by me after my arrest and one of the last to say goodbye. He was a true friend through thick and thin.

"I love you, man. I'll come see you as soon as I can. Keep your head up." He said as he patted me on the back.

I moved around the room and hugged my brother's friends, Jake what-did-the-five-fingers-say-to-the-face, who I had Rick Jamesed several years before, John, Seth, and Greg. They had each become like brothers to me and I knew that I would miss them while I was gone.

I moved on to Michael, a childhood friend who was always there for me when I most needed a friend. Then Grant, my eighth grade teacher who cared for each of his students as if they were children of his own. As I had grown older, we grew to become friends. "This too shall pass." He reminded as I hugged him goodbye.

Nick, the son of my mom's new boyfriend, approached me. He was a year younger than me and when we met, we quickly became friends. Eventually we would become stepbrothers.

I turned to my brother, Blake. He had never questioned me when I was arrested. As a true brother, he immediately stuck up for me and had my back as I had always had his. We pulled each other in and embraced in each other's tight grip, as brothers in arms. Neither of us wanted to let the other go.

"Bubble O, I love you, buddy." I said.

"I love you too."

I looked to my mom, but she waved me on. She wanted to be the last to say goodbye.

I turned to my sister, Sydney. Her expectant arms were outstretched, reaching up toward my shoulders that were barely within her grasp. I lifted her from the floor as I hugged her. She was only fourteen, a little girl. But she would be twenty-one, a full-grown adult, by the time I was released from prison.

"Make sure you write me, Syd. I don't want you growing up without me." I said, attempting to hide the pain within my voice.

She smiled at me with tears in her eyes. I tilted her chin up with my thumb and forefinger.

"You promise?"

"I promise. I'll write you every day."

"Okay." I smiled. "I love you."

I turned to my cousin, Lynsey, who was two years younger than me and more like a sister than a cousin. "And the same goes for you. You better write me too L-Bo."

She hugged me, then wiped fresh tears from her eyes. "Don't worry. I will, I promise. I love you"

"I love you too."

I turned and looked at Claire. She was crying tears that said I love you and tears that said goodbye. I touched her cheek with the palm of my hand and brushed away a tear with my thumb.

"I love you, Claire." I said as I looked into her beautiful, bright eyes.

"I love you too." She replied.

I kissed her once softly, then held her in my arms. I held her as if I knew the moment I let her go, I would lose her forever. With reluctance, I pulled away and kissed her again, one last time.

"Here, Claire." I unclasped the thin, braided rope of white-gold that was affixed with the St. Christopher medallion that had hung from my neck every moment of nearly every day for more than three years. "I want you to keep this for me." I put the necklace around the nape of her neck and fumbled with the clasp until I was satisfied that it was securely fastened. I kissed her on the cheek, then turned away.

I walked toward my mom. As my mother, she had earned the right to have the last goodbye. She had brought me into the world and loved me before I even knew what love was. Her tears had smeared eye-liner in streaks down her face like dark trails of broken dreams. I could feel her grief as she looked at me with love that only a mother can understand. And as I looked at her, her pain shot through my shattered heart. The worst effect of my punishment was not what would happen to me, but the pain that I caused the people who cared for me. I had never intended to hurt them, only help. But I had hurt them still. I had once believed that if I did the wrong thing for the right reasons, then good would find a way. But I had learned that good intentions were not enough to prevent the consequences of my actions from reaching the ones I loved. I wished that somehow my heart could take away all of their pain. But I knew only time could heal their wounds. I rested my forehead against my mom's forehead and we stared into each other's bleary eyes. No words were needed to exchange our thoughts. We both understood what the future held.

"How am I going to do this?" I finally asked. I didn't want to leave home and willingly surrender myself to the punishment of years in prison, but I knew that I had to face the consequences for my actions. Eventually, after my debt to society was paid, I would be able to face the world, free of guilt, free of shame, as a free man, ready to move forward with my life – on the right path, at last.

"You can do it, Charlie. I know you can." My mom encouraged through the tears that glistened within her eyes.

I nodded and tried to take strength from her words. I hugged her again, but she wouldn't let me go. I patted her back and tried to pull away, but she held me tight.

"You be strong in there." She insisted.

"Don't worry. I will, Mom. I love you."

"I love you too." She said, then finally, she let me go.

I took a few steps toward the door, then stopped. I looked at each of them one last time, remembering each of them as they were. I breathed the moment in deep, trying to take in everything, the love, the warmth, the sadness, the tenderness, and the hope.

I reached for the door and opened it slightly, then I turned to face them again.

"I love you all." I said

I smiled as they responded with love and warm wishes, then I stepped out into the rain. I threw the hood of my grey sweatshirt over my head and walked to my dad's car. I climbed into the huge vehicle and closed the door.

"Hey, Charlie. You ready?" My dad asked.

"I guess." I answered, and we drove away.

Few words were exchanged as we made our way through the rain slicked streets of Lexington. The air was dense with precipitation outside the car, but inside the car was thick with tension. He hadn't forgiven me for the choices I had made. And I hadn't forgiven him for his. We had both silently agreed to disagree.

I allowed my eyes to relax on the road ahead as I listened to the rhythmic slide of the windshield wiper and the falling rain. I had no idea what awaited me in the very near future. I could only speculate about how prison would be. From what I had seen in movies and on television, I imagined the gangs, the stabbings, the murders, and the rapes. I hoped the violent portrayal was only a gross exaggeration provided to entertain, but I knew that for better or worse, I would soon know the truth.

We drove past a cemetery with endless rows of weathered headstones. We crossed an overpass above the train tracks, several factories and warehouses, then we came to a clearing. Out of the passenger-side window, I could see Masterson Station park. It was an immense field of rolling hills with horse trails and soccer fields scattered throughout.

I looked into the distance and I could see two people enduring the rain. A man watched over a young boy. The boy kicked soccer balls into a goal as the man cheered him on and encouraged his every step.

Then from within the car, I heard a sniffling sound. I turned toward my dad, and for the first time in my life, I saw him cry. Several tears had rolled down his face like the wandering rain on the window behind him.

"Can you believe it?" He asked. "It seems like just the other day you were playing soccer out there."

"I know." I answered. "I can still see it."

"Back then, did you ever think you'd end up in prison?"

"No. I never thought I would be one of those people."

"Did you even know there was a prison on the other side of the fields?"

"No, but I wish I had."

On the horizon, I could see the dark monstrosity of the prison looming beneath the dreary sky. My dad turned his behemoth of a car onto a narrow road that led into the heart of the prison. As we drew closer, the massive building grew larger and larger. At its highest point, it appeared to be six stories tall and the remainder of the complex seemed to be at least three or four. It was built of stone and red brick masonry from an era long ago. Yet still, like an indestructible force, it stood before me. Around the entire perimeter, two fences towered taller than three tall men and each fence was barbed with endless rolls of razor wire.

My dad followed a sign and parked in the area designated to receive inmates. He pushed a button and I heard the car doors unlock, but neither of us moved. The rain drummed a soft percussion on the steel and glass around us. The dashboard clock showed five after twelve. It was time to go, past time to go, so I reached for the door.

"Charlie, wait." My dad said, stopping me as I held the handle. "Before you go, I just want you to know that I'm proud of you."

I looked at him, confused, and my look gave him reason to continue.

"I know why you did what you did. I don't understand why you had to turn to crime, but I understand what you were trying to do."

I was still confused as to what he was trying to explain.

"I was so caught up with fighting your mom for money that I didn't even realize what you all were going through. I'm sorry you were forced into a situation where you felt like you had run out of options. I know you were only doing what you thought you had to do to help your mom and your little brother and sister."

For the first time in several years I felt like we understood each other.

"I'm just sorry it had to end up this way." He said. "I never thought I'd see the day when my oldest son went to prison. If I could, I would trade places with you."

I let go of the handle and sat back in my seat. "I wouldn't let you do that." I answered. "I know we've both made some bad choices in the past, but it was my choice that led me here, not yours. So I have to be the one to do this. I wouldn't trade places with you even if I could."

He nodded thoughtfully then reached across his seat to embrace me. "I love you, son."

I hugged him in return. "I love you too, Dad. And I'm sorry – for everything."

"I'm sorry too." He replied. "But I think we're going to be alright. No matter what, me and you are always going to be on the same team. I think we both forgot that for a while, but we're family. We're always going to be there for each other. Oh, and I almost forgot. I took some of the money from the refinancing and took care of your portion of that lawsuit from the librarian for you."

"Really? Wow. You didn't have to do that."

"I know. But I wanted to."

"That was really nice of you. Thank you." I shook his hand and looked into his eyes, hazel, the same color as my own. "It's time for me to go, Dad. I love you."

"I love you too, Charlie."

Then I opened the door and stepped into the rain. I pulled my hood up to cover my head and walked toward the large gate that opened to a car port. It was big enough to load and unload several full size busses filled with unfortunate souls. Behind me, I heard my dad's door open and close. I knew he was standing there, watching me walk away. I felt an urge to look back, but I couldn't. I knew that if I looked back, I wouldn't be able to go forward.

I stepped through the gates and inside the carport. I was surrounded on three sides by fence and razor wire. I walked to another gate, a much smaller gate, and I knew it was the entrance to the prison. I found a small box that appeared to be a two-way intercom and pressed a button.

"Hello?" I spoke into the box.

There was no response. I held my breath and hoped that somehow there had been a mistake, but my hopes were cut short when a door within the masonry was opened. A man emerged. He wore dark blue pants and a matching jacket. I knew he was an officer of the prison, coming to receive me. I looked to the sky. Grey clouds hung low, content in their stillness as the rain came down. I let the rain fall against my face and I took a breath, a long, deep breath that reached the bottom of my lungs. It was my last breath as a free man. It tasted sweeter than any breath had ever taster before. I exhaled and I accepted my fate. A gate opened ahead of me, then another. The man told me to follow.

Our time will not last forever. Each and every second we are given is precious. There will come a point in each of our lives when time runs out, a time when there is no escape and the odds are absolute. We can only hope that we lived each and every moment to the fullest.

A door opened. A set of stairs led down, down underground to a dark corridor lined with metal bars, cells.

They say the instant before our time expires, our life flashes before our eyes. The flash is like a one shot impression of all the experiences, the relationships, the emotions and the feelings of an entire lifetime, the joy and the pain, compressed and compacted into one over-loaded instant. Each choice that is made, whether good or bad, is only another stroke on the canvas of life, the ultimate work of art. Regardless of the life we choose to live, rich, poor, sinner or saint, each life is unique. No two will ever be the same.

I stepped through the doorway and walked inside.

When time runs out and the impression of an entire lifetime flashes, the effect is always the same – Life is beautiful.

Author's Note

This book was handwritten during my time in prison. Often written under the glow of a tiny L.E.D. book-light as I lay in my bunk at night. I mailed draft after draft to my brother and sister over the years, and it is because of their dedication that the piles of handwritten pages have been transformed into this book. For their help, support, love, and seemingly unending patience, I cannot thank them enough.

Throughout my years in prison, I have had more than enough time to reflect on the actions and choices of my teenage years. I felt much older at the time, but looking back, I was scarcely more than a child, and a misguided child at that. I am unable to take back what was done years ago, or to retrieve the years of my life that I have paid in consequence for my actions. I can only admit my faults, express how sorry I am for the past, and be thankful for the opportunity to redeem myself in the future.

Special Thanks

This story has taken me a lifetime to live and years to write. Without the generous help and support of an innumerable amount of people along the way, neither would have made it this far. I cannot even begin to describe how much the support through the time of my arrest and the years for me in ways great and small, thank you.

Blake Allen, Sydney Allen, Lynne Dunn, Tom Allen, Granddaddy "Bill" Allen, "Granny" Betty Allen, Fred Almgren, Steve Adams, Sarah Acthison, Bob Allen, Brennan Bandy, Lisa and George Barber, Will Barton, Mike and Karen Bowen, Railey Brown, Joe Bryant, Myra and Worth Blackwelder, David Buchanan, Alden Crissey, Ben Chandler, Cameron Currie, Clinton Childress, Nick Dunn, David Dunn, Christine Dunn, Taylor Dunn, Myke Dabney, Sam Dick, Craig Dunn, Keith Drach, Lauren Elza, Dr. Chuck and Mitzi Eckerline, Rafeal "Flo" Flores, Dr. Jim Green, Chase Hillenmeyer, Seth Hillenmeyer, Stephen Hillenmeyer, Karen Hillenmeyer, Jana Hurt, Billie Hurt, Barbara Hanna, Jeremy Hampton, Stephan Morgan, Lynsey "Lbo" Jones, Laura and "Steve-o" Steve Jones, Jordan Jones, Conner Jones, Collin Jones, Will Jones, Freya Kelly, Hunter and Ted Kessinger, Steve Keller, "Mammaw" Lois and "Pappaw" Skeeter Leake, Bryan Leake, Adam Leake, Jake "The Snake" Locknane, Stanley Marcinek, Keeley Martin, Chelsea Martin, Barbara Martin, Paul Martin, Mark May, Greg Mcdonald, Julie Mcgill, Stinson Miller, Tom Musselman, Henry and Betty Nickles, Pat Nash, Kiki Noble, Big Buzz and Little Buzz Nave, Nick Nickles, Aunt Martha Otte, Bill Owen, Omar Prewitt, Robert Preston, Dr. Bob Rush, Ray Rush, Laura Beth Rider, Bill and Susan Rambicure, Grant Southworth, Joy Simpson, Tubby and Donna Smith, Matt Spicer, Katherine Swinford, Carlos Scott, Matt Smith, Nikki Schwartz, Marian Sims, Travis Sutherline, Savannah Thompson, Michael Tarnofsky, Logan Twerdy, John Tribble, Lisa and John Vandermale, Carl "Los" Warner, Nova Wheeler, Ethan Wills

And to those who prayed for me and always passed along kind words through family and friends, both were felt and greatly appreciated, thank you all.

In Loving Memory of

Ryan Bowen
1985-2003

Bill Allen
1920-2008

James "Skeeter" Leake
1928-2009